ANNALS OF THE NEW YORK ACADEMY OF SCIENCES

VOLUME 83, ART. 5   PAGES 761–916

January 20, 1960

Editor in Chief

OTTO V. ST. WHITELOCK

Managing Editor

FRANKLIN N. FURNESS

Associate Editor

PETER A. STURGEON

SOCIAL AND CULTURAL PLURALISM IN THE CARIBBEAN*

Conference Co-Chairmen: DOROTHY L. KEUR AND VERA RUBIN

Consulting Editor: VERA RUBIN

CONTENTS

* This series of papers is the result of a conference on *Social and Cultural Pluralism in the Caribbean* held and supported conjointly by The New York Academy of Sciences and the Research Institute for the Study of Man, New York, N.Y., May 27 and 28, 1959.

KRAUS REPRINT CO.

Millwood, N.Y.

1978

Library of Congress Cataloging in Publication Data

Main entry under title:

Social and cultural pluralism in the Caribbean.

    Reprint of art. 5, v. 83, 1960, of the Annals of the
New York Academy of Sciences.
    1. Caribbean area–Social conditions--Addresses,
essays, lectures. 2. Pluralism (Social sciences)--
Addresses, essays, lectures. I. Rubin, Vera D.
II. Series: New York Academy of Sciences. Annals ;
v. 83.
[HN192.5.S6 1978]   309.1'729   76-51870
ISBN 0-527-84390-3

*Reprinted with permission of the New York
Academy of Sciences*

KRAUS REPRINT CO.
A U.S. Division of Kraus-Thomson Organization Limited

Printed in U.S.A.

SOCIAL AND CULTURAL PLURALISM

M. G. Smith

Nigerian Institute of Social and Economic Research, University College, Ibadan, Nigeria

In this paper I attempt to define the concepts and conditions of social and cultural pluralism and to indicate their importance for social theory and research. In order to focus attention on theoretical issues I avoid descriptive materials as far as possible.

J. S. Furnivall was the first to distinguish the plural society as a separate form of society. Furnivall was a banker with considerable experience of the colonial Far East. He summarized this experience as follows: "In Burma, as in Java, probably the first thing that strikes the visitor is the medley of peoples —European, Chinese, Indian, and native. It is in the strictest sense a medley, for they mix but do not combine. Each group holds by its own religion, its own culture and language, its own ideas and ways. As individuals they meet, but only in the market-place, in buying and selling. There is a plural society, with different sections of the community living side by side, but separately, within the same political unit. Even in the economic sphere, there is a division of labour along racial lines" (Furnivall, pp. 304).

Anyone with Caribbean experience will recognize the force and value of Furnivall's remarks, but during the years since he introduced it the idea of pluralism has undergone little refinement or systematization, although the term "plural society" now enjoys wide currency. Perhaps for this reason sociologists have tended to shy away from the concept, yet it is essential for comparative sociology, it is easily developed and applied, and without it a rigorous analysis of certain societies is extremely difficult, if not impossible. I shall therefore try to give this concept a suitable theoretical form.

Since he was an economist, it was the plural economies of the Far Eastern colonies that attracted Furnivall's attention. Furnivall saw clearly that this economic pluralism was simply an aspect of the social pluralism of these colonies, and he said so in the passage already quoted. However, I wish to take the argument back one step further, since this social pluralism is also correlated with cultural pluralism, and since the plural society itself develops in rather special, although by no means unusual, conditions. Accordingly, I shall begin by considering the most general problems of social science, namely, the nature of culture and society and their interrelation. To do so I shall quote some recent thinking on these topics.

Ever since Tylor defined culture as all those "capacities and habits acquired by man as a member of society" (p. 1), there has been a fairly general agreement on the nature of culture. For the early anthropologists, culture was the proper subject matter of anthropology and, despite the work of L. H. Morgan, it was only with Émile Durkheim and his school that the nature of society and its relation to culture became an important focus of interest. By then Tylor's definition had become entrenched, and social organization was generally treated as one dimension of culture. The problem of defining society was thus complicated by the requirement that this definition should fit prevailing views of

763

culture. For this reason, among others, Durkheim's method and theory at first failed to win wide support.

It is easy enough to define society generally, and Radcliffe-Brown's (1950) description of it as "the network of social relations" is perfectly adequate, social relations being distinguished by recurrent mutual adjustments. However, even this sort of definition tends to reduce society to social structure by telescoping quite different levels of abstraction. The real difficulty crops up when we try to define societies generally so as to distinguish between them. Since Tylor's view of culture implies that any particular culture is borne by a particular society, it is difficult to see how we can distinguish between cultures, either, unless we have some agreed definition of societies.

By ignoring this anthropological concern with culture as primary and all-inclusive, sociologists tend to escape the difficulties of definition that arise from having to fit culture and society together; however, in trying to distinguish societies, they face much the same problems as do the anthropologists, and their solutions are not very different. Thus the current sociological preference for the study of social systems avoids the problem of defining societies themselves. Marion Levy makes this point very clearly, and bases his version of structural-functional theory on a definition of societies as theoretically self-sufficient systems of action, the members of which are mostly born into their respective units (p. 113). This definition has three features of special interest here. First, Levy's action has obvious affinities with that behavior that anthropologists regard as the content of culture. Second, the theoretically self-sufficient system is generally the most inclusive of its kind. Third, the view of societies as relatively closed reproductive units raises certain difficulties. In these terms, each Nuer tribe might well be a separate society.

Faced with this problem of distinguishing between societies, Radcliffe-Brown's response was an analytic evasion rather similar to the social system approach. In his view, "If we take any convenient locality of a suitable size, we can study the structural system as it appears in and from that region, i.e., the network of relations connecting the inhabitants amongst themselves and with the people of other regions" (p. 193). Radcliffe-Brown then equates "single societies" with the "structural systems observable in particular communities" (p. 194). Despite this, he constantly encountered the problem of differentiating homogeneous and heterogeneous societies. Since he chose to study structural systems rather than societies, and since he conceived these systems as functional equilibria, they were homogeneous by assumption, and their heterogeneity was ruled out. Nevertheless, Radcliffe-Brown offered a useful criterion for distinguishing structural systems. In a homogeneous system each status and role has a uniform definition. When identical statuses and roles are defined differently we have a plurality of structural systems (Fortes, p. 36).

For Raymond Firth, "No society can be given a definite limit," and he holds that "fields of social relations, not clear-cut societies, must be the more empirical notion of social aggregates" (p. 28). On the other hand, Nadel, like Marion Levy, found it necessary to distinguish between societies, and he defines them as "the relatively widest effective groups," effectiveness being judged by "the quantitative range of institutional activities entered into by the group . . . and the nature and general relevance of these activities" (p. 187). Nadel then points out that "mostly, when we look for a society, we find a political unit, and when speaking of the former, we mean in effect the latter" (p. 188). There is an obvious correspondence between Marion Levy's "theoretically self-sufficient system of action" and Nadel's "relatively widest effective group"; both tend to be defined politically.

Since I am concerned to distinguish between homogeneous, plural, and other types of society, I cannot avoid this problem of defining a society; neither can I ignore questions of the relation between society and culture. It is obvious that when societies are conceived as structural systems in equilibrium, their homogeneity is assumed, and heterogeneity is difficult to define, classify, or analyze. In consequence, one general model, namely, that of homogeneous structural systems, is applied to quite different types of society, thereby obscuring their differences, misleading their analyses, and blocking the development of social theory. It is perhaps worth noting here that the two main methods of field investigation, namely, community studies and sampling, both encourage assumptions of unity in the systems with which they deal.

Even so, their failure to distinguish societies has neither deterred anthropologists from distinguishing cultures nor from continuing to define culture in terms of society and vice versa. The current view is neatly stated by Firth: "The terms represent different facets of components in basic human situations. If, for instance, society is taken to mean an organized set of individuals with a given way of life, culture is that way of life. If society is taken to be an aggregate of social relations, culture is the content of those relations. Society emphasizes the human component, the aggregate of people and the relations between them. Culture emphasizes the component of accumulated resources, nonmaterial as well as material, which the people inherit, employ, transmute, add to, and transmit" (p. 27). David Bidney (1953), in his recent review of anthropological theory, shares Firth's view.

The failure to develop an agreed definition of societies ultimately may have the same basis as the continuing definition of culture and society in terms of one another. Analyses based on notions of system tend to avoid the problem of how a culture and a society are related. As we say, Tylor initially defined culture as behavior learned in society but, oddly enough, social organization, which was taken to represent society, was regarded by Tylor, Malinowski, and others as one dimension of culture. The modern view, as stated by Firth (p. 27), is equally unsatisfactory, since it implies that a culture and a society are always conterminous and interdependent. This view also obstructs the recognition and analysis of culturally heterogeneous units.

In discussing their interrelation, Nadel, like Firth, at first treats culture and society as conterminous. "Society, as I see it, means the totality of social facts projected onto the dimension of relationships and groupings; culture, the same totality in the dimension of action" (pp. 79, 80). Nadel is here using the term "action" in much the same sense as Marion Levy or Talcott Parsons; but later on he distinguishes between the boundaries of culture, with its complex of language, idea systems, and activities, and society, with its complex of groupings and relationships. At this stage, culture and society cease to be conterminous for Nadel, since his category of "all-culture" includes forms of action such as language, building, or art styles, which are independent of social boundaries.

Nadel rests this distinction upon his concept of institutions as "standardized modes of co-activity" (p. 108), for example, marriage, blood revenge, family, property, chieftainship, and the like. Although he claims that Radcliffe-Brown's definition of institutions is most like his own, it is probably to Malinowski that Nadel was most indebted for this concept. In fact, Nadel's institutions, like Malinowski's, involve a charter of values, a code of rules, set forms of social grouping and personal relationships, a set cycle of activities, a material apparatus, and a purposive character. These are the distinctive features of Malinowski's institutions, regarded as the "concrete isolates of organized behavior" (pp. 52, 53).

Nadel shows that ideas, activities, and modes of grouping are interdependent elements of institutions, that they form a common system, although they can be separated for analysis, and that their interrelations can be studied. He then distinguishes between "regulative" and "operative" institutions and between those institutions that are "compulsory," "alternative," and "exclusive" (p. 120), and between institutional and residual or noninstitutional forms of action, which he groups in four categories, namely, unique historical events, autonomous idea systems such as language or art styles, recurrent abnormalities such as suicide, and customary conventions and mores. Nadel includes these noninstitutional actions in his concept of culture. For him the society consists of institutional social relations and groupings, and the main body of culture is also firmly rooted in the system of institutions.

The correspondence between Nadel's classification of institutions and Linton's (1936) analysis of culture into core, alternatives, and specialties is clear. Linton's core consists of Nadel's compulsory institutions, and his specialties include Nadel's exclusive institutions, but Linton's scheme incorporates mores, conventions, language, and art styles as well.

This review of anthropological thinking provides the background for my argument. I think the views and positions just quoted are as representative as they are significant. The theory of pluralism seems to develop naturally on this basis.

In my view, only territorially distinct units having their own governmental institutions can be regarded as societies, or are in fact so regarded. Delegation of authority and governmental function is quite general and has many forms, but we do not normally treat an official structure as an independent government unless it settles all internal issues of law and order independently. By this criterion we can identify delegation and delimit societies. It often happens that a subordinate population group is permitted to exercise certain functions of internal administration; one does not thereby distinguish it as a separate society. However, colonial governments that discharge the full range of governmental functions within their territories regulate societies quite distinct from those of their imperial powers. In northern Nigeria the scattered communities of nomadic Fulani do not constitute a single Fulani society, but belong to the various emirates in which they reside; likewise, the general concept of Hausa society breaks down into the separate Hausa societies of these emirates.

I hold that the core of a culture is its institutional system. Each institution involves set forms of activity, grouping, rules, ideas, and values. The total system of institutions thus embraces three interdependent systems of action, of idea and value, and of social relations. The interdependence of these three systems arises from the fact that their elements together form a common system of institutions. These institutions are integral wholes, as Malinowski would say, and their values, activities, and social forms are mutually supporting. The institutions of a people's culture form the matrix of their social structure, simply because the institutional system defines and sanctions the persistent forms of social life. To define the social structure, we must therefore analyze the institutional system. Likewise, to define a system of social value or action, we must first identify and analyze the institutional framework.

It follows from this that a population that shares a single set of institutions will be culturally and socially homogeneous. Provided that it is also politically distinct, it will also form a homogeneous society. The homogeneity of this unit will be evident in the uniformity of its social structure, ideational systems, and action patterns. To determine the forms and levels of integration within such a unit, we must pursue the method of institutional analysis.

It also follows that institutional diversities involve differences of social structure, ideational systems, and forms of social action. These differences may conceivably hold for a single institution, such as the family, for an entire institutional system. Territorially distinct units that practice differing institutional systems and that are politically separate are culturally as well as socially distinct. In short, institutional differences distinguish differing cultures and social units. When groups that practice differing institutional systems live side by side under a common government the cultural plurality of this inclusive unit corresponds with its social plurality, and the network of social relations between these culturally distinct groups is wider and more complex than those within them. In short, culture and society are not always conterminous or interdependent. We do in fact find societies the component sections of which have dissimilar ways of life and modes of social organization. Such societies exhibit cultural and social pluralism simultaneously.

Institutions have been treated as cultural forms by some writers and as social forms by others. Actually, they combine social and cultural aspects equally. Their social aspects consist of set forms of groupings and relations. Their systems of norm and activity, together with their material apparatus, properly belong to culture. Although institutions form the core of culture and society alike, they do not exhaust either. For our purpose, the important thing to note is that a group's institutional homogeneity involves its cultural and social homogeneity, while institutional pluralism involves corresponding cultural and social pluralism. A society the members of which share a common system of basic or "compulsory" institutions but practice differing "alternative" and "exclusive" institutions is neither fully homogeneous nor fully plural. Such units are socially and culturally heterogeneous.

It is possible to compile an indefinite list of institutions if we adopt a very narrow definition. However, institutions dealing with the same phases of life tend to form a systematic cluster, and to forestall confusion I shall speak of these clusters as subsystems. Thus marriage, family, levirate, extended kinship forms, and the like together constitute the kinship subsystem. Likewise, government is the subsystem of explicitly regulative institutions, such as law, parliament, police, and civil and military administration. Each of these institutional subsystems has many links with the others; thus the kinship institutions have prominent economic, educational, recreative, religious, and governmental aspects. We need not predicate any pre-established harmony of institutions, as functional theory has tended to do. The available evidence suggests that consistency, interdependence, and coherence are necessarily greater within each institutional subsystem than between them. This set of institutional subsystems forms the institutional system, and this can vary widely in its mode and level of integration and equilibrium. Societies differ in their complement and distribution of institutional forms. Some lack such institutions as the army, the priesthood, chieftainship, markets, or age sets, but any given institutional system tends towards an internal integration and thus some closure. Thus in a culturally divided society, each cultural section has its own relatively exclusive way of life, with its own distinctive systems of action, ideas and values, and social relations. Often these cultural sections differ also in language, material culture, and technology. The culture concept is normally wider than that of society, since it includes conventions, language, and technology, but the presence of two or more culturally distinct groups within a single society shows that these two aspects of social reality may vary independently in their limits and interrelations.

To analyze a society that has a single uniform culture, we must define the component institutions and their interrelations. As already pointed out, this procedure includes the analysis of action patterns, ideational systems, and social structure. To analyze a society that contains culturally distinct groups we must make similar analyses of the institutional systems of each component group and then determine their interrelations within the inclusive unit. The culturally distinct components of a single society are its cultural sections. They are distinguished by practicing different forms of institution. Generally these cultural sections are highly exclusive social units, each constituting an area of common life, beyond which relations tend to be specific, segmental, and governed by structural factors. Under these conditions the boundaries of cultural and social sections correspond, and the discontinuity of value systems is most extreme. However, it sometimes happens that some members of different cultural sections associate more regularly with one another than with the sections to which they belong. In such cases the social and cultural sections have somewhat different boundaries, and their margins may be dynamic.

This brings me to the problem of defining the type and level of institutional variation sufficient to distinguish cultural groups. It is obvious that modern societies are culturally heterogeneous in many ways. They contain a wide range of occupational specialties, they exhibit stratification and class differences, they often contain ethnic minorities, and their rural and urban populations have somewhat different ways of life. Some writers describe modern society as pluralistic because of its occupational diversity. I prefer to say that it is culturally heterogeneous, and to reserve the term pluralism for that condition in which there is a formal diversity in the basic system of compulsory institutions. This basic institutional system embraces kinship, education, religion, property and economy, recreation, and certain sodalities. It does not normally include government in the full sense of the term for reasons given below. Occupations are simply specialties, in Linton's sense. The development of occupational groupings and institutions multiplies the host of specialties within the culture, but the resulting diversity leaves the basic institutional system untouched. Such a florescence of alternatives anchored in a common system of basic institutions therefore presents conditions of cultural and social heterogeneity without pluralism.

The same thing is true of class differences, which are differences within a single institutional framework. Their compatibility within this framework is essential for their comparison and ranking. Thus we can neither incorporate Hausa class patterns into our own system, nor can we amalgamate the two, simply because our own institutional system and social values differ radically from their Hausa counterparts. Class patterns represent differing styles of life, but the conceptual difference between such life styles and culture as a way of life is profound. Life styles can and do change without involving any change in the institutional system. Within class-stratified societies, such as those of the Hausa or of Britain, the various strata or classes hold common economic, religious, familial, political, and educational institutions, but the condition of cultural and social pluralism consists precisely in the systematic differentiation of these basic institutions themselves.

Within each cultural section of a plural society we may expect to find some differences of stratification or social class. These cultural sections themselves are usually ranked in a hierarchy, but the hierarchic arrangement of these sections differs profoundly in its basis and character from the hierarchic status organization within each severally. The distribution of status within each cultural section rests on common values and criteria quite specific to that group, and this medley of sectional value systems rules out the value consensus that is prerequisite for any status continuum. Thus the plurality is a discontinuous status order, lacking any foundation in a system of common interests and values, while its component sections are genuine status continua, distinguished by their differing systems of value, action, and social relations. Accordingly, insofar as current theories assume or emphasize the integrative and continuous character of social stratification, they may apply to each cultural section, but not to the plurality as a whole. In class systems, for instance, social mobility and acceptance presuppose adoption of Linton's alternatives, that is, of new class conventions, linguistic habits, and life styles; in conditions of cultural pluralism, however, intersectional mobility involves adoption of a new institutional system, and for that reason it can rarely occur within an individual lifetime.

It is especially important to distinguish between pluralism and "class" stratification because of the profound differences that underlie their formal resemblance. Whereas the assumption of integration may be valid for a class system, it cannot normally hold for a plural hierarchy. In general, social stratification occurs without corresponding pluralism as, for example, among the British, the Hausa, or the Polynesians. There is also no inherent reason why all cultural sections of a plural society should be ranked hierarchically. It has been shown by van Lier (1950) that the Japanese, Chinese, Indian, and Negro sections of Surinam have parallel social status. As I have pointed out elsewhere (1959), status models must perform certain social functions, and they cannot do so if they are unduly complex. Consequently, the status structure of a very complex plurality will often equate two or more distinct cultural sections. The point here is that cultural difference and social stratification vary independently. Thus they can neither be reduced to one another, nor can they be equated. Cultural pluralism is a special form of differentiation based on institutional divergences. It is therefore a serious error to equate pluralism with "class stratification," as my colleagues Lloyd Braithwaite (1952) and Raymond Smith (1956) have done for Trinidad and British Guiana, respectively.

Like social classes, the rural and urban populations of a given society tend to differ in their life styles rather than in their institutional systems. However, as Redfield (1954) has pointed out, the institutions of a developing urban population may come to differ sharply from those of the rural folk. This is a rather special case that involves pluralism only if the basic institutional system is affected. Otherwise the result is a condition of social and cultural heterogeneity.

The problems presented by ethnic minorities are somewhat more complex, largely because this term has been ambiguously applied to racial, national, linguistic, and cultural groups. Let us therefore consider specific cases. The Greeks, Italians, and Irish of New York each have their own religious and family practices, perhaps their own languages and sodalities also. If their institutional systems diverge from the general American model so as to be incompatible with the latter, then they must be regarded as cultural sections. Institutional incompatibility is indicated by differences of grouping, norms, activities, and functions. We have simply to ask, for instance, whether the paternal or maternal, the judicial or the priestly status and role have the same definitions and institutional contexts among differing groups, and whether these role incumbents could be exchanged without violating social practice. If they can, the groups share a common institutional system; if they cannot, the groups do not. Differences in the definitions of these specific statuses and roles imply differing forms of social grouping, of institutional action, and of ideational system. They cannot occur in conditions of institutional uniformity.

By this criterion, it seems clear that marriage and the family vary among Greeks, Italians, and Irish in content rather than in form, in their affective quality rather than in their social function, sanctions, and norms. Likewise, the Greek, Italian, and Irish variants of Christianity share common basic forms of organization, ritual, and belief. Their compatibility is evident as well in their common origin as in these common elements. We do not normally distinguish groups that observe different totems, or the same totem in different ways, as practicing different systems of totemism, and I think there is no case for treating Christianity otherwise. Unless ethnic traditions present incompatible institutional forms, they are, like social class patterns, stylistic variations within a common basic way of life, analytically similar to Linton's alternatives.   Thus ethnic variations, like class styles, may produce cultural and social heterogeneity, but do not involve pluralism.

In certain parts of the United States it is possible that the Negro population practices a distinct institutional system in my sense of the term.   There is evidence that certain Negro communities in the South differ sharply in their social, religious, and economic organization from those of the adjoining whites. Assuming this to be the case, we must regard such Negro-white populations as plural communities.   They are communities, but not societies, even if they embrace entire member states of the Union.   As events in Little Rock, Ark., have shown, these member states are not independent units, and therefore do not form separate societies.   The point here is that federalism permits the presence of plural communities within a nation state that may not itself be a plural society.   I discuss this point more fully below.

The whole process of Negro acculturation in the United States, the Caribbean, and other parts of the New World presupposed basic institutional differences between Negroes and whites.   It stands to reason that some sections of the American Negro population will now be less fully acculturated than others. As a result, the American Negroes are culturally diverse and may be subdivided institutionally into two or more sections, the acculturated extreme consisting of those who have adopted white American culture as far as the present color-caste arrangement permits, while the opposite extreme consists of those whose religious, kinship, economic, and associational institutions are furthest removed from white norms.   It follows that the American Negroes do not form a separate cultural section.   They are a subordinate social segment of a culturally heterogeneous society, and may differ among themselves institutionally.   Some groups of American Negroes belong to plural communities; others do not. Such a complex situation cannot be handled adequately in terms of race relations alone; pluralism and its alternatives must be defined institutionally rather than in racial or ethnic terms.   Cultural heterogeneity has many forms and bases, while cultural pluralism has only one, namely, diversity of the basic institutional system.   Plural societies are by no means the only alternatives to homogeneous societies.   The United States and Brazil are heterogeneous societies that contain plural communities and evince pluralism without themselves being plural societies.   Neither color-caste nor class stratification implies basic institutional differences and, in my view, the term ethnic minorities should be reserved for those national groups that share the same basic institutions as the host society, but preserve distinctive styles.

Several other points should be made before we leave this subject of institutional variation.   As we have seen, each institutional subsystem tends to be integrated with other institutional subsystems.   For this reason, it is rare for the institutional differences between groups to be limited to one particular institution.   If these differences are at all significant, they will generally be associated with like differences in other institutions, and the cumulative effect will be basic cultural and social differences between the groups concerned.   Such differentiated groups form separate cultural and social sections.

Institutional differences vary in degree, even when the institutions under comparison also differ in kind.   Thus the kinship institutions of West Indian folk and elite form two distinct kinds of system, but the difference between these two systems is less than that between one based on patrilineal descent and polygyny and another based on bilateral kinship and monogamy. Although both paired comparisons reveal differences in kind, and thus belong to the same order, one set of differences exceeds the other. Clearly, the more obvious the set of institutional differences, the easier their identification and analysis. In this sense pluralism is a dimension, some societies being more sharply divided than others or having more subdivisions. Likewise, within a plurality, two sections may differ less obviously from one another than from a third; provided they all have different systems of basic institutions, however, all three are structural units of identical analytic status.

Since institutions are integral units, the elements of which are activities, ideas, and social relations, their differences involve differing systems of idea, action, and social grouping. To determine whether such differences exist in a given population is a simple matter of empirical research. Such study focuses on the institutional forms of grouping, idea, and action within the population. It seeks to determine their uniformity or difference by the criterion of compatibility already discussed and to define their distribution. Given precise indices and hypotheses, the problems of social integration and change are also open to field study.

Even in a plural society, institutional diversity does not include differing systems of government. The reason for this is simple: the continuity of such societies as units is incompatible with an internal diversity of governmental institutions. Given the fundamental differences of belief, value, and organization that connote pluralism, the monopoly of power by one cultural section is the essential precondition for the maintenance of the total society in its current form. In short, the structural position and function of the regulative system differ sharply in plural and other societies. Institutionally homogeneous societies develop a variety of institutional motivations toward conformity with social norms; institutionally split societies lack these common motivations and tend to rely correspondingly on regulation. The dominant social section of these culturally split societies is simply the section that controls the apparatus of power and force, and this is the basis of the status hierarchies that characterize pluralism. Since the units of this hierarchic arrangement are the cultural sections, ranking applies initially to sections rather than individuals, and within each section it is governed by other status factors.

In such situations the subordinate social sections often seek to regulate their own internal affairs independently of their superiors. Thus, in Grenada, The West Indies, the peasants traditionally avoided the official authorities by settling their disputes through local "peacemakers" or magicians, by ignoring official forms of land transfer, marriage, divorce, wills, registration, and the like, and nowadays by appealing to their sectional leader, E. M. "Uncle" Gairy, for assistance in the most varied circumstances (Rottenberg, 1955). Such evasive adjustments are not necessary among the Bantu on South African reservations, who have their own officials appointed and controlled by the dominant whites. These Bantu are permitted to observe their traditional law as long as it does not conflict with the Union law. In Grenada, where there is only one legal code, the problem of the lower section is to maintain its customs by systematic evasion; the people there are fairly skillful in this respect, but it still remains true that, even within plural societies, we shall not find two equal and independent sets of governmental institutions.

Cultural pluralism is not confined to plural societies, although it is their basis. Furnivall noted this point long ago: "Outside the tropics a society may have plural features, notably in South Africa, Canada and the United States . . . but in general these mixed populations have at least a common tradition of Western culture. . . . There is a society with plural features, but not a plural society" (p. 305). This passage reveals some theoretical confusion; it would be difficult to name a more extreme case of a plural society than contemporary South Africa. Moreover, Furnivall seemed to think that plural societies were confined to the tropics. Nevertheless, I think that his main point here is very sound; in Brazil and the United States we have societies that evince cultural pluralism, but that are clearly different from plural societies. In Canada the French dominate Quebec, while Anglo-Saxons control the other provinces. Even if the French and British Canadians practiced different institutional systems, their provincial separateness would mean that the Canadian Federation is an association of groups differentiated territorially and institutionally. If this unit were dominated by a distinct cultural minority, it would then present a special form of plural society, the critical feature of which is that within it the cultural sections live side by side, a condition that in the Union of South Africa has given rise to *apartheid*.

In Brazil and the United States the culturally and politically dominant tradition is that shared by the overwhelming majority of the population. Under such conditions, even culturally distinct groups are minorities at the national level, although they may well include some local majorities. As national minorities, they present no threat to the current social order and, as long as their customs are tolerated by the dominant majority, these minorities may persist undisturbed. It is therefore necessary to distinguish such societies as Brazil and the United States from another and far larger group in which the dominant cultural section constitutes a small minority wielding power over the unit as a whole. Under such conditions, this dominant minority is inescapably preoccupied with problems of structural maintenance and economic and political control. For this reason it may actively seek to discourage acculturation among the subordinate majority, since the current incompatibility of their institutional systems is held to justify the *status quo*. This has happened in the British West Indies on several occasions, and is presently the major issue in British East and Central Africa. It is this latter group of societies that should be distinguished as plural societies. They are structurally peculiar, and they form a field worth special study. Federal constitutions may modify the significance of community pluralism when the sectional proportions of the community are reversed at the national level. They do not modify the effect of pluralism in the Union of South Africa because the dominant whites are a minority at both levels.

It is probably best to summarize my argument before proceeding. I have tried to show that the institutional system that forms the cultural core defines the social structure and value system of any given population. Thus populations that contain groups practicing different forms of institutional system exhibit a corresponding diversity of cultural, social, and ideational patterns. Since any institutional system tends toward internal integration and consistency, each of these differentiated groups will tend to form a closed sociocultural unit. Such pluralistic conditions are far more widespread than are plural societies, the distinctive feature of which is their domination by a cultural minority. Pluralism is quite distinct from other forms of social heterogeneity such as class stratification in that it consists in the coexistence of incompatible institutional systems. Plural societies depend for their maintenance on the regulation of intersectional relations by one or other of the component cultural sections. When the dominant section is also a minority, the structural implications of cultural pluralism have their most extreme expression, and the dependence on regulation by force is greatest. A society whose members all share a single system of institutions is culturally and socially homogeneous. A society having one basic institutional system in a number of styles or one basic system and a number of institutional alternatives and specialties is culturally and socially heterogeneous. Since social integration develops institutionally, the structural conditions of societies vary according to their homogeneous, heterogeneous, or plural characters. Thus pluralism has three aspects of special significance for us: (1) on the theoretical plane, it directs attention to the need for refinement and variety of analytic models by presenting conditions that cannot be handled adequately with conventional models of homogeneous equilibrium systems or integrative stratification orders; (2) methodologically, there are the problems of studying such units holistically rather than in community segments, of classifying them structurally, and of assessing their relative integration in objective terms; and (3) analytically, the functional organization and development of such units also pose special problems that require historical study.

How do plural societies and other culturally pluralistic units originate? Furnivall thought that they were limited to the modern colonial tropics and were products of Western economic expansion. However, the Norman conquest of Britain, and the Roman conquest before it, certainly established plural societies, and there are many other instances that cannot be attributed to Western economic activity. Thus in Maradi, Nigeria, the former Habe rulers of Katsina, after being driven out by the Fulani in 1807, established a successor state that is also a plural society, since its Moslem rulers form a minority controlling pagans whose kinship, economic, magicoreligious, educational, military, and political institutions are quite distinctive. In Uganda we also find plural societies founded before the Europeans arrived on the scene. Modern economic forces may account for colonial pluralities, but these are not the only ones. Perhaps the most general answer to this question of origin is migration, which also accounts for the development of ethnic minorities. This migration may be forced, as in Habe Maradi or West Indian slavery, or semivoluntary as in the movement of indentured East Indian labor into the West Indies, or voluntary as in the British penetration of Kenya and Burma or the Dutch colonization of South Africa. It may involve conquest and consolidation, but this is not always the case.

It is a major error to conceive the conditions and problems of pluralism directly in terms of race relations. To do so is to mistake the social myth for reality, and thus to miss the structure that underlies it and gives it both force and form.   It is quite true, by and large, that modern plural societies are multi-racial, and that these racial groups tend also to be culturally distinct, but this is by no means always the case, as the cultural diversity of the American Negroes and the distinction between *evolué* and *indigène* in Africa makes clear.   It often happens that racially distinct groups form a common homogeneous society, as for instance among the Hausa-Fulani of northern Nigeria.   Conversely, we sometimes find culturally distinct groups that belong to the same racial stock expressing their differences in racial terms.   This seems to be the case in Guatemala, Haiti, and among the Creole folk and elite of the British West Indies.   History provides us with many other examples, such as the Normans and Anglo-Saxons, the English and the Scots or, most recently and most elaborately, the Nazi ideology.   Race differences are stressed in contexts of social and cultural pluralism.   They lack social significance in homogeneous units.   As the Caribbean slave literature shows most clearly, the function of racism is merely to justify and perpetuate a pluralistic social order.   This being the case, the rigorous analysis of race relations presupposes analyses of their context based on the theory of pluralism.

In class-stratified societies deference is demonstrated or exacted interpersonally, while in plural units it is often generalized by the dominant group and enforced on the subordinate sections.   Such generalized obligatory deference is an important mode of social control.   Normally, dress, manner, or speech serve to place individuals sectionally but, where racial differences obtain, they usually act as the most general indicators, being the most resistant to change. In this way the dominant minority seeks to perpetuate its dominion and the plural structure simultaneously.   Racist ideology seeks to symbolize and legitimize intersectional relations.

Another common sociological error is the reduction of cultural and social pluralism to social stratification.   Such equations misstate the character and implications of institutional differentiation where this is not entirely ignored. Thus the Haitian literature debates whether the Haitian cultural and social sections are castes or classes; Braithwaite applies both labels to the sections in Trinidad; Tumin (1952) treats the Ladino and Indian sections of Guatemalan society as castes; and Lord Olivier (1936) treats the Jamaican cultural sections as classes.   Both Tumin and Olivier presented accounts of smooth change within well-integrated societies.   Both analyses were discredited by violent upheavals in Guatemala and Jamaica shortly after the publication of the two works. The recent development of racism in Trinidad also questions Braithwaite's analysis.   We cannot adequately analyze plurality as an integrated stratification order.

It is also misleading to suppose that the persistence of plural units is due to the predominance of common values between their cultural sections.   Such common values and integrative mechanisms can hardly be claimed for contemporary Kenya, Hungary, the Union of South Africa, British Guiana, Algeria, or Nyasaland.   However, before their current disorders, did the value cohesion and regulative systems of these populations differ significantly from the present? Social quiescence and cohesion differ sharply, and so do regulation and integration but, if we begin by assuming that integration prevails, it is virtually impossible to distinguish these conditions. Here again, pluralism indicates the need for greater refinement in our structural models and social theory.

It is especially difficult to isolate the positive effect of common values in culturally split societies that owe their form and maintenance to a special concentration of regulative power within the dominant group. In the Congo the Belgians tried to solve the problems of political control and social justice intrinsic to these conditions by neutrality in its most extreme form. Accordingly, they denied all cultural sections the franchise, and this appearance of cultural impartiality was highly applauded for the stability it seemed to offer (INCIDI, 1957). The reality was somewhat different, as the Belgian legislation affecting polygyny shows clearly, and recent events have shown the total inadequacy of this solution also. Whatever the form of the political system, the differing sectional values within a plural society are a profound source of instability. Since stratification is now assumed to be an integrative order, it is therefore misleading to represent the intersectional relations of a plural society in these terms.

Since the plural society depends for its structural form and continuity on the regulation of intersectional relations by government, changes in the social structure presuppose political changes, and these usually have a violent form. In desperation, the subordinate cultural section may either practice escapist religious rituals or create a charismatic leadership as the organ of sectional solidarity and protest. This sort of leadership develops only where people are desperate in the face of overwhelming odds. We have numerous examples of charismatic leadership in the West Indies.

The consequence of this mode of political change is often an increased instability, since the uncircumscribable powers of charismatic leaders are incompatible with modern bureaucratic organization and Western parliamentary practice. Either the charisma is routinized by ministerial roles and bureaucratic procedures, in which case the people may lose their leader, or both will probably proceed along the dictatorial path.

Recently the British have created several regional federations by uniting colonial pluralities. It is hoped that these federations will provide favorable conditions for the development of their populations, but these federal associations permit the elite minorities of formerly distinct societies to assist one another in controlling their subordinate social sections, as recently happened in Nyasaland, for example. Federalism may modify pluralities if these are absorbed into larger units with a different structure and composition, but these new colonial federations have much the same sectional compositions as their constituent units. Thus they face two critical tests. First, it remains to be seen whether the associated colonies will transfer decisive governmental power to their federations and thus cease to be separate societies. Second, it remains to be seen whether the federal form and association will facilitate structural changes within the component units.

Since institutional systems tend to be integrated, societies that include two or more institutional systems differ structurally, functionally, and in their modes of development from those that do not. Social science cannot ignore such societies, nor can it deal with them fully if they are treated as homogeneous units. Since the sociology and cultural constitution of these societies are separately unintelligible, both must be studied together to provide an adequate analysis. In this paper I have tried to put forward a theory of pluralism that may serve to guide field work and analysis alike. The utility of this theory depends on its capacity for development.

Acknowledgment

I am very grateful to Phyllis Kaberry, University College, London, England, for detailed criticisms of this paper in its draft form.

References

BIDNEY, D. 1953. Theoretical Anthropology. Columbia Univ. Press. New York, N. Y.

BRAITHWAITE, L. 1952. Social stratification in Trinidad. Social and Economic Studies. 2(2 & 3): 3–175.

DURKHEIM, E. 1893. The Division of Labor in Society. (Translated by G. Simpson, 1933.) Free Press. Glencoe, Ill.

DURKHEIM, E. 1895. The Rules of Sociological Method. (Translated by S. A. Solway & J. H. Mueller, 1938.) Free Press. Glencoe, Ill.

FIRTH, R. 1951. Elements of Social Organization. Watts. London, England.

FORTES, M. 1953. The structure of unilineal descent groups. Am. Anthropologist. 55(1): 17–41.

FURNIVALL, J. S. 1948. Colonial Policy and Practice. Cambridge Univ. Press. London, England.

INCIDI. 1957. Ethnic and cultural pluralism in inter-tropical countries. Proc. 30th Conf. Inst. Study Differing Civilizations. Brussels, Belgium.

LEVY, M. 1952. The Structure of Society. Princeton Univ. Press. New Brunswick, N. J.

LINTON, R. 1936. The Study of Man. Century. New York, N. Y.

MALINOWSKI, B. 1944. A Scientific Theory of Culture and Other Essays. Univ. N. Carolina Press. Chapel Hill, N. C.

MORGAN, L. H. 1877. Ancient Society. Holt. New York, N. Y.

NADEL, S. F. 1951. The Foundation of Social Anthropology. Cohen & West. London, England.

OLIVIER, S. 1936. Jamaica, the Blessed Island. Faber & Faber. London, England.

RADCLIFFE-BROWN, A. R. 1950. Structure and Function in Primitive Society. Cohen & West. London, England.

REDFIELD, R. 1954. The Transformations of Primitive Society. Cornell Univ. Press. Ithaca, N. Y.

ROTTENBERG, S. 1955. Labour relations in an underdeveloped economy. Caribbean Quart. 4(1).

TUMIN, M. M. 1952. Caste in a Peasant Society. Princeton Univ. Press. Princeton, N. J.

TYLOR, E. B. 1871. Primitive Culture (1958 ed.). Harper. New York, N. Y.

SMITH, M. G. 1959. The Hausa system of social status. Africa. 29(3).

SMITH, R. T. 1956. The Negro Family in British Guiana. Routledge & Kegan Paul. London, England.

VAN LIER, R. A. J. 1950. The Nature and Development of Society in the West Indies. Inst. for the Indies. Amsterdam, Netherlands.

Discussion of the Paper

CHARLES WAGLEY (*Columbia University, New York, N.Y.*): Smith has given us a clear and thoughtful statement of the concept of social and cultural pluralism that serves admirably to set the general problem for the papers that follow. He has also clarified and refined the concept of a plural society at several crucial points. If I understand him fully, he has distinguished sociocultural differentiation resulting from social stratification from that resulting from cultural pluralism or the presence in a society of social groups carrying distinctive cultural traditions and living by different basic institutions and cultural values. He has shown that cultural pluralism is quite distinct from racial or ethnic differences, although it may well be accompanied by such differences. Very significantly, he has shown that, in a plural society, the various cultural sections share in common a set of political institutions by which the dominant section welds them into one society. I find myself in close agreement with Smith on these and many other important points that he makes in his excellent paper.

Smith's point of view shares much, I believe, with the point of view expressed by Marvin Harris and myself in a recent book on ethnic minority groups.[1] In that book we attempted to show that minority groups are subordinate segments of a complex state society set off from the other segments of that society by physical or cultural traits that are held in low esteem by the dominant segments. In addition, ethnic minorities are generally self-conscious social segments having a membership determined by a rule of descent and tending by necessity to be mainly endogamous. It would seem, then, that any society containing minority groups would perforce be a plural society. Smith thinks, and I agree, that this need not necessarily be true. The social and cultural sections of a plural society certainly are also minority groups, when the term is used, as Harris and I have used it, not in a numerical sense. However, not all minority groups are social and cultural sections. Ethnic groups or minorities may be set off from the other segments of the society simply by phenotypical physical appearance or by persistent symbols of group unity and not by basic institutional or value differences. Put another way, a minority group may become thoroughly acculturated to the dominant institutions and values of the society and yet, through a rule of descent and through endogamy (either self-imposed or imposed by other groups), remain a distinctive unit within the society.

Still, the similarity between ethnic minority groups and what Smith has called cultural and social sections of a plural society leaves room for some speculation as to their historical relationship. It is precisely the historical dimension that Smith has neglected in his treatment of the concept of plural societies.

As Harris and I have stated, "Only with the development of the State did human societies become equipped with a form of social organization which could bind masses of culturally and physically heterogeneous 'strangers' into a single social entity"[1] (p. 242). The ideal nation-state, in which the national society was physically and culturally homogeneous, has seldom been realized; most states as they expand and take form have been culturally heterogeneous, and, to a certain extent, still are. States have generally taken form by expansion of their frontiers, sometimes into contiguous territory and sometimes, as in the case of European colonial expansion, to distant regions of the earth. In the expansion of states, they incorporated "strangers" or peoples of different basic (and sometimes conflicting) cultural institutions and values. Furthermore, as Smith has indicated, large numbers of culturally distinct people have entered into states by migration, either voluntary, semivoluntary, or forced. Again, as Smith points out, this process has not been limited to the expansion of modern Europe, but occurred very early in Europe, in the Middle East, and in Africa. Smith might have added to his examples both Peru and Mexico in the New World.

Sometimes these strangers have shared in a general way the broad cultural traditions of the people who form the dominant segment of the nation of which they are now a part. This was the case with most of the immigrants into the United States. Most of them have been acculturated and assimilated with relative ease, and even those groups that have remained distinct share many of the basic institutions and values of the nation. Often, however, such strangers spoke different languages, had contrasting cultural values and traditions, were accustomed to a simpler level of technology, and even differed strikingly in phenotypical appearance from the other groups within the nation. As long as a state is made up of several groups that are numerically significant and that retain their cultural distinctiveness in terms of historically derived basic institutions and values, then that state society is a plural society, as I understand the concept. When, however, such strangers lose their cultural distinctiveness and are merely set off from the other segments of the population by symbols of group unity, by differences of socioeconomic status, or by phenotypical appearance, the state-society is no longer a plural society, although it is a state-society containing minority groups and/or social classes.

If this is true, then it seems to me that what we have called a plural society is an earlier form, or an earlier stage, of a state-society with ethnic minorities. In other words, are not the cultural and social sections of a plural society the forerunners of ethnic minorities?

Let me illustrate this point. If I understand Smith correctly, Brazil is not now a plural society. I may add that at one time in their history, both Brazil and the United States *were* plural societies. At the end of the Sixteenth Century, Brazil, for example, contained three social and cultural sections: a handful of Portuguese colonials, a mass of domesticated Indians, and *mestiços* who not only lived by very different basic institutions and values, but who spoke a different language. At that time Brazil also contained a large number of African slaves who at least in the first generations differed culturally from both the Portuguese and the Indians. By the Twentieth Century the Indian groups had become extinct or so reduced in number as to be relatively insignificant in terms of the total population, and the people of African origin have come to share, on the whole, the culturally and politically dominant traditions of the nation.

On the other hand, Guatemala is cited as an example of a plural society. This is true because Guatemala contains one and one-half million people (well over 50 per cent of the total population) who live by Spanish-Indian institutions and values and speak an Indian tongue, in contrast to the basic institutions and values of the politically dominant Ladinos. I think that we must all agree that Guatemala is still a plural society, but every year Indians become Ladinos, and Indians come to share more in the basic institutions and values with the Ladinos. How long will Guatemala continue to be a plural society?

I wonder if Smith would classify Mexico as a plural society. By far the majority of all Mexicans share the dominant national cultural institutions and values. Only about 15 per cent of the population may be considered as Indians (based upon linguistic criteria) and, in terms of their basic institutions and values, a social and cultural segment distinct from the dominant culture. How large must such a segment be to qualify a society as pluralistic? If we look back into the Mexican past, however, there was a time when Mexico was more clearly qualified as a pluralistic society; at the end of the Eighteenth Century only 0.5 per cent of the Mexican population was European or Negro. Some 30.9 per cent were *mestizo*, and more than 60 per cent were Indians. It is safe, I am sure; to interpret these figures as representing different basic cultural institutions and values. It is inescapable that Mexico was once clearly a plural society and that it has become less so in the last 150 years.

It seems to be not fortuitous that Furnivall described plural societies in the colonial regions of southeast Asia, where the numerical strength of the population, the distinctiveness and the variety of cultural traditions, as well as the colonial policies of the European nations themselves have acted as barriers to the emergence of new national institutions and values. We have excellent examples of plural societies in the new nations of Africa. It may be that such plural societies will persist for many years to come, but if the history of complex national states teaches us anything, the various sections will in time come to share the basic institutions and values of the nations, as other strangers have come to share those of the nation-states in which they live.

Finally, I propose to comment upon the applicability of the concept of plural society to the Caribbean region. It seems to me that it might be a useful concept for such societies as those of Trinidad and British Guiana, which contain numerically significant sections of East Indians who, in greater or lesser degree, retain their historically distinctive values and traditions. I cannot see, however, how the concept of plural society can be applied to such societies as those of Jamaica and other islands of the West Indies. Granted that there are vast differences in behavior and even differences in institutions and values between the peasants, local elite, and British colonials, it seems to me from my rather cursory acquaintance with Caribbean society and culture that these segments share most basic institutions and values. Certainly, as compared to the differences between European, Chinese, Hindus, Moslems, and the indigenous peoples in Burma and Java, or as compared to the differences between Indian and Ladino in Guatemala, Caribbean societies seem remarkably homogeneous. In fact, except where there are significant sections of East Indians, the Caribbean seems to contain no more pluralistic features than, say, Brazil, Venezuela, and even Portugal, where there is a tremendous gulf between the behavior, the familial institutions, and many cultural values of the peasantry and of the elite. In short, I rather wonder about the usefulness of such a concept as plural society for the Caribbean region, although, as indicated above, I find it a useful tool for other regions of the world. It seems to me at this time that, like Brazil and the United States, and even more than Mexico, Caribbean societies have already gone through the stage of a plural society.

References

1. WAGLEY, C. & M. HARRIS. 1958. Minorities in the New World. Columbia Univ. Press. New York, N. Y.

VERA RUBIN (*Research Institute for the Study of Man, New York, N. Y.*): Smith, in his paper, observes that the theory of pluralism seems to develop naturally from the basis of anthropological thinking; this, despite his quite justifiable criticism that anthropologists continue "to define culture in terms of society and vice versa." This conceptual problem stems, as Smith notes, both from the encyclopedic definition of culture that is still our scientific stock in trade, and from the global extension of the concept of society in sociological usage. A taxonomy that covers the social organization of a town, a tribe, a territory, at times a single family, strains at the conceptual seams. Webster, for example, lists twelve distinct definitions of society.[1] Kluckhohn has already noted the conceptual difficulties in the identification of society with culture,[2] and Smith's position is a scholarly contribution to this effort at theoretical clarification. Nevertheless, the distinction between society and culture is still elusive in Smith's formulation, and the circular definition seems to underlie the concept of pluralism, as when he states that "a group's institutional homogeneity involves its cultural and social homogeneity, while institutional pluralism involves corresponding cultural and social pluralism."

From this point of view, despite Smith's denial, the functional theory of institutional harmony is also implicit in the plural concept, and both culture and society seem to be viewed at a static zero point rather than in process. It is perhaps a logical step from the concept of culture as a complex whole to the functional model of society as a "perfectly balanced whole."[3] Part of the conceptual confusion arises, I believe, from our professional preoccupation with primitive societies that are relatively homogeneous and where society and culture may indeed be conterminous, and from the functionalist tendency to favor closure in cultures and to polarize equilibrium and disequilibrium as social forces. Smith confronts us with the methodological problem of studying modern societies, which, as he observes, are culturally heterogeneous and marked by ethnic and class diversities in styles of life. Smith has written previously that "where this condition of cultural plurality is found, the societies are plural societies. Where cultural homogeneity obtains, the societies are homogeneous units"[4] (p. 5). Smith, equating society with culture, now matches cultural with social heterogeneity in societies that have "dissimilar ways of life and social organization," and introduces these as intermediate systems between the primitive and the pluralistic, citing the United States as an example. Such societies, in his view, are culturally heterogeneous but not pluralistic because "life styles can and do change without involving any change in the institutional system." It is difficult to determine, however, from Smith's formulation, when an institutional variation is a life style and when it is a "basic way of life." As Smith maintains that "in a culturally divided society each cultural section has its own relatively exclusive way of life"[4] (p. 11), the boundary line between cultural heterogeneity and cultural pluralism seems blurred. Again, dealing with the process of Negro acculturation in the United States, Smith proposes the concept of plural communities, rather than of plural societies. This seems a heuristic device for fitting the facts into his model of cultural heterogeneity rather than of pluralism. The facts of the social structure of Negro life in the United States, however, would hardly fit Smith's definition of society in terms of status and role equivalences and of corresponding value systems.

Smith has written extensively on the proposition that "the kinship institutions of West Indian folk and elite form two distinct kinds of system"[4] (p. 22), and has based his typology of the West Indies as plural societies on institutional differences of this order. I quote from a recent publication by another writer on this subject: ". . . people in the different classes have distinctive courtship patterns; tend to marry within their own class and develop distinctive patterns as far as stability, fidelity and dominance are concerned after marriage.   The upper classes viewing much of the sexual behavior of the lower classes as morally abhorrent often consider it their moral duty to impose their own code as far as possible on people in the lower classes under their domination or influence."[5]   This passage happens to refer to class differences in behavior and beliefs in the United States, although it is quite reminiscent of Smith's discussion of distinctions between the "culturally different sections" of West Indian society, neither of which understands or approves the kinship institutions of the other.

Much has been written of the West Indian family and its variant types, but usually in terms of differences at a given point in time rather than in reference to developmental periods in the life of the individual and of society.   In the United States the age of marriage is delayed as one goes up the class scale; in the West Indies there are also class correlates of the age of legal marriage, and he rates of marriage are actually much higher than the statistical indices of illegitimacy would indicate.   This developmental aspect of marital unions among the lower classes where the so-called West Indian family forms predominate tends to be overlooked in theoretical polemics over the origins of the institutional variations.   Recent demographic studies by George Roberts[6,7] have done much to clarify this point and to place the vital statistics of Caribbean class differentials in rates of marriage in their time dimension rather than in a pluralistic scheme.   Recent family studies have also placed these variations in a sociocultural developmental cycle.[8,9]

This means, not that legal marriage is absent, but that it is delayed by perceived functional requirements.   In fact, the "Western" ideal of marriage is so well accepted that it has become functionally tied to a specific set of social and economic attributes, such as a costly validating feast, independent ownership of a house and furnishings, male authority, and the social role of the wife Legal marriage is present as the ideal and becomes normative, given the socioeconomic prerequisites that may come with a later age or with the requisite status of the male.[8,9]   In another context, Meyer Fortes has recently stated: "When it is recognized that these so-called types are in fact phases in the developmental cycle of a single general form for each society, the confusion vanishes."[10]

Whether we look at differences in the family complex, in education and occupation, and so forth, a review of the expanding literature on social class organization in the United States seems to parallel Smith's model for a pluralistic framework, point for point.   The studies made clearly reveal correlations between social class affiliation and cultural forms in the institutions that Smith has cited in various papers.   These correlations include differences in material culture, associations, recreational patterns, types of crime, years of schooling and even, apparently, the epidemiology of mental disorders.[11-16]   Nevertheless, Smith does not consider the United States a pluralistic society, but a culturally heterogeneous one.   Why should this matter be treated as pluralistic in the Caribbean but heterogeneous in the United States?   In terms of some of his criteria of pluralism, such as racism, resort to escapist religious cults, the rise of charismatic leaders, instability, and coresidence, parallels surely exist in both areas. It is relevant therefore to ask Smith: When is a culturally heterogeneous society also pluralistic? Furnivall's observations in southeast Asia and Smith's formulation for the Caribbean would tend to indicate that the concept of pluralism is applied exclusively in the special conditions of conquest or of colonial societies in which an intrusive foreign minority is politically dominant and remains culturally as well as socially exclusive from the indigenous population. Aside from the political implications, which are dealt with in other papers, I propose to examine this briefly from the functional point of view of social structure and value systems in the Caribbean, since Smith holds that where the boundaries of cultural and social sections correspond, the discontinuity of value systems is most extreme. However, Smith is of the opinion that in the West Indies the medley of social value systems rules out the value consensus that is prerequisite for any status continuum, and goes on to say that to determine whether such differences exist is a simple matter of empirical research.

Recently an island-wide study was undertaken of the attitudes and values of secondary school youth representing all segments of the population in Trinidad.* Trinidad is one of the most heterogeneous of Caribbean societies, but has been described along a continuum ranging from assimilationistic to pluralistic. Observed behavior reveals many common cultural denominators but, with some knowledge of the area, it is obvious that extremes of sociocultural differentiation exist. The survey data reveal the expected diversity in value systems by social class and ethnic background. However, a significant degree of common aspirations and values related to the core culture is also evident. The replies, which are unstructured, fall into three types: regularities by social class, regularities related to ethnic background, and regularities related to the common goals of mobility regardless of class or ethnic background. For both East Indian and Creole youth in Trinidad there is a core of modal values related to levels of aspiration, to perception of the opportunity structure, and to status symbols in a national frame of reference. This is evident in most of the areas of the institutional system that Smith defines as the core culture: kinship, education, religion, property, sodalities, economy, recreation, and law. The choice of occupational alternatives falls largely into the same clusters. In the kinship subsystem, marriage and family life are universal choices, with emphasis on the family of procreation. Concepts of household authority overwhelmingly indicate equality as an ideal. This pattern differs from the matricentric lower-class Creole family types, the ideally paternalistic Creole middle-class family, and the paternalistic East Indian family structure. The modal value of the youth, regardless of class or ethnic background, reflects the Western concept of bilaterality in family authority.

Similarly with regard to kernel-of-truth hypotheses about national character: the Creole is supposed to prefer immediate gratification to sacrifice for long-range goals, while the East Indian is supposedly more willing to sacrifice

* The survey in Trinidad was carried out in 1957 by myself and Ira Greiff, Fellow of the Program for the Study of Man in the Tropics, which is a joint program of the Department of Anthropology of Columbia University and the Research Institute for the Study of Man (RISM), New York, N. Y. Intensive analysis of the data, with the assistance of Marisa Zavalloni of RISM, is currently under way.

for long-range goals. The autobiographies of these young people make it quite clear, however, that there is a high correlation between achievement goals and the perceived need for self-reliance, and that sacrifice of immediate gratifications for future rewards cross-cuts all social and cultural segments of the group. Existential differences in material culture are also cross-cut by common aspirations for material achievement beyond the level of the parents and shared goals of Westernized styles of life.

It would be a serious error, of course, to overlook ethnic and social class differences in ethos; however, if only the polarities of ethnic differentiation were to be abstracted, one would make the equally serious error of overlooking the convergence of values and shared collective goals. It is necessary to take an over-all view, then, whether we are to be concerned with theory or methodology or social action, as Smith suggests. Undeniable social tensions exist in the society, accompanied by conscious clinging to distinctive cultural symbols and ethnically based aspirations. Nevertheless, the political changes taking place and the broadening opportunity structure are creating integrative mechanisms for the society. Smith points out that institutionally homogeneous societies develop a variety of institutional motivations towards conformity with social norms. This need not necessarily presuppose cultural homogeneity. In a society where status may be achieved and where channels for mobility are broadened, the ideal values tend to be perceived as desired forms of behavior and, ultimately, to be incorporated in the ways of life of different segments, although multicultural traditions may persist at different levels of integration.

Smith has previously taken a historical view of the development of social structure in the British Caribbean and has noted that in the 1820s "Acculturation by adoption of white behavior and institutions was a necessary aspect of the preoccupation with improvement of status for coloured males."[17] In a colonial society the problems of assimilation and social mobility are closely linked, yet this assimilative process in the West Indies has been going on for more than a century, and the emergence of a mulatto middle class, although relatively small, was indicative of the adoption of a Westernized value system where the means of status achievement were available.

The present situation in the British West Indies is one of rapid change in social structure, national identifications, and value systems as a concomitant of the changing political situation. Since these are significant for the formation of a national society and a national culture, the study of social process calls for a study of emergent collective goals in terms of individual and group motivations.

Finally, Smith's view of cultural homogeneity as a condition of societal homogeneity may seem Utopian in the sense that such a society would not only eliminate cultural differences but provide a harmonious setting in which there is no conflict of interests. Such a Utopia is neither in the line of evolutionary trends to greater complexity and heterogeneity, nor is it a necessary prerequisite for an integrated social order. We may have racial and cultural pluralism in a single territorial unit without conflict where there is an opportunity through communication and through channels of mobility for core values and desired statuses to be diffused to the various segments of the social structure.

The "institutional" differences that Smith describes for the "three culturally distinct sections"[17,18] are differences of a subcultural order similar to those characteristic of heterogeneous societies.   Even in the case of Trinidad, where the most striking diversity may be found, the differences are essentially cultural.   The East Indians have been dependent on the sugar estates, and the estates dependent on the East Indians as a labor force, for more than a century. East Indian and Creole are involved in the same economy and the same political and legal structure, and are reacting to the same societal imperatives: they are part of a national system of action, culturally distinct in many ways, but socially interdependent.   In Smith's exposition of pluralism, the institutional system is used as the framework of both culture and society.   Although there is necessarily interdependence and overlapping of socio-cultural phenomena, a tautological model cannot serve to distinguish conceptually different entities. This task still remains for social science to undertake.

Whether the theoretical model of pluralism is a useful research framework for examining the unity and diversity of the Caribbean remains to be established.   I believe, however, that a conceptual model that limits research to either an assimilationistic or a pluralistic framework can provide only limited explanations of culture change.   Meanwhile, we are fortunate to have Smith's stimulating paper, which challenges us to hard thinking about the nature of society and the nature of culture.   How do we define them?   How do we study them?

References

1. WEBSTER'S NEW INTERNATIONAL DICTIONARY OF THE ENGLISH LANGUAGE. 1946. 2nd ed., unabridged.   Merriam,   Springfield, Mass.
2. KLUCKHOHN, C.   1954.   *In* Toward a General Theory of Action.   Parsons and Shils, Eds. Harvard Univ. Press.   Cambridge, Mass.
3. RICHARDS, A.   1957.   Man and Culture: an Evaluation of the Work of Malinowski.   R. Firth, Ed.   Routledge & Kegan Paul.   London, England.
4. SMITH, M. G.   1957.   Ethnic and cultural pluralism in the British Caribbean.   Working paper for the 30th study session.   Intern. Inst. Differing Civilizations.   London, England.
5. PACKARD, V.   1959.   The Status Seekers. : 153–154.   McKay.   New York, N. Y.
6. ROBERTS, G.   1955.   Some aspects of mating and fertility in the West Indies.   Population Studies. 8(3).
7. ROBERTS, G.   Mating and Fertility in Trinidad.   In preparation.
8. CLARKE, E.   1957.   My Mother Who Fathered Me.   Allen & Unwin.   London, England.
9. SMITH, R. T.   1956.   The Negro Family in British Guiana.   Routledge & Kegan Paul. London, England.
10. FORTES, M.   1958.   *Introduction to* The Developmental Cycle in Domestic Groups. : 3. J. Goody, Ed.   Cambridge Univ. Press.   Cambridge, England.
11. WARNER, W. L.   1944.   Who Shall Be Educated?   Harpers.   New York, N. Y.
12. HOLLINGSHEAD, A.   1945.   Elmtown's Youth.   Wiley.   New York, N. Y.
13. WHYTE, W. F.   1956.   Streetcorner Society.   Univ. Chicago Press.   Chicago, Ill.
14. CLAUSEN, J. A.   1956.   Sociology and the Field of Mental Health.   Russell Sage Foundation.   New York, N. Y.
15. HOLLINGSHEAD, A. B. & F. C. REDLICH.   1958.   Social Class and Mental Illness.   Wiley. New York, N. Y.
16. SUTHERLAND, E. H.   1940.   White collar criminality.   Am. Sociol. Rev. 5.
17. SMITH, M. G.   1953.   Social structure in the British Caribbean about 1820.   Social and Economic Studies. 1(4): 55–79.
18. SMITH, M. G.   1955.   Framework for Caribbean Studies.   Univ. Coll. West Indies Extra-Mural Dept.   Mona, Jamaica, West Indies.

THE RANGE AND VARIATION OF CARIBBEAN SOCIETIES

David Lowenthal

American Geographical Society, New York, N. Y.

Pluralistic circumstances affect Caribbean societies in a variety of ways. No society is altogether plural or even heterogeneous; if it were, it would not be a society at all, but only an assemblage of functionally unrelated communities. No society entirely lacks institutional diversity; if it did, it would be so homogeneous that it could not survive in any environment. Between these theoretical extremes, however, there is a continuum of possible sociocultural configurations. Some societies exhibit more, or different, evidences of pluralism than others. Aspects and combinations of pluralism vary from place to place in intensity, in structure and interrelatedness, in degree of formal institutionalization, in the extent to which they are locally apprehended, in historical stability, and in functional import. In any particular society, for example, one or more determinants of social stratification, such as color, descent, wealth, occupation, age, or sex, may inhibit freedom of choice or expression more or less completely in various realms of activity.

Elsewhere in this monograph Smith has set a theoretical framework; I shall consider how to assess the varieties of sociocultural diversity that actually do occur within West Indian societies. I limit myself to the islands because I know them best, and because their insularity suggests a manageable scheme for analysis. I use the word "diversity" rather than "pluralism" advisedly. The distinction Smith makes between heterogeneous and plural is a valid one, but it is difficult to use. At just what point do differences in ways of life become so incompatible as to make a minority a separate cultural section? How does one decide whether stylistic similarities conceal fundamental diversities? Are the basic institutions the same in one society as in another, and have they always the same relative importance? How much social mobility, actual or perceived, makes a plural society merely heterogeneous? How large must an institutionally distinctive minority be to qualify the whole society as plural rather than merely pluralistic, and does the size of the group effectively measure its significance?[1] It appears to me that nonplural societies grade imperceptibly into plural ones. In any case, diversity is a necessary element of pluralism. This paper concerns both concepts.

To compare societies, one must first decide what one means by a society. No functional hierarchy of social groups properly fits circumstances throughout the West Indies. The role of the family, the estate, the parish, the society, the empire, or indeed of any social or territorial unit, is here crucial, there trivial; its scope or size here extensive, there narrow. Smith's definition of societies as "territorially distinct units having their own governmental institutions" establishes sufficient and perhaps necessary criteria, but does not actually identify them; how potent or inclusive need governmental institutions be to qualify a social unit as a society? I shall instead experiment with an arbitrary geographical measure.

To my mind, the most apposite realm for societies in the West Indies is the island. There are obvious exceptions: Hispaniola and St. Martin, for example, both divided by sovereignty. However, the island does less violence to social reality, involves less Procrustean chopping and stretching than any other topographic category, because insularity is a basic fact of life. An island is a world, to use Selvon's title.[2] The network of social relations seldom survives the sea. Polynesians and Melanesians, more at home with the ocean, make it a highway instead of a barrier; but for West Indians (save, perhaps, in French Martinique and Guadeloupe) the island is in most contexts the most compelling areal symbol. A man who says, "I am a Jamaican," or "I am a Barbadian," is very likely expressing the broadest allegiance he knows.[3]

Each of the smaller islands also has special characteristics, a unique self-image, and a particular view of all the others. What is more, large and small islands are equally conscious of their individuality. Jamaican and Montserratian parochialisms are much alike, although one country has 1,700,000 people and the other only 14,000. Physical insularity intensifies a sense of belonging within each island, whatever its size. To be sure, Jamaicans who live in the Blue Mountains are unlike inhabitants of the Cockpit Country, and those who dwell in Kingston have little in common with people on Frome sugar estate at the western end of the island. However, these differences do not divide Jamaica into one hundred separate Montserrats; indeed, not even into two or three.

Communities do exist, of course, along with neighborhood self-consciousness, but these microcosms are hard to identify; self-sufficient in no respect, they are socially and culturally integrated with island society as a whole.[4-6] West Indian communities cannot be understood as worlds in themselves. To be sure, community organization and subregional ties are more important in some islands than in others, though not necessarily in the largest or most populous of them. Barbados, with 230,000 people, is practically one geographical community, despite fairly rigid class barriers, owing to its excellent road network and its historic cultural homogeneity. Dominica, on the other hand, with only 65,000 people, has considerable village and local self-consciousness because population centers are isolated by difficult topography and poor communications and, in part, because of the collapse of the plantation economy that once supported island-wide social institutions. In Jamaica and in Trinidad, physical and social distance notwithstanding, island feeling prevails over local and sectional interests, partly because island radio and newspapers, island government and politics, are omnipresent. However, these unifying forces are weaker in an island such as St. Vincent and practically nonexistent on Bequia, in the Grenadines. One can walk around Bequia in a day, but its 4000 inhabitants include 3 mutually exclusive communities. On the other hand, the web of kinship brings the 8000 people in nearby Carriacou into a close network of associations.

The administrative status of these and other tiny islands is no gauge to the local state of mind. Many constituent parts of The West Indies federation are themselves island groups: Trinidad includes Tobago, St. Kitts includes Nevis and Anguilla, Antigua has Barbuda, St. Vincent and Grenada share the Grenadines, and both Jamaica and the federation are involved with the Cayman Islands and the Turks and Caicos Islands. Long association or political expediency might promote unit solidarity, but most of these unions are fortuitous or recent; a man from Tobago is apt to think of himself as a Tobagonian, not as a Trinidadian. The primary geographical identification is that with the island, no matter how small or dependent it may be. St. Kitts and Nevis are only 2 miles apart and are economically interdependent (Nevis grows food for Kittician sugar plantations), but the inhabitants of each island seldom have a good word to say for the other, and both snub Anguillans, who are 60 miles away and a different kind of folk entirely, in their own view and in reality. Grenada and its dependency, Carriacou, likewise have little in common; the difference between the hierarchical social structure of the former and the egalitarianism of the latter is just one of many vital contrasts.[7] At the same time, Carriacou and its own tiny dependency, Petit Martinique, are quite dissimilar; the Petit Martiniquaise would seldom call himself a Carriacouan any more than he would a Grenadian. Only the smallest islands and those used as resorts by the "mainlanders" lack this overriding sense of individuality. One scholar termed Lesser Antillean feeling "a case of insular psychology gone mad."[8]

A sense of individuality does not, of itself, suffice to make an island a society. West Indian islands are not discrete social organisms; they are both more and less than this. There are inter-island family and economic ties throughout the eastern Caribbean. Many small-island elite live elsewhere: Martiniquaise own Guadeloupe *sucreries*, important Tobagonians reside in Trinidad, and Petit Martinique is governed by a Grenadian District Officer who visits once a week from Carriacou. However, the social institutions of Jamaica (not just its government) are similarly truncated with respect to Port of Spain and London. Similar qualifications limit most societies. Only the largest nations are entirely self-governing, and even these have myriad links with other peoples: property owned abroad, social, economic, and religious enclaves and exclaves.

The choice of islands as social units is statistically as well as methodologically convenient. There are 51 Caribbean islands of whose essential social integrity I am reasonably certain: each of them is an "enduring, cooperating social group so functioning as to maintain and perpetuate itself."[9] The units range in population from Cuba, with 6,500,000 people, to Mayreau, one of the St. Vincent Grenadines, with 250. Almost nine tenths of the 18,700,000 West Indians live in societies larger than 1,000,000 people. Eight per cent inhabit societies ranging from 100,000 to 1,000,000, 4 per cent in societies smaller than 100,000. The picture is quite different when one takes social units as the measure. Only 5 societies (one tenth of the total) have more than 1,000,000 people; 5 others have between 100,000 and 1,000,000 each, while 41 societies are smaller than 100,000. Most of these (53 per cent of all the social units in the West Indies) have fewer than 10,000 people each, even though together these small-islanders comprise less than 0.5 per cent of the Caribbean population. Of the islands having populations of less than 10,000, two thirds have less than 2500 inhabitants apiece. In other words, more than one half of all West Indians live in a society larger than 3,000,000 (Cuba or Haiti); but the mean population per society is 366,000 (one half again as many as Barbados), while the mode is a society of only 7000 persons (about the size of Anguilla).

The small size of most West Indian societies has a significant bearing on individual heterogeneity and pluralism. Unless they are completely cut off from the modern world, social groups with fewer than 100,000 people face many special problems: a "colonial" relationship with some larger territory or, in the case of The West Indies federation, with a federal government; a dearth of trained men and of leaders for external as well as for local governmental positions; a lack of cultural focus; and a narrow, conservative outlook and sometimes pathological sensitivity to criticism, exacerbated by small-island feuds and a claustrophobic absence of privacy. Common metropolitan bonds, like economic interests, and analogous social cleavages result in superficial but trivial similarities. Jealousies, rivalries, fears, and, above all, mutual ignorance, tend to make each small island a museum in which archaic distinctions are carefully preserved. It is precisely because so many of the West Indian islands are isolated and miniscule that they exhibit pluralistic features. Geographical and sociocultural heterogeneity reinforce each other.

Colonial status, a frequent feature of pluralism, is likewise linked both with insularity and with small size. It is no accident that, of the 51 West Indian societies, only the 3 most populous are politically independent: that is, ruled by their own elites, not by outsiders. The next largest one, Puerto Rico, is semi-autonomous. The remainder are in effect colonial, whatever their formal status. A high proportion of the smallest territories (those with populations under 40,000) endure double colonialism as dependencies of dependencies. Indeed, some of the Grenadines are dependencies of dependencies of dependencies. However, neither government nor size is an infallible indicator of sociocultural heterogeneity, much less of pluralism.

There are, however, several more direct approaches to an appraisal of the range of West Indian societies. One method, inherent in Smith's paper, is holistic and functional: to assess the general condition of each society and rank it according to intensity of pluralism, that is, the degree of incompatibility or antagonism between the different cultural sections. This approach demands analysis not of institutional differentiation but rather of the strains to which it leads: the extent to which government is maintained by force rather than by consent; the degree to which the activities and aims of each cultural section offset or negate those of other sections. What is crucial is the relationship between the cultural sections.

Not every disagreement or difference is evidence of pluralism, however, nor is discord an infallible yardstick. Horizontal plural societies, in which cultural sections are not hierarchically arranged, display little strain if there is little contact between the sections. On the other hand, apparent agreement on goals and values in stratified societies is not necessarily an indication that pluralism, much less tension, is absent. The fact that each cultural section in British West Indian societies parades loyalty to the Crown, avoids manual labor when possible, admires white skin, and fancies Christian marriage as an ideal does not indicate that they share a basic way of life or common institutional systems, but rather that each strives to advance by emulating the perceived behavior of the ruling section and by discrediting its own circumstances and ways of life. Cultural unity may mask institutional diversity. What is more, horizontal and vertical pluralism have disparate origins, careers, and terminations. When differences between nonstratified sections become intolerable, partition, as in Israel and to some extent in Canada, is a likely result, while stratified societies, such as that of Haiti, are more apt to suffer revolution.

When one considers that some West Indian societies (notably Trinidad, British Guiana, Surinam, and St. Croix) contain important horizontal as well as vertical sections, and that the character and role of each is constantly shifting, the difficulty of judging the intensity of pluralism becomes evident.[10] A pragmatic, comparative assessment of the incompatibility of sociocultural sections demands prophecy as well as omniscience.

A second approach involves a holistic but synthetic type of analysis. This is to ascertain the extent of sociocultural heterogeneity in each society and then compare the societies with each other, starting, perhaps, with pairs of approximately equal size: Barbados and Guadeloupe, Aruba and Antigua, St. Croix and Montserrat, Bonaire and Bequia, St. Barthélemy and Providencia, Union and Saba. This method raises several questions. For one, heterogeneity is not pluralism; cultural diversity often coexists with institutional unity. Nevertheless, without heterogeneity there can hardly be pluralism; they are correlated. To rank societies according to their degree of internal diversity is certainly relevant to a study of pluralism.

A more serious difficulty is that no one has devised a formula for adding up different sorts of diversity. How many points does one allot to this or that amount of ethnic heterogeneity, how many points to various differences in rural and urban living patterns, how many to property and kinship systems? Social and cultural elements can hardly be combined quantitatively for any society, let alone for more than one. Any general comparison must be essentially impressionistic, as much a work of art as a product of science. This is probably why it is seldom undertaken in the Caribbean, or elsewhere, except by travelers, novelists, and poets. Social scientists usually find the task temperamentally disagreeable. Nevertheless, we need more such studies by competent observers, especially studies comparing British, French, and Dutch dependencies.

The third approach is particularistic and synthetic. This method is to examine specific aspects of society and culture and to study the range and variation of each throughout the West Indies. This approach yields no generalizations about any particular society as a whole, but it has its uses, nonetheless, and it has the advantage of being possible. It has been tried, for various traits, at various levels of sophistication, and with various degrees of success by Proudfoot[11] for the British and American dependencies; by Kruijer[12] for St. Eustatius, St. Maarten, and St. Thomas; by the Keurs[13] for the Netherlands Windward Islands; by M. G. Smith[7] for Grenada and Carriacou; and by Cumper[14] for the British Caribbean generally. Two kinds of study are needed: detailed comparisons of all facets of life in a few societies, and broad surveys of particular traits and institutional subsystems for the whole area. Class and color configurations; the roles of minor ethnic groups; metropolitan policies, influences, and images; ecological and economic patterns; religious, legal, and educational systems; mating and kinship; and other aspects of culture and society should be separately scrutinized for each and compared for all West Indian societies.

Let us consider color-class stratification. The classic white-colored-black system of status ranking,[15-17] significant in many West Indian societies, is unimportant in others.   In Cuba, the Dominican Republic, and Puerto Rico, where Negroes are a fairly small minority, the elite is hardly distinguishable, in terms of color, from most of the lower class.   Many of the smallest West Indian societies are virtually homogeneous with respect to race and color: Carriacou, San·Andrés, St. Eustatius, Barbuda, and Mayreau being almost entirely Negro communities, and St. Barthélemy being almost entirely white.

Elsewhere the pattern and the significance of color heterogeneity vary profoundly.   Warner views status systems based on color as the most inclusive and rigid form of social stratification, one in which the position of the individual is fixed and determined by birth.[18]   In few Caribbean societies, however, do color-class differences retain these castelike attributes; all have some measure of mobility and assimilation.   The white békés of Guadeloupe and Martinique, an endogamous and genealogically self-conscious group, form a closed elite (closed to metropolitan and other Antillean whites as well as to gens de couleur) at the summit of an otherwise open class structure.   Until recently the mulatto elite in Haiti occupied a similar position.   In many of the smaller islands, such as Saba, Bequia, and La Désirade, black, colored and, when present, white groups tend to form separate communities rather than ranked sections within the same community; despite some status difference, each group is essentially classless.[19]   In still other societies (St. Croix, St. Thomas, Aruba) special economic circumstances such as tourism or oil refining, together with continual in- and out-migration and skewed age and sex distributions, obscure the color-class pattern and diminish its functional significance.

Even where color-class hierarchies clearly operate, it is difficult to estimate how important they are.   Barbados is most self-conscious about color-class distinctions, but other British Caribbean social hierarchies may well be more rigid.   Too little is known of the different character and varying roles of the elite in, for example, Barbados, where many whites are not members of it; in Trinidad, where it is deeply divided by nationality; and in Grenada and Dominica, where it is becoming predominantly light-colored.   We need comparative studies of the elites of each society in terms of their ethnic and social origins, numbers, proportions to the total population, residential patterns, occupational and economic roles, uniformity or diversity of circumstances, internal solidarity, extent of identification with the whole society (higher in Barbados, for example, than in Trinidad and St. Vincent), affluence relative to others, control of political, educational, and religious institutions, and stereotypes and self-images of the rest of the population.

We also need comparative studies of peoples partly or wholly outside the stratified social order.   The extent to which East Indians in Trinidad, British Guiana, and Surinam have been Creolized is debated in this monograph, as it probably will be perennially, but few will deny that these East Indians constitute a separate cultural section.   This is not true of East Indians in other West Indian societies, who are generally assimilated to, sometimes integrated with, the Creole lower class.[20]   Is it because these East Indians are much smaller minorities (7 per cent in Guadeloupe, less everywhere else)?   East Indian minorities (predominantly urban, to be sure) in other parts of the world maintain separate social organizations.

The same is substantially true of other ethnic minorities in the West Indies. The Chinese, Portuguese, and Syrian communities, together do not account for 3 per cent of the population of any West Indian territory, but in many of them they play significant roles.[21]   Their virtual monopoly of retail trade in some societies represents, for the Creole majority, a social truncation as serious, perhaps, as the truncation of political functions involved in colonial relationships.   On the other hand, the presence of certain minorities may serve to ease other status relationships.   If Syrian merchants, for example, are accepted to any extent by the elite, the middle class is also apt to find areas of acceptance; on the other hand, rejection of these "foreign" elements may promote an awareness of common outlook among Europeans and Creoles.*

It is interesting that all these West Indian minorities have achieved a measure of economic success; however much or little they fit into the general social order, they are not at the bottom of it.   There are no West Indian counterparts to the Negroes and Puerto Ricans in northern cities of the United States, the eta in Japan, or the Albanians in Belgrade, who perform certain menial tasks that are virtually badges of caste.   Until recently the few Javanese in Paramaribo, Surinam, were the only garbage collectors and sewer cleaners, but today they abjure such occupations.   Convicts used to perform similar services in French Guiana until the termination of the penal establishment there.

Data are needed from each West Indian society about all of these minorities and about their relative and absolute numbers, their economic roles, and the extent to which they remain aloof from, or merge into, the general social order.

The extent of linguistic differentiation within West Indian societies similarly illustrates their diversity.   Language is both a symbol of and an adjunct to status.   What proportion in each society speaks the "standard" tongue, and on what occasions?   How different is the Creolese variant in pronunciation, vocabulary, and grammar?   How do various sections of the population feel and act about the use of patois?   There are several fundamentally different situations.[22,23]   In most societies the patois is a dialect of the language of the educated, but in Dominica, St. Lucia, Curaçao, and Surinam the local patois has no relation whatever to the official prestige tongue; the two are mutually unintelligible.   Linguistic differentiation is thus formalized, and the gulf between social classes is greater than in societies where the patois is a variant of the metropolitan language.   The opposite is true where the lingua franca derives from a European language that is more widely spoken in the region than the local official language.   In the English-speaking Netherlands Windward Islands and, to some extent, in San Andrés and Providencia, linguistic differentiation tends to break down rather than to reinforce social stratification, because the values associated with the language of the majority outweigh the prestige associated with metropolitan Dutch or Spanish.

To describe the range and diversity of social institutions and cultural forms is not enough, however; one must also account for them.   How is it that pluralism affects one society more than another?   How can one explain heterogeneity in one place and homogeneity in another?   Why are certain traits diverse in this place and uniform in that one?   Answers to such questions

* I am indebted to Rhoda Métraux, Institute for Intercultural Studies, New York, N. Y., for this suggestion.

require comparative analysis, to avoid oversimplified or excessively functional explanations.

Let me illustrate with data on the European Guianas.[24] Here, I think, comparisons have special validity because these territories are contiguous, because their inhabited areas are remarkably alike physically, and because their settlement for a long time followed similar models, particularly in Surinam and British Guiana, which were drained and diked for plantation agriculture along the same lines until the late Eighteenth Century.

Ethnic heterogeneity characterizes both British Guiana and Surinam, principally because many indentured laborers were brought in after the emancipation of the slaves. One half the population of each territory today is of Asian origin, virtually all Indian in British Guiana, while three tenths is Indian and two tenths Javanese in Surinam. However, Surinamese society is generally less integrated. In British Guiana, East Indian ways of life have become more and more similar to those of other rural or urban folk, while in Surinam the Creoles, Hindustanis, and Javanese for the most part have their own villages, languages, and even customary garb. British Guianese East Indians refer to their compatriots in Surinam as "good" Indians, that is, closer adherents of old-country fashion and ritual (personal communication from C. Jayawardena). Unlike British Guianese, Surinamers do not hesitate to assert their separate ethnic interests; political parties are avowedly divided along racial and religious lines; there is scarcely any sense of a general Surinam society. Occupational and rural-urban ethnic differentiation are also more pronounced in Surinam. Three fourths of the Creole population is urban, compared with less than one half in British Guiana, and most of Surinam's rural Creoles are concentrated within a few districts.

Several factors help to account for these differences. For one, slavery lasted twenty-five years longer in Surinam than in British Guiana. In the interim many slaves fled the country and, when emancipation finally came, in 1863, the Negroes still left on Surinam estates were not willing to wait out an additional decade of indenture. In British Guiana, many former slaves pooled their savings to buy up estates and turned to subsistence agriculture; in Surinam, most of them moved off the land.

The delay of emancipation also retarded the introduction of indentured workers. East Indians began to enter British Guiana as early as 1841, but did not reach Surinam until after 1873, and the Javanese came there still later, between 1891 and 1939. Neither group in Surinam has had as long to become assimilated as have the East Indians of British Guiana. Moreover, the East Indians of Surinam (known there as Hindustanis) have found acculturation more difficult for lack of a continuing tie with certain British institutions and aspects of culture. Besides, there is little in common between the Hindustanis and the Javanese. Many of the latter are still first-generation immigrants, for the most part content with their alien status as Indonesian citizens, and are regarded as clannish and unenterprising by Europeans, Creoles, and Hindustanis alike.

Dutch colonial policy is partly responsible for the fact that Surinam's rural villages are, by and large, more homogeneous racially than those of British Guiana. Until after the Second World War the Surinam government promoted residential segregation by leasing abandoned estates to ethnic groups. This practice is now disavowed, but efforts to promote integration have had little success, perhaps because many people still believe, at heart, that the different races simply will not work or live well together.

The linguistic situation displays similar segmentation. In British Guiana English is both the vernacular and the prestige language of the educated, but in Surinam the common Creole tongue (*Taki-Taki*, an amalgam of African, English, and other elements) is utterly unlike the official, upper-class Dutch. Dutch is unimportant elsewhere in America, and *Taki-Taki* is incomprehensible outside Surinam, so it is little wonder that Javanese and Hindustanis prefer to retain their own, more widely spoken, languages. Even the Creoles are divided, some prefering Dutch, others promoting *Taki-Taki* as their "own" tongue, that is, as an appurtenance of nationalism. Lacking a viable common language, Surinam is unlikely to reach a level of social or cultural integration comparable to that in British Guiana, even should Surinamers desire it.

These features represent, of course, only one aspect of social organization in the Guianas. Analogous contrasts can be drawn with respect to the varieties of stratification within the Creole groups and the roles of the European and other minorities. Whatever point of departure one selects, society and culture can be understood best, as Furnivall remarked of colonial practice, when studied both comparatively and historically.[25]

References

1. HALLOWELL, A. I. 1957. The impact of the American Indian on American culture. Am. Anthropol. **59**: 201–217.
2. SELVON, S. 1955. An Island is a World. MacGibbon & Kee. London, England.
3. LOWENTHAL, D. 1958. The West Indies chooses a capital. Geographical Rev. **48**: 336–364.
4. SMITH, M. G. 1956. Community organization in rural Jamaica. Social and Economic Studies. **5**: 295–312.
5. SMITH, R. T. 1956. The Negro Family in British Guiana. Routledge & Kegan Paul. London, England.
6. WAGLEY, C. Recent studies of Caribbean local societies. *In* The Caribbean: Natural Resources. A. C. Wilgus, Ed. Univ. Florida Press. Gainesville, Fla. To be published.
7. SMITH, M. G. Kinship and Community in Carriacou. To be published.
8. WHITBECK, R. H. 1933. The Lesser Antilles—past and present. Ann. Assoc. Am. Geographers. **23**: 25.
9. WEBSTER'S NEW COLLEGIATE DICTIONARY. 1947. Society (def. No. 7). Merriam. Springfield, Mass.
10. BROOKFIELD, H. C. 1958. Pluralism and geography in Mauritius. Geograph. Studies. **5**: 3–19.
11. PROUDFOOT, M. 1954. Britain and the United States in the Caribbean; a Comparative Study in Methods of Development. Faber & Faber. London, England.
12. KRUIJER, G. J. 1953. Saint Martin and Saint Eustatius Negroes as compared with those of Saint Thomas: a study of personality and culture. West-Indische Gids. **35**: 225–237.
13. KEUR, J. & D. KEUR. Windward Children. van Gorcum. Assen, Netherlands. To be published.
14. CUMPER, G. 1949. Social Structure of the British Caribbean (Excluding Jamaica). Parts 1, 2, 3. Extra-Mural Dept., Univ. Coll. West Indies. Mona, Jamaica, West Indies.
15. SMITH, M. G. 1955. A Framework for Caribbean Studies. : 47–50. Extra-Mural Dept. Univ. Coll. West Indies. Mona, Jamaica, West Indies.
16. SMITH, M. G. 1957. Ethnic and cultural pluralism in the British Caribbean. Intern. Inst. Differing Civilizations. Lisbon, Portugal.

17. BRAITHWAITE, L. 1953. Social stratification in Trinidad. Social and Economic Studies. **2:** 5–175.
18. WARNER, W. L. 1957. The study of social stratification. *In* Review of Sociology: Analysis of a Decade. : 234–235. J. B. Gittler, Ed. Wiley. New York, N. Y.
19. LASSERRE, G. 1957. La Désirade, petite île guadeloupéenne. Cahiers d'Outre-Mer. **10:** 325–366.
20. LASSERRE, G. 1953. Les "Indiens" de Guadeloupe. Cahiers d'Outre-Mer. **6:** 128–158.
21. FRIED, M. H. 1958. The Chinese in the British Caribbean. *In* Colloquium on Overseas Chinese. : 49–58. M. H. Fried, Ed. Intern. Secretariat, Inst. Pacific Relations. New York, N. Y.
22. LE PAGE, R. B. 1955. The language problem of the British Caribbean. Caribbean Quart. **4:** 40–49.
23. EFRON, E. 1954. French and Creole patois in Haiti. Caribbean Quart. **4:** 199–213.
24. LOWENTHAL, D. 1960. Population contrasts in the Guianas. Geographical Rev. **50:** 41–59.
25. FURNIVALL, J. S. 1948. Colonial Policy and Practice: a Comparative Study of Burma and Netherlands India. : 9–10. Cambridge Univ. Press. Cambridge, England.

METROPOLITAN INFLUENCES IN THE CARIBBEAN: THE NETHERLANDS ANTILLES

Dorothy L. Keur

Hunter College, New York, N. Y.

Geographic Location

The Netherlands Antilles comprise 6 islands divided geographically into 2 groups; the so-called A-B-C group (Aruba, Bonaire, and Curaçao) and the Windwards (St. Maarten, St. Eustatius, and Saba), lying south and east of the Virgin Islands in the arc of islands designated by the British as the Leeward Islands. The A-B-C group, lying just north of Venezuela, is 550 miles distant from the Dutch Windwards geographically and even further in ethos. I discuss here the Dutch Windwards in regard to the role of the mother country in their life and pluralistic culture, since lack of space prevents consideration of the very different and much more complex situation in Curaçao and Aruba.

Past History

Beginning in the Fifteenth Century, for about 200 years the history of the Dutch West India Company made a permanent imprint on the character of the Dutch Windwards. With the company's particular form of mercantilism and emphasis on commerce and lucrative trade (especially foodstuffs, salt, contraband arms to the American revolutionists, and above all, slaves) there resulted a less intensive and extensive plantation economy than elsewhere in the Caribbean. Merchant members of the company and some independent entrepreneurs may have become wealthy, but whatever the profits, they were not utilized for the local development of island plantations. Moreover, ecologic conditions abetted this trend away from cultivation by providing a great salt pond for ready exploitation on St. Maarten, extremely steep topography on Saba, and serious periodic droughts on St. Eustatius, forming natural barriers, though not culturally insurmountable ones, to successful cultivation of cash crops. The islands are also too small in area to support any sizable white planters' group. Dutch St. Maarten is 13.5 square miles in area, St. Eustatius 8.2, and Saba only 6.

Today no such Dutch aristocracy remains to form a stable part of island society. Hence the natives are deprived of a source of important contact with interpreters of certain aspects of Netherlands life. Both Negroes and non-Dutch white natives now refer, somewhat nostalgically and certainly in idealistic terms, to those "fine old Dutch families," who used to own most of the land and ruled it with a firm but just hand. Memory accords high prestige to these bearers of the "great" past and their traditional Dutch culture. The present upper class of whites on St. Maarten, largely non-Dutch in provenience and called somewhat derisively "the Up Street whites," are regarded as economic opportunists and interlopers, clearly distinguishable from "the real Dutch."

On St. Eustatius ("Statia") history has had a peculiarly strong unifying effect on all classes except for the immigrants from the neighboring island of St. Kitts.

On Statia the islanders love to speak of the "Golden Rock" days when their island was the acknowledged great emporium of the Caribbean, when as many as 200 sailing vessels sometimes stood in the roadstead at one time, and when the population reached a total of 25,000 (at present it is approximately 1000), and when the island was very rich. Despite the fact that 97 per cent of the present population are descendants of slaves, they strongly identify themselves with the former greatness and wealth of their island and, very incidentally or unconsciously, with the history of the metropolitan country. Moreover, some blame all their difficulties today, and certainly their economic ones, on that perfidious British Admiral Rodney who, in 1780, dealt a blow from which, it is true, the island never fully recovered. The Statians regard this glorious period of history primarily as their own, and as part of their heritage.

Present Government and Personnel

The psychological distance from the metropolitan country is further increased today by the important political and economic role of Curaçao and Aruba. The relative proximity of the A-B-C group, at least within the West Indian area, and the very large proportion of Windward Islanders who have worked, studied, been hospitalized, or visited relatives there, have drawn attention to these islands as to a magnet. This circumstance has blocked off more direct contact with the Netherlands proper. The complexity of life in industrialized Curaçao or Aruba is well understood, but of the few native islanders who have visited the Netherlands proper for higher education or medical services only three or four have returned to describe Dutch life in meaningful terms.

The metropolitan government has become increasingly paternalistic in policy and, in effect, has taken over many of the functions originally considered the duties of the plantation owners. Hence health and medical services, old-age pensions, and government-sponsored work at relatively high wages are now accepted, expected, and even demanded by a large proportion of the native population. In this respect, however, most natives are cognizant of the generosity of the Netherlands and/or the Netherlands Antillean government seated in Curaçao, in contrast to the French or British. The average annual amount paid by the central governments to these 3 small islands per capita is $164.00, while the revenue raised by them amounts to about $2\frac{1}{2}$ per cent of this expenditure.

Such paternalism acts as a two-edged sword, however, since it fosters an increased sense of superiority in the Dutch or Curaçaoan administrators, who are inclined to speak of "these people, so like children," or "they are so childish." At the same time, resentment is felt by the more ambitious and aggressive natives who feel that they can achieve no advance or that they are being suppressed. Actually, there is a great lack of training for leadership and a dearth of leadership opportunities for natives at the present time. The exception to this is membership in the new island councils, first elected in 1951. Those elected to this office thus far, however, have suffered badly from lack of training, and some have resorted to downright demagoguery.

Over all, there is an aura of mutual suspicion, reserve, and lack of understanding between personnel representing the metropolitan government and the natives. Part of this is due to Dutch national character traits. On the whole, the Dutch are honorable, fair, and dispassionate, but rather inflexible and unbending. As one native expressed it, "The Dutch are always right, but if not, you mustn't tell them." The Dutch seem lacking in the kind of glamour possessed by the French, who so easily stimulate people to shout *"Vive la France"* and wave the tricolor. At least, this was observable on French St. Martin. The native of Dutch St. Maarten commonly calls himself "a St. Maartener," while north of the boundary separating the Dutch part from the French the more usual assertion is "We are French." It is only when conflict arises with the French or British that the Dutch islander seems proud to claim affiliation with his metropolitan country in such an expression as "We Dutch are much better off than you."

Another not inconsiderable factor affecting native attitudes is the impermanence of the Dutch officials and professionals, who speak constantly of their coming furlough. They are given six months' leave in a six-year period of service. With few exceptions, they regard their years in the Dutch Windwards as a period of exile, albeit a voluntary one, and with a salary higher than a comparable position would yield at home. An atmosphere of the purely temporary pervades their work. This attitude greatly affects their relationship with the natives, who have seen many teachers, agricultural agents, doctors, and heads of police come and go. They are conditioned now to take the good with the bad, and all with a shrug of the shoulder. The result is a lack of any enduring personal relationships that might build good will and bridge the gap between the mother country and what the Dutch refer to as their "West."

The Nature of the Population and Social Structure

The past and present constitution of the population is an important factor in the attitudes toward, and the reactions to, the metropolitan country. On St. Maarten, at present, there are about 85 per cent Negroes; on Saba, 50 per cent; and on St. Eustatius, 97 per cent. The present Caucasian or white segments of the population are largely island-born and, curiously, non-Dutch in origin. Their provenience is now difficult to establish, but it is very probable that the great majority are north European in origin, possibly descendants of privateers, buccaneers, and colonists forced to flee other islands after conquest by an enemy.

The class structure differs considerably on the three islands, but it is notable that on none of them is there a mulatto social class. There are mulattoes, judging from the phenotypes to be seen, although they appear to be few in number. They equate, with but very few exceptions, with the so-called colored classes. The reasons for this are somewhat obscure, but certainly one contributing factor is the lack of a deeply entrenched, numerous, or long-enduring plantocracy. The absence of a mulatto class has deprived the islands of one potential source for a trained elite that might have helped to close the gap between native and Netherlander. Small communities of non-Dutch whites, such as the groups that settled at Simson's Bay on St. Maarten and at Mary's Point and Hell's Gate on Saba, have remained completely aloof until the last decade or two. They have fostered racial segregation, social fragmentation, and withdrawal from affairs of the metropolitan government.

On Saba in particular, where the former largely white population has been steadily decreasing over the last fifty years and now constitutes about 50 per cent of the total, the class lines drawn are strongly color-conscious. Whites are ranked above Negroes; the small number of Dutch personnel are at the top. Native Saban whites tend to view with alarm the growing political power of Negroes, but they are also critical of the central government. The strong cleavage here makes the task of government very difficult, impeding any effective program of cooperation between the metropolitan personnel and the Sabans. No matter what decisions are made, they are bound to displease a large segment of the population.

Only 3 per cent of the total population of Statia is white; members of only two or three Dutch families were born in the Netherlands. The Dutch may well be at the top of the social ladder, but the upper Negro or "colored" class is close at their heels. The few remaining leaves on the tree of plantocracy (about 6 old ladies who are native to the island) equate with the Dutch in class position, although they are more benevolently tolerated by the colored groups. On Statia the Dutch feel themselves "boxed off," and there is a minimum of mutual understanding.

On St. Maarten the situation is much more complicated, but the Dutch are generally recognized as dominant in position and power. Here the social pattern is fragmented into competing and antithetical groups. Several of these groups, of both races, are jockeying for higher position in the political and economic scale, with attendant mutual ill will and suspicion. The Dutch are not personally involved in this struggle. They are regarded largely with indifference, and there is a minimum of intercommunication.

Dutch Culture and Customs

There is actually very little that strikes the eye or ear as Dutch. This is certainly not the case in Curaçao, where much has been transferred and only lightly readapted from the Dutch climate to the tropical environs. The imprint of Dutch material culture on the Windward Islands is a shallow one, evidenced in a number of minor traits. Perhaps the most widespread and influential are the Dutch insistence on cleanliness and the social hygienic and medical practices, resulting in a healthy populace. In general, the islands are very clean. Saba, in particular, is notable for the good care given to its houses, both inside and out. Consultation Bureaus, held weekly for mothers and babies under one year of age, are patterned exactly on the Dutch model. The yearly calendar of special and feast days is adopted from the Netherlands. Two days are allotted to Christmas, Easter, and Whitsuntide. The special day of prayer and the day of thanksgiving for deliverance from hurricanes are patterned on similar days pertaining to the harvest in parts of rural Holland. Some attempt is made to keep alive the Dutch tradition of the visit of St. Nicolas and his attendant, Black Piet, on December 5, but there is little feeling for this saint among the natives. Indeed, the gay role of Black Piet is not understood, and it is thought demeaning to people of color, so that a white boy must be blacked for the occasion, which is usually celebrated in only one of the schools.

The method of voting by selecting one candidate on a party list, first set up for the election of the island councils in 1951, is taken from the party list system practiced in the Netherlands.

The Dutch form of civil marriage has been adopted and is popular; so much so that common-law unions, while known and accepted, are not very frequent. Civil marriage carries no special prestige and no feast is required, as with the church "blessing," but it often results in added government subsidies.

Also the Dutch law as administered by the judge of the circuit court provides a sense of stability and immutability. It engenders respect. "You can't change *that*, man" is often said of it. Nevertheless, the native police are generally recognized as quite ineffective since they are likely to be relatives or political pawns, or both.

The total culture complex emerges as a many-faceted mosaic, with relatively few elements of the pattern typically Dutch in the sense of manifestations of the metropolitan country.

Language and Education

The major problems of language and education demand separate mention and treatment, which lack of space prohibits here. Understanding of the mother country, and consequently the efficacy of its administration, are seriously impeded by the language barrier. Dutch is the official language and is spoken by the administrative staff, heads of police, doctors, priests, and teachers from Curaçao or the Netherlands. It is assiduously taught in the schools and, in the fourth year, an attempt is made to teach all subject matter in Dutch. However, English (and a form of Creole English) continues to be the language of the people, apparently dating from the early days of settlement by non-Dutch whites. Most older natives speak only English. "Why shouldn't we? It is our mother tongue" was an explanation given by a white St. Maartener. Pupils in school learn Dutch readily enough, but seldom will voluntarily speak it outside the school walls; it quickly falls into disuse in the postschool years, except among the few who continue their education in other parts of the kingdom. This anomalous linguistic situation arouses some suspicion and increases insecurity in the native populations, since it is felt that one cannot be quite sure of understanding governmental laws and regulations or of exactly what the administration is "up to" or what it "might put over."

The most important direct bearers of Dutch culture today are the schoolteachers from the Netherlands. They comprise most of the teaching personnel of the highest two or three classes and the heads of the schools. Nuns of the Dominican order, born and trained in the Netherlands, make up the greater part of the staffs of the Catholic schools, implemented by native islanders who teach the lower grades. In the so-called public (that is, "openbare"*) schools, the heads and perhaps one additional teacher are young men from the Netherlands, and subject matter and lesson plans are comparable to the system used there. The history of the mother country is taught with considerable thoroughness. Pupils must learn, for example, the name of the murderer of William the Silent, Prince of Orange in the Sixteenth Century. On Saba, the history book still

* Nondenominational.

in use in the public school in 1957 began with the sentence, "One hundred years before Christ, the Germans came to our land." Pupils learn of the Dutch climate; they hear of oak and pine trees; they have been asked to write a composition on iceskating. Something of the greatness of Holland's Golden Age of Art is imparted. However, even at best, among conscientious and sympathetic teachers, the culture they represent seems so removed and remote from the absorbing daily concerns of island life as to be quite unimportant. Transitional material to make meaningful intercultural connections is totally lacking. In the postschool years, concepts of Dutch life and culture fade rather rapidly, yet there has been, in the last two decades, a noticeable and increasing trend toward higher education, with more and more pupils applying for the subsidies offered by the government. This is especially true of the upper-class Negroes. There is a recognition that higher education is a good and desirable thing, for prestige, and so that "we can amount to something here."

The image of the metropolitan country is amorphous, except for the concept of the queen and the ruling House of Orange. The visit of Queen Juliana in 1956 and the crown princess in 1957 both engendered a strong feeling of pride that the members of the ruling family, so overwhelmingly rich and powerful, cared enough for the islanders personally to visit them. When a Dutch naval vessel appears in the roadstead, this too, though to a much lesser extent, evokes pride in the power and greatness of the mother country, but under ordinary circumstances any display of chauvinism is weak and lackadaisical. Although antagonism may be shown to Dutch-born personnel, there seems to be no feeling of antipathy to the metropolitan country itself, yet there is no feeling of devotion. The image of the Netherlands is blotted out by the strongly defined silhouette of Curaçao against the tropic sun.

METROPOLITAN INFLUENCES IN THE CARIBBEAN: THE FRENCH ANTILLES

Michael M. Horowitz

Columbia University, New York, N. Y.

Martinique, Guadeloupe, and French Guiana are unique in the West Indies, being the only countries politically integrated with the *métropole*. Since the enactment of the law of *assimilation* in 1946 they have become full *départements* of France, of a status equivalent to that of any in the mother country. Also, Martinique and Guadeloupe are the only ones that have had in recent years both extreme right and left wing-controlled local legislatures, the former during the period of Vichy rule and the latter immediately following the end of World War II.

Although integration occurred when it did for immediate and specific reasons, the idea was not a new one. Both Richelieu and Colbert had planned to make of the islands settlements of French peasants who would provide for their own subsistence and protect the interests of France in that part of the New World (Delawarde, 1935; Mims, 1912). The settlers were, for the most part, indentured laborers, contracting to work 3 years in return for their passage and 300 pounds of tobacco (Debien, 1951). The crop inventory included provisions, tobacco, indigo, and cotton. During this early colonial period, lasting roughly from 1635 to 1670, the main lines of social organization were established, "for the colonists brought with them not merely their tools, farming techniques and language, but also a social tradition based on the *ancien régime* seigneurial system with its relationships between the lord and the peasant laborer, its notions of elite endogamy, and its rather relaxed concern for peasant marriage and the legitimacy of their children" (Horowitz, 1959). There was no question then that the colonists were and would remain citizens of France.

During the latter half of the Seventeenth Century the landholding colonists learned that great riches lay in providing sweetening for the metropolitan table. The effect of sugar cane on the local scene was monumental, touching every facet of life. The most striking change was the substitution of African slaves for the European indentured laborers. Also signi..cant was the fact that the capital requisites for cane production in land, slaves, and equipment precluded the further entry of former indentured workers into the landholding group. A third result of the devotion to cane was the complete economic dependence of the islands on the mother country. The classic colonial mercantile relationship, in which the colony provided a raw product for the *métropole* and received from the latter all manufactured goods and even, in this case, food, followed the extension of sugar cultivation in the French West Indies.

The society included three main groups: white landowners, colored slaves, and freed men of color. The latter group remained small during the first century of colonization (in 1736 there were only 901 freedmen, 13,917 whites, and 54,742 slaves), but in 1848, the year of general emancipation, freed men of color constituted 32 per cent of the total population of 113,357 (Baude, 1948). Those freed were often the children of estate owners and female slaves. In the early days children received at birth the status of their fathers, but since manumission meant a loss of revenue because the masters paid a head tax on each slave, the state initiated the Roman system of *partus sequitur ventrum** in 1674, when the king repossessed the islands from the French West India Company (Labat, 1931). Père Delawarde (1937) reports that the presence of such place names in Martinique as Rue Mulâtre and Fonds Gens Libres indicates that illegitimate children were occasionally presented with small parcels of land in the hills, land unsuited for cane cultivation.

Intertwined in French parliamentary debates are the notions of political assimilation for the colonies and racial equality. A priest pleaded before the revolutionary assembly in these words: "I hope that the National Convention will apply the principles of equality to our colonial brothers from whom we differ by color only" (Sablé, 1955, p. 48). The assembly formally ended slavery, and Martinique and Guadeloupe became *départements* of France in October 1793. The liberal sentiments of the revolution were never transcribed into action in Martinique, for the slaveowning whites, declaring loyalty to the Crown, supported the British occupation of the island and maintenance of the regime. Martinique remained under English domination until the Treaty of Amiens in 1802. The overseas departments reverted to colonial status following Napoleon's accession to complete power and the new constitution of twenty-second Frimaire in the Year VIII (1799). This attempt to satisfy the interests of the white colonial aristocrats was met in St. Domingue by the revolt of Toussaint L'Ouverture and the establishment of the state of Haiti. As Sablé (1955, p. 56) notes wisely, the error lay in identifying the interests of the sugar plutocracy with those of France.

In 1848 the liberal forces that achieved the final abolition of slavery in the French colonies attempted to increase colonial representation, but the reactionary Second Empire provided for the traditional rule of Algeria and the overseas territories. The question of political integration was raised again during the Third Republic. On November 24, 1874 the General Council of Martinique requested that the colonies be considered integral parts of France, and that all laws in force in the *métropole*, and only these laws, be applied. This request was repeated in 1882, with the statement that the "humiliating differences which exist between the colony and a French *département*" should be done away with and that "Martinique be constituted as soon as possible a French *département*" (Sablé, 1955, p. 89–92). Similar resolutions were heard from Guadeloupe, but in Réunion, in the Indian Ocean, where the local legislature remained dominated by the plantocracy, the demand was for continued colonial status.

Demands for assimilation continued throughout the seventy years of the Third Republic and were silenced only by the Vichy regime. For the first time in almost one hundred years the majority of the populations of Martinique and Guadeloupe were effectively disenfranchised. The plantocracy reasserted itself in the political sphere, and the Church, rightly or wrongly, was identified by the people as being sympathetic with the rule of Henri Philippe Pétain and his local representative, Georges Robert. The blockade by allied warships prevented the exportation of sugar and rum and the importation of foodstuffs.

* The offspring follows the womb.

Famine was an ever-present possibility, and the islands were able to survive only through doles of food from the United States. With the establishment of the Fourth Republic, reaction to the physical and social deprivation of the war was swift and sure: both Martinique and Guadeloupe voted overwhelmingly Communist, electing Communist deputies to represent them in France. In 1946 Aimé Césaire, deputy from Martinique, presented again the demand for the complete integration of the colonies of Martinique, Guadeloupe, French Guiana, and Réunion into France. This time the proposal was accepted by the National Assembly, and the four colonies joined the *métropole* as *départements d'outre-mer*, of status equal to those in the mother country except for certain modifications relating primarily to customs and social security.

To summarize, the possibilities for the colonies to enter the *métropole* as political equals have always been high during periods of liberal ascendance in France: 1789, 1848, 1870, and 1943. Assimilation has been opposed by those, both in France and in the colonies, who feared the extension of the franchise to the socially deprived, generally those of African descent.

Under the Fourth Republic the leading official on the island was the prefect, appointed by Paris. Each island elected three deputies and two senators to the National Assembly. The islands are subdivided into communes with popularly elected mayors and municipal councils, and each commune elects a representative to the departmental legislature (*Conseil Général*).

The most important benefit received from departmentalization is the application in the French West Indies of the extensive social security system of the mother country. Of these, the most significant are, *Assistance Médicale Gratuite*, providing free medical and pharmaceutical care to most of the population; *Allocation Familiale*, aid to families of salaried personnel; and *Assistance à la Famille*, which covers those who are not employed for wages (as agricultural tenants and small proprietors).

We have argued elsewhere that the traditional color-class pyramid—a white aristocracy, a colored middle and professional class, and a black proletariat—is an inadequate description of the complex stratification system in Martinique, which is better characterized "as a society of two estates, one composed of the white descendants of the former slave-owners, the other of everyone else. Paralleling this is a seigneurial class system of land-owners and laborers, each with a well-developed consciousness of purpose and ideology. In such a society, with little possibility of expansion of managerial positions through industrialization, there is no true middle class, but merely persons playing intellectual and commercial roles which provide services to the extremes. The strategic point is membership in one estate or another, with actual occupations of interest within the context of a given estate" (Horowitz, 1958).

The intellectual and professional group, composed almost entirely of persons of color, has been articulated most closely with events in the *métropole*. Many of them have continued their education in French universities, and a large number of these never return to the West Indies. The image of France dominates their self-conception, and they tend to derogate the cultural possibilities of their natal lands. Whereas Haiti has been able to develop a certain nationalistic identification among some of its intellectuals, French West Indians have remained devoted to France. In general, France has encouraged this, although one occasionally meets a man who explains, "I was French, before going to France. There I learned that I was a Martiniquan." Despite the prejudice that is sometimes manifested against the West Indian in the *métropole*, many persons have achieved important positions in education, art, the military, and government. A large percentage of the civil servants in the French African administration is West Indian.

The vast majority of professional and bureaucratic positions in the *départements d'outre-mer* is filled by persons of color. This is a relatively recent phenomenon, for even after emancipation most of the doctors, lawyers, officials, and professors were white. The eruption of Mt. Pelée in Martinique in 1902, however, destroyed most of the persons who filled these roles. People of color gained access to them for the first time. In Guadeloupe the situation was quite different.

Martiniquan estates are still owned by resident white families, descendants of the slaveowners. These persons, scarcely represented among the professionals, constitute an economic elite and control, not merely most of the productive lands, but also the import-export trade and the larger retail businesses. Constituting no more than 2 per cent of a total population of about 240,000, they maintain the strict endogamy that Conrad Arensberg (1957) attributes to the marital notions of the prerevolutionary aristocracy. They are for the most part opposed to the departmental status, which they view as a threat to their own control. Many supported the Vichy regime and wish for a political change that would modify relationships in the colonial direction. They too, are oriented toward France, but to a France of the *ancien régime*.

In Guadeloupe, on the other hand, the estates are owned by absentee metropolitan corporations, and somewhat more land seems to be controlled by peasant proprietors. The Guadeloupian aristocrats never recovered from the failure of sugar cane to compete with beetroot in the Nineteenth Century. While in Martinique the existence of the owning family on the plantation tends to perpetuate the paternalism often associated with this arrangement, in Guadeloupe there is no such buffer, and the interests of class are much more clearly defined. Both Communism and the trade unions are more active in Guadeloupe than in Martinique.

Most West Indians are rural proletarians, but the cane laborer in the French Antilles is also a citizen of the *métropole*, a voter, and indeed has been enfranchised since the Third Republic. In spirit they are no less Frenchmen than are the professionals, although their identification is of a different kind. The working classes of Martinique and Guadeloupe maintain a way of life that was introduced into the islands by the indentured *engagés* of the Seventeenth Century and that was taught to the later-arriving Africans who worked side by side with them, although the latter, of course, introduced much that was specifically their own.

The laborers form the strength of the Communist and Socialist parties that dominated French West Indian politics during the Fourth Republic. They exhibit the French and Italian ability to vote Communist on a Sunday afternoon after having attended mass in the Catholic Church, which they find no necessity to renounce. The working classes have received the most tangible benefits of departmentalization through the extension of an elaborate range of social security and minimum wage guarantees.

In short, French West Indians feel themselves to be French, although the particular identification made varies with socioeconomic status. Political integration merely formalized an arrangement that had existed for three quarters of a century. However, political integration did little to alleviate the economic problems with which these territories were burdened, problems that were the inevitable results of 300 years of colonial mercantilism. Simply, Martinique and Guadeloupe are committed to restricted agricultural activity, producing mainly cane sugar, rum, and bananas for a market that can obtain them much cheaper elsewhere. Fauvel (1955) argues that assimilation actually aggravates the situation, claiming that the extension of minimum wage legislation militates against any possibility of local industrialization. The already excessive costs of transportation to and from these islands where natural resources are most limited cannot support a wage level known to Europe. On the other hand, Jackson (1958) feels that integration will permit the involvement of the French Antilles in the European Economic Community, to the benefit of both the islands and France. The other possibility that is beginning to be considered on both islands is for an economic alignment with the West Indian Federation (Guérin, 1956). This position will gain momentum to the extent to which the West Indies proves itself to be an economic success. Of course, we have no indication that the federation would welcome its French neighbors, nor that the latter would accept the specific role assigned to them in a rational market.

One other identification must be mentioned briefly, and that is of some of the intellectuals with the emergent states in Africa, or with a philosophy that has been called *négritude*. The chief spokesman for this viewpoint in Martinique is Aimé Césaire, deputy and former head of the Communist Party, who wrote in 1956: "In the same way one may speak of a great family of African cultures that merits the name of Negro African civilization and that binds together the separate cultures of each of the African nations. Furthermore, one realizes that, because of the vicissitudes of history, the range and extent of this civilization have far outspread Africa, and thus it may be said that in Brazil and in the West Indies, and not only in Haiti and the French Antilles, and even in the United States there are, if not centers, at least fringes of this Negro African civilization" (p. 191).*

Education is an important determinant of the self image. Primary and secondary school facilities are superior to those found in the other West Indian islands, with the possible exception of Puerto Rico. Organization and curricula are identical to those in the *métropole*, for academic education is oriented toward the baccalaureate examinations given during the last year at the *lycée*. Almost all schooling is public and secular, although there are Catholic high schools that tend to recruit their students largely from the ranks of the white plantocracy (Leiris, 1955). The "bacc" is a much coveted degree, for it is the means of entry to prestigeful positions in the civil service and the professions. Each year many West Indians receive scholarships to the metropolitan universities

* Editor's translation.

for studies especially in law, medicine, dentistry, pharmacy, and education. Most French West Indian politicians are schoolteachers. The difficulty is that the islands provide too few positions for all those who studied in France, and many are obliged to remain there or to emigrate to other parts of the empire, especially to Negro Africa.

The populations of these *départements* are, for the most part, literate in standard French, but the language of ordinary communication is Creole. In the rural areas and in the proletarian sections of the cities French is rarely spoken except in church and at school. Among the bourgeoisie and the professionals, however, Creole is likely not to be spoken, and children are taught that speaking Creole is uncultured, being merely the language of the laborers. For example, a child will be told, *"Tu parles comme un nègre."** Two indices of the degree of literacy among these peoples are the quantity of local publications and bookstores. In Martinique, for example, regularly published newspapers are sponsored by the communists, the socialists, and the Gaullists, by the Chamber of Commerce, the Church, the unions, and the league for public schools. In addition to literary and artistic reviews, a motion picture journal, an athletic news, a scandal sheet, and many other publications appear regularly. The bookstores in the smaller towns and the cities stock classics and important modern works as well as pulp, and sell the most recent books of such West Indian authors as Zobel, Joyau, Gratient, and Césaire.

Except for a handful of Adventists and the East Indian adherents to the syncretic cult of Maldevidan, the Roman Catholic Church has no serious competition in the French Antilles. Martinique and Guadeloupe each have a bishop and, although the islands are still considered "missionary regions," there is considerable local entry into the clergy.

The image of France is also reflected in athletic activity, where soccer is the dominant sport. Recently, however, basketball has achieved an enthusiastic following, and films of the Harlem Globetrotters are among the most popular of the cinema offerings.

I have been concerned with outlining some of the effects that France has had on her former colonies of Martinique and Guadeloupe. Space does not permit a discussion of these effects on the other French Caribbean lands. French Guiana has always been the neglected stepchild, mistreated more because of an unfortunate horror-provoking reputation than because of any organic complaints. The combination of the penal colony and the several disastrous attempts at settlement, plus exaggerated reports of unhealthy climate, have discouraged serious plans for development. However, occasionally there is some proposal for resettling part of the burgeoning populations of Martinique and Guadeloupe on the South American mainland, similar to suggestions often voiced for the exploitation of British Guiana and British Honduras (Heyrel, 1957). It is still uncertain whether the expenses involved in development could be recouped from the increased productivity of the land.

The other areas, all dependencies of Guadeloupe, include Marie Galante, Désirade, Les Saints, St. Barthélemy, and one half of St. Martin. As there have been no serious investigations of these islands, we cannot discuss them here. We suggest that St. Barthélemy might be of considerable help in coming

* "You are talking like a Negro."

to terms with the Caribbean, since its population is almost entirely of European descent and could provide important comparative information.

References

ARENSBERG, C. M. 1957. Discussion of methods of community-analysis in the Caribbean. Caribbean studies: a symposium. : 97. V. Rubin, Ed. Inst. Social and Economic Research. Jamaica, B. W. I.

BAUDE, P. 1948. L'Affranchissement des Esclaves aux Antilles Françaises, Principalement à la Martinique, du Début de la Colonisation à 1848. : 92, 93. Imprimerie Officielle. Fort-de-France, Martinique.

CÉSAIRE, A. 1956. Culture et colonisation. Présence Africaine. : 190–205.

DEBIEN, G. 1951. Les Engagés pour les Antilles (1634–1715). : 47–68. Imprimerie F. Paillart. Abbeville.

DELAWARDE, J. B. 1935. Les Défricheurs et les Petits Colons de la Martinique au XVIIe Siécle. Paris, France.

DELAWARDE, J. B. 1937. La Vie Paysanne à la Martinique. : 63. Imprimerie Officielle. Fort-de-France, Martinique.

FAUVEL, L. 1955. Les conséquences économiques et sociales de l'assimilation administrative des Antilles françaises. In Developments Towards Self-Government in the Caribbean. : 186. W. van Hoeve Ltd. The Hague, Netherlands.

GUÉRIN, D. 1956. Les Antilles décolonisées. Présence Africaine. : 167–179.

HEYREL, J. 1957. La Martinique et Son Avenir. : 97–101. Les Editions Françaises. Paris, France.

HOROWITZ, M. M. 1958. Culture, class and politics in Martinique. Ann. Meeting of the Am. Anthropol. Assoc., Washington, D.C. : 8.

HOROWITZ, M. M. 1959. Morne Paysan: Peasant Community in Martinique. : 19. Ph.D. dissertation. Columbia Univ. New York, N. Y. University Microfilm. Ann Arbor, Mich.

JACKSON, M. H. 1958. The economy of the French Caribbean. The Caribbean: British, Dutch, French, United States. : 121–124. A. C. Wilgus, Ed. Univ. Fla. Press. Gainesville, Fla.

LABAT, R. P. 1931. Voyages aux Isles de l'Amérique 1693–1705. : 219. Editions Duchartre. Paris, France.

LEIRIS, M. 1955. Contacts de Civilisations en Martinique et en Guadeloupe. : 75. UNESCO. Paris, France.

MIMS, S. L. 1912. Colbert's West India Policy. Yale Univ. Press. New Haven, Conn.

SABLÉ, V. 1955. La Transformation des Isles d'Amérique en Départements Français. : 48, 56, 89–92. Editions Larose. Paris, France.

METROPOLITAN INFLUENCES* IN THE CARIBBEAN: THE WEST INDIES

Lambros Comitas

Columbia University, New York, N. Y.

Despite decades of intraregional political and economic isolation and the vast expanse of sea separating them from each other, a group of ten British colonial units in the Caribbean has federated, under the suzerainty of Great Britain, into a new nation. The West Indies, as this federation calls itself, forms a thousand-mile chain that curves northward from Trinidad, at the northeastern tip of South America, to Jamaica in the Greater Antilles. Linking these two are Grenada, Barbados, St. Vincent, St. Lucia, Dominica, Montserrat, Antigua, and St. Kitts-Nevis. These ten small units and their even smaller dependencies are inhabited by about three million people, five sixths of them found in Jamaica, Trinidad, and Barbados. The density of population is high everywhere, averaging 375 persons per square mile for the entire region, but billowing to an almost incredible 1400 for Barbados. Racially, the area is populated primarily by the Negro descendants of former slaves, by a much smaller white group that has lost some of its formal political power but that still retains social and economic dominance, and by a numerically intermediate colored group that is a physical and cultural amalgam of the Negro and white. In Trinidad there is a large, fast-growing minority of East Indians, and throughout the federation, small but usually important clusters of Chinese, East Indians, Syrians, and Portuguese are to be found.

Except for Barbados, the cultural inventories of each island have been modified, disrupted, and changed by the all-too-frequent substitution of one European ruling power for another during a period of ferment that lasted well into the Nineteenth Century. Each island society has had its own unique historical development and, consequently, a differing political and economic relationship with Great Britain. Jamaica, for instance, is on the verge of complete self-government; Barbados has a new constitution that has not yet clarified the role of the governor but, like Trinidad, it is fast approaching self-government. The smaller units, especially the recipients of grants-in-aid from Great Britain, remain on the crown colony level, with concomitant metropolitan restraints. It is evident from even a short description such as this that there are differentiae operating on the various levels of this new but not quite independent nation. Notwithstanding these discordances, the British West Indies hold numerous social and cultural characteristics in common. We turn now to these similarities and to the influences that created them.

---

* The word "influence" is used within the context of this paper in a special sense. Webster defines influence as "the act or the power of producing an effect without apparent *force* or direct *authority*; as, influence by suggestion." [1] If this definition is taken literally, it follows that we are permitted to deal only with the unpressured or unforced effects of the *métropole* on its colonies and not with the obvious sociocultural results of the domination of Great Britain. However, except for institutions and cultural elements that have readily identifiable derivations, it is extremely difficult to distinguish between imposed effects (those accomplished through the use of authority) and unpressured effects (those accomplished without such use). As a practical operational necessity, it becomes essential, therefore, that we interpret the word "influence" quite broadly and subsume under it all those effects produced by the *métropole* in the colony with or without the use of authority.

The development of the British West Indies is mirrored in the changing colonial policies of the *métropole* through the past three centuries. These policies, a reflection of the economic theories of their times, had varying degrees of impact on the region. The first and most important, having created the conditions that produced the original social structure of the area, was that doctrine called mercantilism, a system aptly described as the economic counterpart of nationalism. The nation state of the Seventeenth and Eighteenth Centuries "acting in the economic sphere sought by methods of control to secure its own unity and power"[2] and pursued strength in the conquest and exploitation of colonies. Ideally, the colony was to be an appendage of the *métropole*, founded to produce goods and markets necessary to the mother country. Consistent with this theory, the West Indies, after a short, unsuccessful experiment with small-plot agriculture, turned to the intensive cultivation of sugar cane. A crystallization of factors, including the man power demands of this particular crop, the rigors of a subtropical climate, and mercantilist aims in general, demonstrated the desirability of a large, strong, but manageable work force. This growing need found an ideal solution in African slave labor and led directly to the great slave importations to the New World, the middle leg of the nefarious triangular trade. Amassed from various West African tribes with differing cultures and languages, these slaves were forced into a new and difficult way of life that included the abandonment of their native tongues for English or dialects of it. The law regarded them as property. This legal dehumanization denied the slaves even the potentially ameliorative benefits of education and Christianity.

In contrast, the few whites who migrated from the *métropole* to the West Indies were more similar in cultural background to one another than were the Africans, and they entered a social milieu in which they were dominant. With the exception of a number of indentured white laborers found especially in presugar Barbados,[3] the whites arrived as owners, managerial personnel, or free men seeking their fortunes, but each endowed with those personal rights guaranteed all English-born subjects. Structurally, this situation permitted the introduction of many of the traditional social forms of the *métropole*, especially in the domain of law and government, but these elements were modified where necessary to fit the unique West Indian conditions. For example, dominance, a prerequisite of any slave system, generated privileges, so that the new Caribbean societies developed patterns not found in the *métropole*. Among these newly acquired privileges were seigneurial rights to slave women and concubinage, patterns that contributed heavily to the growth of a mixed, colored population. Thus the economic and political motivations of the metropolitan power were responsible for a West Indian social structure composed of two sharply differentiated units, whites and blacks, masters and slaves, and straddling both could be found the budding of a third or colored population.

Later shifts in metropolitan economic policy modified this basic formula. At the end of the Eighteenth Century mercantilism was displaced by *laissez faire*, which extolled the economic utility of free competition and assumed noninterference of government in economic matters. Adam Smith and his disciples proved to their satisfaction that colonies were not profitable and, with the gradual acceptance of this hypothesis, the metropolitan government shed itself of the responsibility for the development of its colonies.[4]   Within this framework, the pleas and arguments of humanitarians such as William Wilberforce found more receptive audiences.   Their initial objective, the abolition of the slave trade, was gained in 1807 and the second, emancipation, was enacted in 1833.   These legislative acts of the British Parliament affected each island of the West Indies differently.   In islands such as Antigua and Barbados, where most of the arable land was already in sugar, the change from slave to wage labor was essentially a legal one only; social conditions remained close to those existing before emancipation.   In islands such as Jamaica, which still had unsettled areas in their mountainous interiors, the newly freed slaves left the plantations and sought refuge inland.   Where this occurred, a major structural modification ensued; the movement to the hills led to the formation of a quasi-independent peasantry.   Partially due to this depletion of the organized work force, the introduction of indentured East Indian labor seemed necessary for the plantocracy, especially in Trinidad.   Despite these changes, with slavery legally abolished, the rudiments of a peasantry developing, and the growing colored population becoming socially and culturally defined, political and social inequality remained the characteristic leitmotif of the British Caribbean.

Early Twentieth Century reaction to *laissez faire* took the form of a modern or new imperialism combining tariff protection at home with the acquisition of new colonies.   The expansion and welding of the empire as well as the reforging of the old, neglected colonial links were accomplished under the slogans of imperial preference, defense, and conference.   Metropolitan obligation to the more backward colonies distinguished this new imperialism from the old; overseas possessions, to be useful, could not be allowed to remain ignorant of the innumerable benefits of Victorian and Edwardian civilization.   Materially and socially, this latest shift was of negligible importance to the West Indies, which had become the backwater of the empire.   Its major value lay in that it provided a more permissive atmosphere for the events leading to the West Indian present.

By the turn of the century the rate of population growth was soaring, especially in Barbados and Jamaica.   Opportunities for work were fast diminishing, a low standard of wages prevailed, and the level of housing as well as other necessities of life was deplorable.   Safety valves such as migrations to Panama for work on the canal, to the United States, and to Cuba were insufficient to curb a growing popular discontent that culminated in the late 1930s in riots and disturbances throughout the region.   The West India Royal Commission of 1938–1939, which investigated these disturbances, recognized the qualitative difference of these from past unrest: "... the discontent that underlies the disturbances of recent years is a phenomenon of a different character, representing no longer a blind protest against worsening of conditions, but a positive demand for the creation of new conditions that will render possible a less restricted life."   As a result of this social upheaval, limited political rights were finally gained by the masses.[5]

As we can see, West Indian social structure, formed in response to metropolitan objectives, in no way recreated the structural configuration of the home country.   Nevertheless, much in the West Indies appears British: the schools, legal and political forms, styles in clothing, sports, allegiance to the Crown and royal family and, as is commonly held for Barbados, some traits of character and outlook. Certainly, we must agree that many social institutions and cultural elements are clearly derived from the *métropole*. However, it is not the retention of mere form that is important here, but how the total institution or element, originally developed in Great Britain, actually operates when in a completely different social context, such as in societies having at least three culturally differentiated sections, the white, colored, and black, as they have been defined by Smith.[6,7] For instance, the legal code of the region, St. Lucia excepted, is patterned after that of the United Kingdom. However, unlike Great Britain, law in the West Indies tends to widen the differences between sections rather than to act as an agent of unification. This situation has developed because law has a different function in the West Indies than in Britain. In the Caribbean it promoted the control of the *métropole* and its representatives, the resident whites. One example of how this control was maintained is found in the judiciary. Positions on high courts such as the West Indian Court of Appeal until recently were allotted to the Colonial Judicial Service,[8] which recruited primarily from metropolitan and not West Indian sources. Judges and magistrates for the lower courts came predominantly from the white section and the upper levels of the colored section, the appointees from both categories being trained in the *métropole*. This combination could scarcely envisage change in the social order. Consequently, law and the judiciary were, and to some degree still are, relied upon by the white or dominant section to preserve the *status quo*.

For the colored or intermediate section, law traditionally has been an avenue for mobility. A large portion of the professionals produced by this group has been trained in its prestigeful practice, which guarantees a respectable position in society and opens opportunities for material and political success. While this section has sought some amelioration of the inequities in legal administration, it nevertheless uses the prevailing system for its own purposes. The black section sees law basically as an instrument of coercion. The small minority of this section that lives in the isolated, closed, peasant communities avoids contact with this alien institution, preferring the application of customary sanctions and the use of local "peacemakers." However, the great majority lives in more open villages, in plantation towns, and in the growing urban areas. In these places the courts are used extensively to redress wrongs or to gain prestige within the group itself and are visited by many for entertainment. Only rarely, however, are they employed by members of socially inferior sections to seek redress against members of superior sections.

The constabulary is also very similar to the British model. Organized along metropolitan lines, the police forces have been led by professionally trained metropolitans and by local white and colored, while they are manned by the lower section. As befits a colonial relationship, connections between police and *métropole* have been close and, significantly, the former is one of the last departments of government to be relinquished by the Colonial Office to local authorities. The dominant sections benefit from the police. Many of the minor, as well as a number of the major, legal transgressions of the upper two sections are disregarded, and protection of their interests takes precedence over those of the large majority of the population. In contrast, the subordinate sections attempt to avoid contact as far as possible unless provoked. A Jamaican newspaperman commented recently on the widespread feeling that there is an almost institutionalized abuse of authority by the police of that island and claimed that this situation "stems from the identification of the policeman as an instrument manipulated by foreigners for punishing people, much as 'government' was once a vague, foreign entity that could annoy people. In short this concept of the role of the policeman stems from our colonial era, and accurately reflects the historical reality of that age. The policeman was not ours, responsible to us and meant to help us, just as 'government' was not ours, responsible to us and meant to help us. But the government is now ours, responsible to us and meant to meet our needs and desires. Unfortunately, this political fact, as is so often the case, has not changed a social attitude. The policeman is still liable to act as if John Citizen were a rebellious native and Morant Bay [a revolt in 1865] occurred last week."[9] If we accept the hypothesis of pluralism in the British West Indies, then an explanation of this situation is relatively simple: to maintain a plural society, the dominant section must control the regulative institutions.[7] Law and police are just such institutions. Their outward forms, due to the historical connection, are British, but their functions and content are reworked to meet the different needs of a very different system. The subordinate sections are not altogether wrong when they identify the policeman as an agent of a "foreign" or alien group.

There are other institutions where structure and function in the colonial versions appear quite similar to their metropolitan parent: education in the West Indies, for example, follows the form found in Great Britain now and in the past. Current policy in both places is very similar: primary schooling is to be provided for all, secondary education of high standard for a small fraction of the population, and university training for exceptionally few.[10] Reminiscent of an earlier, sharply class-conscious England are the curricula of West Indian primary schools. These schools, largely the result of missionary activity in the Nineteenth Century, evolved from the teaching of catechism and the Bible to a more secularly oriented emphasis on conventional subjects, principally, the three Rs. The content of these subjects has remained predominantly British rather than West Indian. Little attempt has been made to emphasize subjects with more pertinent and immediate local relevance, a neglect that gives basic education in this region an unrealistic quality. Furthermore, teaching is usually conducted in standard English, although most islanders employ a creolized version of English, and St. Lucians and Dominicans speak a French patois. For the overwhelming majority, schooling stops at the primary level and, in general, this group enters the adult world with precious little preparation.

Although recently they have put some emphasis on science, West Indian secondary schools remain committed to the classics, thus betraying their origins as schools for the sons of colored imitators of the white aristocracy. In the main, a system of external examinations from Great Britain determines their standards and subject matter, and their general organization imitates that of the British public schools. Lack of school places and high cost effectively prevent most West Indians from seeking this advanced education. Consequently the secondary level, for all practical considerations, is reserved for children of the upper sections. It provides a rigorous academic training, but has little connection with the peculiar realities of West Indian life. Even the minute number who manage to receive university training abroad and more recently at the University College of the West Indies in Mona, Jamaica, favor socially preferred fields such as law and medicine. Numerous other subjects of equal importance but of negligible social esteem are almost automatically ignored by all. The point here is that portions of the British educational complex flourish in the West Indies because they actively reinforce the social structure. By keeping rigid barriers between primary and secondary levels and by maintaining metropolitan substance and orientation, West Indian education acts as an enculturative process that blocks the growth of a fully integrated society and tends to perpetuate the present deep schisms.

I have described the effect of the *métropole* on just a few British Caribbean institutions. Needless to say, however, metropolitan influences of one kind or another have permeated almost every phase of West Indian life. In general, the varying degrees of Britishness that West Indian sociocultural elements display result from the differential working of these influences into the social structure. Each section, modified by its own insular setting, blends these British influences in its own characteristic fashion, guided in part by the image it has developed of the *métropole*. To understand the creation of these images, or collective representations, as Émile Durkheim might say, we must know the type and degree of interaction between each section and the *métropole*. For example, the lowest ranked but most populous section has the smallest degree of contact with metropolitans. Indirect sources such as radio, Rediffusion,* and motion pictures are perhaps more instrumental in forming its image of the *métropole*. For many males, a mental picture of this other world depends also on interest in cricket and other sports. It is not uncommon to hear fishermen in a remote Barbadian hamlet discuss English cricket and cricketers with great precision, although unsure about almost everything else metropolitian. In fact, the image or concept of the *métropole* for the large majority does not depend on any direct interaction, but on incomplete observation of very narrow areas of metropolitan activity, a selectivity that almost automatically involves distortion. As the intermediate sections are more likely to live in urban areas, contact with metropolitans is more frequent. Contiguity juxtaposed with envy creates an intense interest in metropolitan behavior and affairs that results in an accumulation of diverse knowledge about this group. However, general lack of interest and social and cultural barriers prevent even the locally resident metropolitan from acquiring an equivalent knowledge of the West Indian. This frustrated interaction, rather like looking through a one-way glass, has left its marks. Of the three, the dominant section has the clearest view of the *métropole* and its inhabitants. Among them, education and travel in Great Britain are common, and transatlantic family connections are maintained. Interaction is fairly free, and differences between dominant and metropolitan whites are relatively minor.

To sum up, then, an attempt has been made to present some of the major

---

* Rediffusion is a wire broadcasting system by which programs are carried by wire into the subscriber's home and heard through a speaker.

metropolitan pressures that affect West Indian society. Local configurations differ from their British models functionally. Discrete social and cultural elements derived from the *métropole* are modified and changed to fit the prevailing colonial societies. This modification is not arbitrary, since consistent regularities can be found in each island society. However, their differing colonial histories have produced some range of modification that gives to individual islands and each local section a somewhat distinct quality.

Acknowledgment

I am indebted to M. G. Smith, Nigerian Institute of Social and Economic Research, Ibadan, Nigeria, for his helpful comments.

References

1. WEBSTER'S NEW COLLEGIATE DICTIONARY. 1956. Merriam. Springfield, Mass.
2. CLOUGH, S. B. & C. W. COLE. 1941. Economic History of Europe. Heath. Boston, Mass.
3. LIGON, R. A True and Exact History of the Island of Barbadoes (abridged). Extra-Mural Dept. Univ. Coll. West Indies. Mona, Jamaica.
4. WICKER, E. R. 1958. Colonial development and welfare, 1929–1957. Social and Economic Studies. 7(4): 170.
5. HEWITT, J. M. 1954. Ten Years of Constitutional Development in Barbados. Cole's Printery. Bridgetown, Barbados.
6. SMITH, M. G. 1953. Social structure in the British Caribbean about 1820. Social and Economic Studies. 1(4): 55–79.
7. SMITH, M. G. 1955. A Framework for Caribbean Studies. Extra-Mural Dept. Univ. Coll. West Indies. Mona, Jamaica.
8. BRAITHWAITE, L. 1957. Progress towards federation. Social and Economic Studies. 6(2): 178–179.
9. RAWLINS, R. 1959. The police and you. Public Opinion, March 28. Kingston, Jamaica.
10. PROUDFOOT, M. 1953. Britain and the United States in the Caribbean. Praeger. New York, N. Y.

SOCIAL STRATIFICATION AND CULTURAL PLURALISM

Lloyd Braithwaite

University College of the West Indies, Mona, Jamaica, West Indies

The discussion of social stratification in relation to cultural pluralism is important because these two approaches to the phenomena of social stratification and to the so-called plural society have for the most part developed quite separately. What is proposed here is to show briefly and, consequently, perhaps inadequately, the manner of approach of those primarily interested in one or the other of these phenomena and to examine concretely the society of of the island of Trinidad. Such an approach would appear to have two merits: first, Trinidad rivals in cultural complexity any other island or territory in the Caribbean and, second, it permits the possibility of examining the limitations of the existing approaches to the problems and of uniting two large areas of sociological interest within some broad framework of sociological theory.

For the purposes of this paper, social stratification is regarded as a form of social differentiation in which social groups or quasi-organized groups (social classes) are differentiated in terms of status within a hierarchically arranged social order. The empirical study of social stratification has had two important points of impetus: one was the study of "socioeconomic status" by sociologists; the other impulse, possibly more important, was given by the attempts of the social anthropologist to describe modern Western society. Strangely enough, it is the anthropological approach to the problems of social class and social status that has stimulated the greatest theoretical interest. Unsurprisingly, these approaches are by no means mutually incompatible; some of the pioneers attempted (some might say reverted to) sociological techniques of objective measurement.

The approach of the anthropologist seems to have sprung largely from a desire to discover, in his study of modern Western society, some principle of social structure that would serve to reduce the complexity of its culture to some order. The principles of social class, status, and stratification are roughly comparable, at first glance, in simplicity and "explanatory value" to those of kinship, locality, age-group, and the others with which the anthropologist is accustomed to deal.

The anthropological concern with the problems of Western society has not been paralleled by a like concern of the sociologists with the problems of colonial societies. Sociologists do not appear to have realized how culture-bound have been their concerns, particularly among empirically minded sociologists addicted to the production of *ad hoc* theoretical schemes. Until recently American sociologists, for instance, appear to the outsider to have been concerned primarily with empirical and quantitative analysis of segments or aspects of American social structure.

One consequence of this is that the analysis and understanding of multiracial and multicultural societies is relatively undeveloped. The comparative research that has been done in the field of race relations, for instance, has been concerned chiefly with the problems of prejudice, discrimination, and the measurement of relevant attitudes and with the so-called race-relations cycle, and much of the export of sociology has been in the international extension of such projects.

Moreover in the United States, where empirical sociology has achieved its highest development, it has been the anthropologists who have worked most clearly and distinctly with the concept of culture. Consequently, sociological concerns have not proved to be particularly relevant to the analysis of multicultural or multiracial societies in which gross differences in culture coincide or coexist with racial differences.

In default of an adequate sociological theory (notions of the plantation, the race-relations cycle, and the concept of the frontier notwithstanding) the phenomenon of cultural pluralism has been fruitfully examined by political scientists concerned with the problem of nationalism and national minorities or by persons interested primarily in problems of colonial administration and, more especially, with those problems that arise where there is a transition to self-government. The dearth of theoretical formulations in this field has been met largely by the concept of the plural society, which has attracted much attention and uncritical use. The notion was transferred from the field of economics, where the "dual economy" of Western enterprise and traditional native production formed a striking contrast.

The chief advocate of the theory of the plural society has been, of course, Furnivall.[1] Although he was interested primarily in problems of colonial administration, his views are by no means those of an orthodox colonialist. Rather, they appear to stem from a somewhat naive acceptance of the radical criticism of the social order. The colonial society, the radical claimed, is held together by force, which is harmful and disruptive in its consequences. The theory really differs from the conventional sterotype portrayal of imperialism only in that it declares that the imperialists are not to blame.

This suspicion as to the genesis of the theory has, of course, nothing to do with its intrinsic adequacy. It is of interest only because the theory of the plural society is logically unacceptable; therefore its widespread acceptance must be explained on other than logical grounds.

The Plural Society

The plural society has been defined by Furnivall as one lacking in social will. According to him, under modern conditions all tropical countries tend to be plural societies. That is, a European or "Western" power creates a superstructure that leads to the destruction of the former established pattern of social relationships. The cultural homogeneity of society (as it existed before Western contact) is replaced by a culturally and racially heterogeneous society. The one common feature that all groups in the plural society share is the desire for economic advancement. Hence arises the lack of a common social will.

It is convenient to bear in mind the brief description of the plural society given by Furnivall in his essay *Tropical Economy*:

"I. The plural society has come into existence because the only factor common to all groups and members has been the economic factor. Trying to cure its defects by purely economic measures is like casting out devils in the name of

Beelzebub. The *first* problem is to find some principle transcending material ends, some moral principle, that *all* can accept as valid.

"II. The economic factor predominates because the colonial power, exercising political control, is primarily concerned for its economic interests. The *second* problem is then to dissociate as far as possible economic and political control; to find some moral and not solely material authority.

"III. The predominance of economic forces is prejudicial to social and individual welfare because these forces sacrifice social to individual demand. The *third* problem, accordingly, is to devise some machinery for the organization of demand.

"IV. The plural society is inconsistent with political welfare because it is unable to stand alone for lack of a common social will. The *fourth* problem therefore is to devise some means of creating a common social will."[2]

The problem faced in creating an autonomous community and self-governing country is thus seen as, basically, one of creating such a social will as will be capable of sustaining a self-governing country. A people must be capable of wanting what it needs and doing what it wants.

It is clear from the foregoing description that Trinidad to some extent falls into the category of a plural society. Here the heterogeneous cultural elements have been drawn together because of the dominant political structure of the British Empire, which facilitates movement on a broad Empire-wide scale.

Furnivall has obviously pointed with a great deal of insight to some of the problems of such a society. However, it can be doubted whether the term plural society is sufficiently clear theoretically to throw much light on the problem.

Indeed, Furnivall claims that all tropical societies are plural societies, and cites the case of the Indians in East Africa and the Syrian merchants in West Africa. However, the mere existence of a national or ethnic minority such as the Syrians in West Africa does not create the characteristic problems of the plural society. In some respects the nation states of West Africa with racially homogeneous groups form a similar type of social structure to that found in a so-called plural society.

Furnivall himself sees that the term "plural society," when used too loosely, becomes debased, and he contrasts a plural society with a society with pluralistic aspects. It is my belief that, rich though Furnivall's insight is, the conceptual framework he employs is not adequate to deal with the phenomenon he is analyzing. Even the terms used by Sorokin[3] of differentiation between unibonded and multibonded groups goes a little further. It at least leads to a study of what are the particular bonds that unite the social groups in question and suggests a range extending from these societies or groups with one single common value to those that share many major values in common.

If we use the more general sociological theory of Parsons and Shils, we get a better picture.[4] A plural society is one composed of such varying groups, each with its own subculture, that only a few cultural symbols are shared by all. Under these circumstances there are consequently tendencies toward disintegration. In those societies usually referred to as plural we see societies in which the dominant ties of particularism and ascription,* especially those of the large kinship group, are largely replaced by those of universalism and achievement.

The position is complicated further by the fact that this is not an indigenous process, but part of the disruption of a subordinate social system by one which is superordinate. To a very large extent the values of particularism and ascription still remain strong, but have an entirely new content: the acceptance of the superiority, as such, of the superordinate system. By and large, however, this process of acculturation implies the introduction and partial acceptance of universal and achievement values in spheres in which particularistic and ascriptive values were previously dominant.

The concentration of the phenomenon of the lack of social will of which Furnivall speaks obscures the really important fact that no society can exist without a minimum sharing of common values, without a certain amount of "social will." This may be responsible for the fact that, although Furnivall shows a great deal of insight into so many of the problems involved in the metropolitan-colonial relationship, he tends to lay too great stress on the economic factors affecting policy and too little on the necessary existence of sentiments favorable to the metropolitan power and the ways and means by which such sentiments are inculcated and encouraged. It is impossible to understand the sociological evolution of colonial societies without taking this factor into account.

A major need of the individual in a subordinate social system whose particularistic-ascriptive values have been torn asunder would appear to be acceptance of another such set of values. Hence it comes about that the first reactions of many colonials is toward the acceptance of the superiority of the scale of values of the superordinate social system. After a time there is a sufficient acquaintance with this scale of values and a sufficiently general incorporation of them into the subordinate society for this relationship of superior to subordinate to be questioned, even when the common yardstick of generally accepted values is used.

When this relationship is questioned, the problem of the integration of the subordinate system also comes into question. When there are heterogeneous cultural elements in the population, the position is particularly acute. With the breakdown of the system of integrative values that holds the subordinate community in position, there are no other system integrative values to take their place.

Furnivall, in his discussion of the political features of the plural society, states that it has these characteristic aspects: the society as a whole comprises separate racial sections; each section is an aggregate of individuals rather than an organic whole and, as individuals, their social life is incomplete. However,

* "Ascription: the normative pattern which prescribes that an actor in a given type of situation should, in his selections for differential treatment of social objects, give priority to certain attributes that they possess (including collectivity memberships and possessions) over any specific performances (past, present, or prospective) of the objects . . . the role-expectation that the role incumbent, in orienting himself to social objects in the relevant choice situation, will accord to the objects' given attributes (whether universalistically or particularistically defined) over their actual or potential performances" (Parsons and Shils, pages 82 and 83).[4]

in point of fact the breakdown of the power and prestige of the metropolitan power shows that these separate racial sections that are thought of as being atomistic under colonialism have a very strong group consciousness of their own. It is true that the breakdown of the integration of the colonial society with the metropolitan society tends to create a set of disparate individuals, but this is a feature of all societies that have accepted the Western democratic scale of values without possessing the political and economic conditions and the psychological attitudes necessary to ensure the working of a democratic regime. The interesting feature about the special case of the multiracial, multicultural, or plural society is that, in addition to this, we have the development and accentuation of antagonism between subordinate groups.

The cases that spring most readily to mind are those of Palestine, Malaya, and India. There can be little doubt that, at the time of transfer of power, neither the proponents of partition nor the advocates of a united India were able to assess at all accurately the explosive forces that they were unleashing. It was the dominant power, directly concerned as it was with the integration of the previous system, that made the most realistic appraisal of the situation. In all the other societies of which Furnivall wrote intimately we see the same disparate tendencies manifesting themselves.

In this connection we must note the emergence of somewhat similar problems in places such as Nigeria, which is not a multiracial society, but a multicultural one. Here, as the society moves in the direction of self-government, the separate self-conscious groups have become somewhat more antagonistic to one another. It is not that the "union is not voluntary but is imposed by the colonial power and by the force of economic circumstances,"[1] it is that the identification with the superior social system has ceased, and subordinate identification (whose strength has not been appreciated, precisely because of this subordination) now assumes a major importance.

The colonial system, far from placing economic considerations first, is in fact dominantly based on ascriptive ones. That is why the characteristic colonial response in revolt takes on a certain common form. The answer to ascription is ascription; to nationalism, nationalism. When the need to replace the system's integrative values becomes paramount, the tendency is to look for similar values elsewhere. If the country has a culturally homogeneous tradition, this is revived, and colonial nationalism tends to result; if the country is a plural society, sectional and racial antagonism tend to preponderate.

This need for system integration throws some light on the much-noted appeal of communism to underdeveloped peoples. Marxism not only furnishes an ideology that allows the acceptance (albeit partial) of universalistic-achievement values to which people have become accustomed with Westernization, but it also makes for system integration. It replaces a fragmented scale of values with an integrated and unified one. It presents a philosophy that appears to have all the answers, and this exerts a powerful attraction on the individual. Even more important, however, is the fact that it permits of a certain degree of identification with a metropolitan power. Hence it comes about that the combination of "nationalism" with communism becomes feasible. The nationalism allows the working off of aggressive feelings against the dominant power in control, while communism allows for the identification with both a foreign and a metropolitan power. Of course, such an identification is not inevitable. Sometimes the separate ethnic groups seek the same psychological comfort from identification with the foreign power from which the ethnic group originally came. To some extent this is the case with the Indians of Trinidad, and to the extent that this occurs the crisis in the integration of the society is deepened. Even in this case, however, there is still often to be found a marked tendency to identify with that metropolitan power which is in opposition to the dominant power. For, insofar as people seek to obtain a new integration of the society as a whole, they find the appeal of communism with its subtle blend of universalism and particularism extremely powerful.

It has been suggested that not merely places with distinctive ethnic pockets, such as Trinidad and British Guiana, but the society characteristic of all the West Indian islands can be described best as a plural society. The danger here is that the differences between the subcultures of the different social groups come to be stressed, and this is contrasted with a so-called unitary or homogeneous society that does not exist in reality, but that is an ideal type to which no society in fact corresponds in total detail.

In a sense every society has pluralistic aspects. Indeed, one of the main problems that recent advances in sociological theory elucidate is the fact that different values and attitudes are necessarily produced by any functioning social system, so that the integration of these diverse values is one of the important tasks of the social system to which energies must be allocated. In addition to this, however, there enter into the functioning of groups geographical and other factors that may correspond with special cultural traits and either raise or lower the prospects of such groups functioning as separate independent entities. The mere existence of cultural pluralism does not necessarily threaten the existence of the social order.

Furthermore, in any social system the values to which people aspire must be in short supply, otherwise we are forced to believe in the possibility of a classless society. If these values were unlimited and in supply as free goods, they would cease to be a central focus of attention. It is for this reason that all attempts to create classless societies, whether in small Utopian communities or on the grand scale, as in the Soviet Union, have collapsed. This fact in itself makes the existence of pluralistic or subcultural elements an inevitable product of any social system.

Nevertheless, societies can be characterized by the number of values that are shared as desirable by all; insofar as they are diverse, we can speak of cultural pluralism. In this sense it is clear that the society of Creole Trinidad could be accurately described as in some sense a plural society.* As shown

---

* Trinidad society (contemporary population approximately 780,000) has been described in terms of social stratification as a society in which the dominant values have been those of racial origin and skin color, and one in which the social ascendancy and high status of the white group was broadly accepted. It was further characterized as a colonial society in which the hierarchic grouping of social classes was reinforced through the subordinate nature of the colonial society in relation to the metropolitan power. However, it was pointed out further that sharp social changes were taking place in that ascriptive values of race were being replaced by those of achievement in the economic and political fields, and one in which the goals of an independent democratic society were replacing the old colonial relationship.

While such an analysis is essential, and later developments have emphasized the validity of this position, it was incomplete in that it ignored much of the cultural complexity of the

elsewhere, the main common value element has been the sharing of the value of ethnic superiority and inferiority.[5] Other values, however, were shared only by the middle and the upper classes, yet others by the whole society except the upper class, and so on. The fact that there was only one common value strongly held by the whole society, of a type inherently productive of tensions, created a certain tendency to "disintegration" within the social system, particularly when this main common value was challenged. This disintegration was reflected in the political life of the community as the lower class, with its own subculture, became dominant, and again in socially deviant behavior, as in the case of the steel-band movement.

We have in the case of the various ethnic-group cultures within the island (the more usual sense in which the term plural society has been used) a more complicated case. With the breakdown of the common-value element ("the political and social superiority of the Englishman and the European") we find the same assertion of disparate tendencies within the social group. There was to be observed, for instance, not merely an increased tension between Indians and non-Indians, but between Hindu and Moslem as well. The splits within the Chinese community, too, became more public and important. Our chief concern, however, is not whether to use the term plural society to characterize either or both situations. The point of substance is that we must be careful not to stress the culturally pluralistic elements of the society without appreciating the fact that there must be a certain minimum of common, shared values if the unity of the society is to be maintained. In the case of Furnivall this led to the neglect of ties of sentiment with the imperial power, to an overstressing of economic elements, and to an over all view of the political structure as essentially one of force. In the case of an analysis of Trinidad society there is also the possibility that these same elements may be neglected.

In the case of Furnivall there seems to be a tendency to misunderstand the existing hierarchy of values by stressing the equality of the plural elements and the importance of the ethnic cultures. This leads to an over-idealization of the subordinate cultures as compared with the dominant scale of values with its corresponding lack of social will. Something of the same sort may be seen in the West Indies by those who stress the pluralistic elements in the situation. We have seen, for instance, the development of the concept of lower-class family life as equally viable with that of the middle and the upper classes. Here one of the basic problems in the integration of the society tends to be overlooked. The concept of pluralism, considered outside of a sociological theory, leads also to a definition of the social system purely in terms of cultural institutions and of the adherence of the different groups to different institutions. The confusion in meanings which surrounds the term "institution" is thus introduced into the confusion that surrounds the term "plural society."

---

island. It was confined to the Creole section (about 55 per cent of the society). There can be no doubt that acceptance of these values was widespread among the rest of the population in spite of the persistence of subcultural patterns. These values are, however, not so firmly implanted among the Indian section (about 35 per cent of the population) largely because of the tenacity of certain aspects of Hindu and Moslem culture. What we therefore see in the case of the acculturation of the Indian ethnic groups is a process of acculturation in which large aspects of Hindu and Moslem culture were shed and the dominant features of the host society, such as we have described, accepted.[4]

One alternative to an analysis in sociological terms of the social structure is to divide these institutions into "core" institutions and "peripheral" ones. However, if these institutions are not defined in "structural-functional" terms, that is, in terms of the functional tasks of the social system itself, they tend to reduce sociology to a mere department of biology. Hence the attempt to create order by the use of an institutional treatment eventually ends by creating even greater theoretical disorder.

In the analysis of social stratification in relation to pluralism, the homogeneity of a culture or social system is differentiated from a plural society by the institutionalists as follows: the homogeneous society shows among different social classes an allegiance to the same forms of institutions, the plural society shows among different social classes allegiance to different forms of the same institution.

Two objections may be raised here. In the first place, it is usually more appropriate to regard social classes as quasi-organized groups. It is not the interaction among themselves as a group that defines the membership of any given social class, but more particularly their place in a hierarchy defined in relation to other groups. Therefore, it is somewhat incorrect to look upon these groups as if they were self-contained societies. The definition of such a group as a society depends upon the interaction among its own members, and it is clear in the case of the West Indies that, while the existence of a subculture shared by so many of the lower class renders concerted action possible, there is in fact very little unity of action precisely because of the fact that such a group is only quasi-organized; it is, in a sense, a category created by the research worker rather than a separately functioning social system. The problem of the plural society is indeed a problem of social structure posed by the existence of marked differences of culture, but a society or social system cannot be defined in cultural terms by merely observing the presence or absence of cultural traits; it must be done in terms of social action, that is, the interaction of social roles. The approach that defines society in terms of culture is fundamentally at variance with the approach that, while recognizing the importance of cultural items, stresses the viewpoint of social action. All the most important developments in sociological theory will appear to revolve around this important distinction about social action.

In the second place, differences in social class must depend on a difference in the spread of certain values among different groups. The important differences may be few or many. The contrast between homogeneity and heterogeneity would tend to ignore this important theoretical point. Furthermore, it tends to encourage a merely quantitative estimate of what are "similar" and "different" in institutional practices and beliefs and to ignore the main point, which is that certain of these values are central and others peripheral to the social system. Thus, notwithstanding the concept of cultural core and cultural focus, sociology becomes reduced to cultural anthropology.

Consequent upon this definition of society in terms of culture or in terms of institutions is the view of the integration of the society as a matter of holding the institutions of the society together. Such a view leads to the conception of the integration of homogeneous societies as essentially different from and less difficult than that of heterogeneous societies. This view of the plural society or the culturally diverse community as essentially unstable appears to ignore some of the most important facts. The most significant of the plural societies, the caste system of India, has shown a stability not shared by "homogeneous" Western societies. Similarly, conditions of revolution and other forms of political instability appear not to depend upon homogeneity of culture alone, although this may be a relevant factor. For instance, the threat to the social order in the West Indies in the postemancipation period appears to lie not only in the cultural differences of the social groups, but in the fact that such differences came to be hinged around and identified with racial and color symbols that were cardinal to the values held by the society. At the same time these values were threatened by the introduction from outside the West Indian community (viewed as a separate social system) of ideas and values as congenial to the subordinate groups in the society as they were uncongenial to the West Indian ruling class; these ideas and values were derived from the superior social system (the United Kingdom) to which there was a common allegiance.

The allegiance to different institutions may or may not threaten the integration of the entire social structure dependent upon a variety of conditions. The shared cultural characteristic facilitates, under certain circumstances, unity of action as organized groups. However, whether such unity of action develops a form that can be contained within the larger social structure depends on the strength or wealth of the shared common values, as well as of a variety of other features. Some of these are discussed below in connection with the differences between the lower class and the Indian community. Among many persons who use the concept of the plural society there is a tendency to underestimate the bonds of sentiment and a stress on the power and authority aspects of the society that leads to the obscuring of some crucial issues. An uncritical use of the term institution vitiates the functional approach. An adequate functional analysis cannot be made on the basis of a classification of institutions that is haphazard or based on external appearance. Structure must be defined in terms of function.

The limitations of the concept of the plural society as contrasted with the unitary society can be seen from the fact that nearly all national societies, even the most homogeneous of them, show significant regional, ethnic, rural-urban, and social class differences among themselves. Another society appears highly unitary when we do not know it, but all the research that has been done in the more highly developed societies has gone to show that a rich cultural variation can subsist within an apparently highly unified national society. Indeed, from an historical point of view, it is the homogeneous society that appears exceptional. In this sense Furnivall, for instance, is forced to classify nearly all the societies he mentions as plural societies. He is forced to rely upon Great Britain as an essentially homogeneous society.* While disagreeing with his formulations, we must agree that Furnivall showed a great deal of insight even when he pointed to the "absence of social will" as one of the characteristics of this plural society. Those areas in which groups of markedly different cultures are found to exist within a larger structure, such as the modern empire state, pose extremely important problems because, as a consequence

---

* Sharp differences in class cultures in British society are clearly recognized both on the empirical and popular levels.

of the breakdown of the belief in European superiority and of European dominance, there is indeed a relative absence of social will. What is needed is the study of a range of societies so that it becomes clear what are the minimum common values that must be shared in order that a viable social structure may exist.

In this respect it should be noted that in Trinidad, although the cultural framework of the Indian and Creole peoples appears to be fundamentally different, nevertheless there are more values held in common than appears at first sight. For instance, the acceptance of the British social system and its scale of values as a superior one led to the partial incorporation of a whole series of values and attitudes characteristic of that system. These values and attitudes are more or less incompatible with the culture of the system of values of the subordinate ethnic groups, and a process of gradual shedding of the latter has consequently taken place.

Thus, although the ascriptive color values were the dominant ones in the island, the universalistic-achievement values of the larger social system also invaded the island society. This was reflected not only in the increasing incorporation of a "democratic" scale of values, but also in the system of administration. The elementary principle of democracy, "each one to count as one and not more than one," was applied to the various groups in a large variety of situations, as in the religious question, in the question of the control of education, and in the suppression of carnival. The dominant demands of the subordinate social groups, both lower-class Creole and Indian, came to be expressed in this demand for equality of treatment, a demand that was at least not incompatible with the new goals that the society has come to accept. The one case in which there was a striking difference of treatment was that of the regulation of marriage. There has never been any attempt to accept the lower-class Creole family structure as worthy of legal existence in its own right, while in the case of the Indian family there was always some respect, and eventually legal recognition, shown to the existing social customs of the group.

That is a reflection of the fact that the Creole populations were accepted as belonging essentially to a national community and therefore could be expected to live up to the more general standards of the society. Such cultural differences as there were did not lead to a conception of a lower class eternally destined to be different from the other classes. Although some biological and other rationalizations developed to justify their inferior position, this did not in fact prevent a definition of the goals of the society as universalistic in the sense that there were no legal barriers to economic opportunity. Following the abolition of slavery the eventual evolution of West Indians toward the acceptance of democratic political participation was logically compatible with with that position. To some, indeed, it seemed its inevitable fulfillment.

On the other hand, the Indian group was considered as almost outside the social system. The dominant conception of the upper group was economic in relation to the Indian problem, but even here the control from abroad tended to modify the purely economic outlook and to that extent incorporated the Indian into a universalistic scale of values; indenture was temporary, and the loss of freedom was compensated by the removal of all those legal restrictions that tended to perpetuate the caste system. Indeed, so much of the culture was shed that the recognition of Hindu and Moslem marriage and divorce created as many problems as it solved.

It is the incorporation of these universalistic values that makes it possible to conceive of a system of common values shared by Indian and Creole alike that may overcome the tendencies toward disintegration already apparent in the social system.

In this respect it is interesting to compare the situation with that in the United States. Although the United States has been conceived as a unitary society by some, there seems to be greater wisdom in Furnivall, who pointed to the United States as an example of his plural society. There, as is well known, wave after wave of different groups possessing somewhat different cultures swept into the country, particularly during the Nineteenth and early Twentieth Centuries. The existence and persistence of these divergent nationalities, while posing special problems of their own, have not hindered the overriding loyalty to the "American way of life" that renders the national system viable; in part, the problem has been met by the theory of the melting pot. All immigrants were to be subjected to a process of Americanization by which their cultural traits were to be replaced by American ways. On the other hand, the resistance of the immigrant cultures to Americanization has led to the conception, in Louis Adamic's colorful phraseology, of "a nation of nations."[6] In other words, the idea of a unitary or homogeneous society has been replaced by the acceptance of cultural pluralism. An interesting analysis of these aspects of the social structure of the United States is made in an article by M. M. Gordon[7] in which he points out that these problems have not been given the attention they deserve. Gordon seeks to go beyond the popular conceptions of the melting pot and the nation of nations. In his opinion there are at least five possible conceptions of cultural pluralism that are nonetheless compatible with an overriding sense of national loyalty.

First, there is the goal of complete assimilation, which is impossible of achievement.

Second, there is a possible recognition of subcultures, of various features of cultural pluralism. Gordon defines a subculture as "a social division of a national culture made up by a combination of ethnic group [used here as a generic term covering race, religion, or national origin], social class, region and rural-urban residence."[7] These subcultures may all be permitted to coexist, but with the contacts between them secondary and not primary, and limited in number. Such groups would have tolerant attitudes toward one another and maintain such relationships as would be necessary to meet the demands of a common legal system and allegiance to a common government. This Gordon calls "cultural pluralism: the tolerance level."[7]

Third, there is a form of "cultural pluralism: the good group relations level." This is characterized as one in which the subcultures continue to exist, but secondary contacts increase in number, and a limited number of primary contacts then takes place. Relations on this level imply employment integration, common use of public accommodations, interethnic composition of civic organizations, and frequent symbolic demonstrations of intergroup harmony to emphasize common goals and values. Primary contacts are not such as to endanger the endogamous system and therefore the ethnic subculture as a whole. This, in his opinion, is the position that obtains in the United States at present.

Fourth, there is the "community integration level." In this there is an acceptance of all ethnic backgrounds as equally valid and a positive encouragement of primary group relationships. This level accepts diverse ethnic backgrounds that presumably need be shed only insofar as they affect social participation. In this respect the goal differs from the previous goal in the acceptance of ethnic approbation as in itself a positive value. This is a goal envisaged as possible in America, because the brotherhood of man takes a higher place in the hierarchy over every subcultural system of the individual nation and of the values of the subculture itself.

Finally, there is conceived as a possibility a mixed type or "pluralistic integrative" level. In this case the common allegiance and common val es remain, but ethnic groups are permitted to retain their special heritage. However, unlike the present position there would be a subcultural system in which the individuals who wished to rise above ethnic affiliation would be allowed to participate.

The limitation of this analysis is that it seems to center its attention so largely upon the United States. It takes into consideration only situations conceivable within that country and within a national framework. There is a much wider range of possibilities which needs to be taken into account. The importance of the phenomenon of the plural society lies precisely in pointing to the minimum common values that must be shared if a viable social structure is to exist: in other words, the implications of cultural diversity for the integration of the social structure and the larger national framework. The introduction of the concepts of the dominant systems and subsystems of culture is insufficient if no basic change in the relationship of these systems is considered.

Nevertheless, this recognition of a variety of situations in a continuum is helpful, and we may consider how far in Trinidad the social structure in any way resembles one or another of these types. The assimilationist ideal was present to a certain extent in the attitudes toward the lower class, since in the postemancipation period it was considered desirable that the exslaves and their descendants should be educated to a truly Christian way of life. In the case of the Indians, on the other hand, although there was intermittent concern for the problem posed by the existence of a large number of heathens and aliens in the social order, there was never any serious concern with stripping the Indians of their cultural heritage and replacing it by something self-consciously new. The acculturation of the Indians took place largely as a "natural" and not as a planned process. The fact that Trinidad society was not autonomous but subordinate to the larger British social system meant that there would not be any conscious attempt at Trinidadization in the same way that people were Americanized. Insofar as Indians adopt the ways of other Trinidadians they are described as being Creolized. However, the Creole culture was considered to be in many respects an inferior one.

On the whole, the relations between the non-Indian and the Indian communities approached in its position most closely Gordon's second category, that of cultural pluralism: the tolerance level. Although a certain amount of friction between Indian and Creole developed, and although there was a tendency to exploit the less sophisticated of the Indians, there was an over-all tolerance of the ethnic group and its culture.

Primary group contacts between the Indian and other ethnic groups were limited. This situation arose not only because of mutual prejudice, but also because of certain special aspects of the culture of the Indian group. The recreational life of Creole society centered around the mixing of the sexes; the particular dietary customs of the Indians made the usual dinner invitation a difficult problem, for the taboos on drinking possessed a great if diminished force among the Indians, while drinking was a major form of recreation among the Creoles.

The secondary contacts of the Indian group, however, eventually produced a middle class possessing many of the attributes of the colored middle class and the white upper class. Even here, however, we are still dealing with a subcultural group since, although its subculture of achievement is middle class, its primary contacts are still mainly with other individuals of the same subculture of origin and ascriptive status. Development along separate lines has continued in spite of the increasing Creolization of the Indian professional class. However many persons still conscious of their Indian origin have sought to retain a certain ethnic exclusiveness in their social clubs while mixing in the rest of Creole society. This has been resented by members of the Creole middle class, who envisage them as seeking to obtain the best of both worlds.

The third phase, cultural pluralism, the "good group-relations level," represents the ideal possibility toward which Trinidadians can now aim. The crucial problem is how far universalistic standards have reached down among the masses of the population so that a common loyalty can override the particularistic ethnic affiliations.

The "community-integration" type of society is clearly not within possibility of achievement in contemporary Trinidad, and the best that can be hoped for is the evolution of the second type into the third and then the fifth type of culturally pluralistic society.

There are two other points in connection with the coexistence of several subcultures within a social structure that must be noted. First, the fact that values are shared does not mean that they are common in the sense of being widespread; there may be a common acceptance of the superiority of a particular scale of values and a particular type of action, although the social groups that hold these values may not aspire to them. This is the case in most caste societies and in all highly stratified societies in which there is little mobility.

On the other hand, in a society in which there are varying cultural traditions there may still be an over-all awareness of the values of the superior group and an acceptance of the desirability of striving for them. In the first case there is a more-or-less total acceptance of the pattern of stratification as more or less permanent; in the second case there is a great deal of ambivalence because of the fact that there is the acceptance of mutually incompatible cultural traditions. Hence there is the characteristic cleavage between the "level of aspiration" on the one hand, and the "level of expectation" on the other. As long as the levels of aspiration and expectation are more or less the same for the lower-class individual and diverge sharply from those accepted as superior, there is no threat to the disintegration of the larger social structure. Again it would appear that, as long as the level of aspiration and the level of expectation are so much at variance that the level of expectation of the subordinate group is unrelated to the values accepted as superior, there is no serious problem. However, when the levels of expectation and levels of aspiration approach those of the superior group the problem of the integration of the social structure becomes acute. Then there arises the characteristic demand for equality of treatment.

In the case of the lower class of Creole Trinidad, the levels of aspiration were "national," the levels of expectation subcultural; in the case of the Indian community, both level of aspiration and level of expectation tended until recent years to be subcultural. In understanding the development of the society special attention must be paid to those groups of both cultures that have most completely incorporated upper-class values. It is through them that the attack against the dominant upper class becomes most vocal. In Trinidad society this revolt showed itself both in Negro nationalist movements that expressed an alternative to the dominant system and, when the revolt became stronger, in the political movements for self-government. These developments are more fully discussed elsewhere, but here it is essential to note that the movements came from those groups that had to a large extent shed subcultural characteristics. As a result of this there is a confusion on the part of the leaders of their own position with that of the masses to whom they turn for support. Consequently, it is not necessary that there be a total acceptance or striving for the upper-class values by the masses for a mass movement to develop. In order that a threat to the stability of the social order may develop there must be merely sufficient of that merging of level of "national" aspiration and level of personal expectation to lead to an identification of the mass of the people with the new leadership.*

To the extent that leadership is unable to establish such roots, it fails through lack of support. The crisis arises when through continued Western rule the disruption of the subcultures is such that they become incorporated into a system of "national" striving. Thus leadership in Trinidad arose directly or indirectly from those groups that had traveled abroad and imbibed the best of Western culture and therefore demanded equality of treatment. The lower-class subculture, with its ambivalent cultural traditions, could never become a focus for the political movement because, when the lower class thought in national terms, it evaluated itself and its problems according to national standards; hence the much-noted political apathy of the mass of the people. When, however, the acceptance of upper-class values came within the level of expectation of a sufficient number of lower-class individuals, there was a response to political leadership. The demand for adult suffrage, in its emo-

* Stonequist, in *The Marginal Man*[8] long ago showed the role of the marginal group in effecting leadership of nationalist movements. However, the insight expressed in that book, because of inadequate theoretical foundation, led to an indiscriminate use of the term "marginal," so that "marginal man" became, like "plural society," a source of more confusion than help.

tional origin, at any rate, was one for economic and social equality on the part of middle-class persons who felt they had been subjected to discrimination.

On the other hand, it is an indication of the difference of the problem of the integration of the Indian group that there has begun to develop a fear of the general economic dominance of the latter. The fact is that the Indian group, far from being a minority, bids fair to become a majority of the population. However, this factor of numerical preponderance applied as well to the Creole lower-class group. Besides this, however, the Indian community, possessing so many elements of a different culture, is less appreciative of the national tradition than is the Creole lower class. This group is growing more powerfully in terms of economic strength and is throwing up a sufficiency of leaders in the economic field. It is conceivable therefore that a tie-up can develop between the economic and political fields that may lead to an eventual challenge to the general economic dominance of the white group.

While the situation is a complex one, it appears that in recent elections overriding loyalty to the Indian ethnic group and its culture has led to the return of Indian members in all those constituencies in which Indians predominate. In the case of the Indian group, however, there has not developed such a disparity between the middle-class leader advocating the Indian cause and the leaders actually thrown up by the masses.

One hypothesis that has been advanced is that the persistence of the caste pattern led to the success of Indians of high-caste origin. If these ethnic values persist over the general universalistic achievement values and democratic political forms to which the society has become committed, then the future of Trinidad is likely to be quite different from that envisaged by those who planned the future and initiated political change.

One feature that may lead us to a too optimistic view of the spread of universalistic ideas is the fact that the principle of equality of treatment developed as between the different subcultural groups in the society. This principle is not necessarily in line with the conception of a democratic universalistically oriented society. The system unit of such a society tends to be the individual and the primary group, that at a minimum is compatible with a continuously functioning social system, namely the conjugal family. The principle of equality of treatment of groups recognizes larger particularistic ties to the ethnic group as a whole, and the individual tends to become subordinated to this ethnic tie. It is this replacement of the individual by the group as the system-unit that differentiates the society whose main principle is equality of rights of the individual from the multicultural society that gives formal recognition to its component cultural groups.

Social Stratification and Subcultural Groups

A discussion of the various groups on the island would show a varying degree of assimilation to the dominant social values and culture. The analysis in terms of social stratification serves the useful purpose of stressing the common values of the society. However, there are of course severe limitations to analysis in terms of social stratification. The basic problem is not whether the approach to the society is through a theory of pluralism or through a theory of stratification, but one of levels of analysis. Insofar as the various ethnic groups in the islands comprise social subsystems of their own, these subsystems are themselves also capable of analysis in terms of stratification and even of cultural pluralism.   For instance, although we have been speaking of the Indian group as a single entity, the relations between Hindu and Moslem are of great importance.   Again, in terms of social stratification the Hindu group can be analyzed in terms of the partial persistence of hierarchically organized caste groups and in the way in which this original form of social stratification (and its associated cultural pluralism) has been modified and subordinated to the more general norms of the society.

What is needed, therefore, appears to be not a commitment to any particular form of approach, but the relation of these forms of approach to some sort of general sociological theory that will render the inevitably partial empirical analyses meaningful.   Without this we are likely to fall into doctrinaire disputation with selective perception and selective presentation of the facts. This is all the more important because, while some features of cultural pluralism (such as urbanism and its effects on the mingling of cultures) will respond readily to quantitative analysis, the most meaningful problems of the plural society are much less susceptible to such treatment.   The basic problem is the implication of cultural pluralism to the integration and viability of the social order, but in the analysis of the phenomenon we may easily find that the group of leaders, numerically small and culturally assimilated, is of critical significance.

References

1. FURNIVALL, J. S.   1948.   Colonial Policy and Practice.   Cambridge Univ. Press.   Cambridge, England.
2. FURNIVALL, J. S.   1945.   Tropical economy. *In* Fabian Colonial Essays.   R. Hinden, Ed.   Allen & Unwin.   London, England.
3. SOROKIN, P. A.   1947.   Society, Culture, and Personality, Their Structure and Dynamics: a System of General Sociology.   Harper.   New York, N. Y.
4. PARSONS, T. & E. A. SHILS, Eds.   1952.   Toward a General Theory of Action.   Harvard Univ. Press.   Cambridge, Mass.
5. BRAITHWAITE, L.   1952.   Social stratification in Trinidad.   Social and Economic Studies. **2**(2, 3): 5–175.
6. ADAMIC, L.   A Nation of Nations.   1945.   Harper.   New York, N. Y.
7. GORDON, M. M.   1954.   Social structures and goals in group relations.   *In* Freedom and Control: Essays Presented to Robert MacIver.   M. Berger, Ed.   Van Nostrand. Princeton, N. J.
8. STONEQUIST, E. V.   1937.   The Marginal Man: a Study in Personality and Culture Conflict.   Scribner.   New York, N. Y.

Discussion of the Paper

SIMON ROTTENBERG (*University of Chicago, Chicago, Ill.*): I am something of a novice among practiced journeymen, for my investment is in reflection on other things than those that constitute the core of this monograph.   I hesitate, therefore, to approach Braithwaite's paper frontally, because I am not confident that I truthfully understand words and phrases to which those of other disciplines are privy, but that are not included in the stock in trade that economists have accumulated.

I prefer, therefore, to make one observation, from an outsider's vantage point, about the nature of pluralism in society and then to turn to a cognate topic, that is, pluralism in the economy. Most of what I have to say, therefore, will be complementary to the Braithwaite exposition.

It seems to me that any given society is, at any given time, homogeneous and heterogeneous in various degrees up to and including complete heterogeneity. Every society falls at once at all points on the continuum between the quality of being one and that of being fragmented into as many parts as the number of its population. This is true because there is available a large number of standards of definition, each yielding a different result.

Harold Laski used to make much of pluralism in the political organization of society. The sovereignty of the state, he said, was not complete, but was constrained by the allegiance paid by the citizenry in limited and roughly defined spheres to nongovernmental institutions and forms of organization.[1] It would have been better, perhaps, to have formulated this proposition in another way. In some areas, for example, any given citizen pays allegiance to the state; in others, to his trade union; in still others, to his political party. Within the areas relevant to each, each is sovereign. If there are some specific areas that are not exclusively relevant to any single institution but are shared by two or several, then the individual chooses among them in such a manner that what the economist calls his utility is maximized.

Society, in its nonpolitical facets, seems to be structured in the same way. A sense may be perceived in which the entire population of the earth constitutes a single society, but introduce some standard of nationality and it fragments to perhaps one hundred societies. Introduce some standard of ethnicism and it becomes some other number of them. By some income test, there is still another number; by an age-class test, still another; if the standard of differentiation is the distinct household, it is some larger number. Indeed, any of these cells can be fragmented further and the number of them multiplied by cross-classification. Income classes, for example, can be differentiated by age classes.

Clearly, just any standard will not do. Six-toed people can be distinguished from five-toed people, but this distinction is fruitless for an understanding of the structure of society, unless peoples of different number-of-toe classes possess a certain sense of likeness with others of their kind and a certain sense of unlikeness with those of other kinds. The points that suggest themselves are that any society is at once unitary (that is, nonplural) and plural, and that there are as many subsocieties as there are standards by which aggregates of people differentiate themselves from other aggregates; that by some test differentiation does not occur; and that, by some other test, differentiation is complete and each "aggregate" is composed of one person.

In terms of the foregoing discussion, all societies are alike, and the distinction between plural and nonplural societies collapses. It can perhaps be revived sensibly by arguing that, implicitly, I have given equal weight to all standards of differentiation, whereas some are more important than others, and that I have acted as though the number of meaningful standards is equal in all societies, whereas there are more of them in some societies than in others. That is to say, the magnitude of the difference between the Ashkenazic Jew and the Sephardic Jew may be less than that of the difference between white and Negro in Mobile, or Greek and Turk in Cyprus, and that we must not treat differences as though they were all of equal magnitude. If there are in fact large and small magnitudes or, in other terms, senses of community that are deeply and superficially felt, perhaps the distinction between plural and nonplural societies revives.

An interesting paradox suggests itself with respect to differences among societies in the number of meaningfully relevant standards of differentiation. This is that the degree of homogeneity of society seems to be an inverse function of the number of standards prevailing in the society. Thus, if in Cyprus all Turks were exactly alike and all Greeks exactly alike, so that only one standard of differentiation, that of national origin, were relevant, Cypriot society would be more plural than if Turks (or Greeks) were differentiated from one another in many discrete ways. This is true because, if there were a multiplicity of standards, some Greeks would resemble some Turks more than they would resemble other Greeks, and the multiplicity of overlapping aggregations would diminish the real cost to individuals of moving among subsocieties. Thus, the more divided a society appears to be, the less divided it really is.

I shall now leave these layman's comments on cultural pluralism and consider pluralism in the economy.

The primary exponent of the existence of plural economies is J. H. Boeke, of the University of Leyden, the Netherlands. The theory appears in various of his published works, but especially in his *Economics and Economic Policy of Dual Societies*.[2] Boeke's experience is largely in what is now Indonesia. There he observed a Western capitalistic society and an Eastern precapitalistic society. The two were, he said, different; an analytical apparatus sufficient to predict aggregate behavior in the one would be unpredictive for the other.

If what is meant is that technically advanced and technically backward sectors exist side by side in the economy, or that capital-intensive and labor-intensive firms both survive, either in the same or in different industries, then, of course, counterparts can be found anywhere, and there is nothing special about Indonesia, or the East, or the low-income countries. The 1954 *Census of Manufactures*[3] in the United States, for example, shows that of a total of 287,000 manufacturing establishments in the country, fully 108,000 had less than 5 employees. The small firms produce a smaller proportion of industrial output than they represent in the number of firms, of course, but it is significant that they are able to survive, and presumably they do so for 2 reasons: first, because they are to some extent in different industries than the large firms, even where the census classifies them into a single category, and therefore, small and large are not competitive with one another in the same product markets; second, because the optimum size of firms is a function of a number of variables, one of which is the talent and capacity of managers and, as long as talent is not equally distributed among people, only some will have abilities appropriate to large firms. One might ask why those with talents for managing large firms do not capture the entire market; the answer is that there are some sizes that are too large even for them, and that unit costs begin to rise when optima are exceeded. The small and technically backward firms survive in competition with large and technically advanced firms even where they confront one another in the same product markets. Where they do not (that is, where they are in different industries) they nevertheless compete with one another for labor and for raw and intermediate materials in factor markets. Thus the small firms cannot escape competition with the large by moving to different output complexes. Still they survive, although the small firms use less capital per worker than do the large ones.

This is the case in the United States. Thus one of the world's most "capitalistic" economies, in Boeke's typology, also has its backward sectors. However, the Western economies, according to Boeke, are not plural; only the Eastern (or "quasi-Eastern," such as the African) are. What, then, is the measure of difference between sectors, such that we can appropriately speak of pluralism? Benjamin Higgins paraphrases Boeke thus: "The pre-capitalistic or eastern sector of a dualistic economy has several characteristic features. One of these is 'limited needs,' in sharp contrast with the 'unlimited needs' of a western society. Accordingly, ... 'anyone expecting western reactions will meet with frequent surprises. When the price of coconut is high, the chances are that less of the commodities will be offered for sale; when wages are raised the manager of the estate risks that less work will be done; if three acres are enough to supply the needs of the householder, a cultivator will not till six; when rubber prices fall the owner of a grove may decide to tap more intensively. . . '.

"Such needs as there are in eastern societies are social rather than economic. It is what the community thinks of commodities that gives them their value.

" 'If the Madurese values his bull ten times as much as his cow, this is not because the former is ten times as useful to him in his business as the latter, but because the bull increases his prestige at the bull races.'

"Speculative profits are attractive to the Oriental, but 'these profits lack every element of that regularity and continuity which characterizes the idea of income.' Similarly there is no professional trading in the eastern village community. Eastern industry is characterized by 'aversion to capital' in the sense of 'conscious dislike of investing capital and of the risks attending this,' ... lack of elasticity of supply. . . ."[4]

Other differences are enumerated, but this suffices. A number of questions now occur to me.

Has the Oriental economy been correctly characterized here? Is it really true that, when the price of coconuts is high, fewer of them will be offered for sale, or is the truth merely that each individual producer of coconuts then engaged in the trade will diminish his output, but that this diminished output will be overcome by the output of others who are attracted by the relatively higher prices from other trades to the coconut trade? For if this is really what happens, it duplicates exactly what economists have observed to happen in Western economies.

Also, if the characterization has been correct, are Oriental economies really different from Western economies? Can we not say about automobiles in the United States what is said about Madurese bulls? If the United States corporation executive values his Lincoln Continental automobile ten times as much as his drill press, this is not because the former is ten times as useful to him in his business as the latter, but because the car increases his prestige in suburbia. Is it really true that "needs" are "unlimited" in Western society? Is it not true that, in the West as in the East, time is a scarce resource and leisure competes for it with income? Is it not true also that in the West, beyond some point, it is considered more worthwhile to spend increments of time for leisure rather than for income? If Orientals engage in sporadic ventures for profit but do not organize on-going businesses, is this not an expression of diversification produced by the limited extent of the market? Does not the equivalent occur in Western economies where markets are limited when entrepreneurs have their eggs distributed in many baskets, with a wide and varied portfolio of business equities? Does the Oriental really eschew capitalization, or does he not capitalize in agriculture, investing real resources in the cultivation of his plot only to harvest the yield in a later somewhat long run? If he shuns risk, do we not observe the same thing in the omnipresence of insurance companies and pension funds in Western economies, and is this not evidence that the West likewise has its shunners of risk? Thus, find a quality in Eastern economies, and a counterpart can be found in the West.

Three and only three assumptive propositions can be made about behavior in the economy. There is only one hypothetical case in which none of the three has relevance, and that is where all goods are free (like air) and can be consumed in any quantity without depriving another of any quantity of it, and at zero real cost. This describes no real world economy anywhere. What then are the three possible postulates? They are, first, that choices among alternatives are made randomly as by the turning of coins or the throwing of dice; second, that choices are made such that utility is sought to be minimized; and finally, that choices are made such that utility is sought to be maximized. I cannot believe that those who see pluralism in economies would accept either of the first two postulates as characterizing behavior in the Eastern sectors of the plural economies; if they reject those two, they are perforce compelled to accept the third. However, if they accept the third their case collapses, for this is equivalent to admitting that predicative propositions, derived from the same assumptive postulates, have relevance to both sectors of the so-called plural economies, and the pretended substance of economic pluralism melts away. This is not to say that there are no differences in tastes among different aggregates of population. One may consume large proportional quantities of rice and another of fish; one may barter kind for kind and another have a common medium of exchange; and one may make transfer payments through a combination of a progressive income tax and disproportionate public welfare payments to the poor, while another makes transfer payments by purchasing brides.

However, these are superficial differences. As long as both systems seek to achieve their ends by economizing, by combining consumption items in such proportions that utility is maximized, and by combining resources in production in such proportions that whatever is sought to be produced is done at the lowest real cost per unit of output, then these allegedly different economies are really more alike than they are different, and the dual economies collapse into one.

References

1. LASKI, H. J.   1921.   The Foundations of Sovereignty.   Allen & Unwin.   London, England.
2. BOEKE, J. H.   1953.   Economics and Economic Policy of Dual Societies.   Intern. Secretariat, Inst. Pacific Relations.   New York, N. Y.
3. CENSUS OF MANUFACTURES.   1954.   U. S. Govt. Printing Office.   Washington, D. C.
4. HIGGINS, B.   1956.   The dualistic theory of underdeveloped areas.   Econ. Development and Cultural Change. 4(2): 99.

PEASANTS, PLANTATIONS, AND PLURALISM

Elena Padilla

Community Mental Health Board, New York, N. Y.

In the history of the social sciences, three concepts, the peasant, the plantation, and pluralism, have developed independently. However, the first two of these were related as soon as historians and social scientists, including human geographers, began to examine local tropical agrarian societies in an historical or in a horizontal perspective.

The concept of the peasant society has a long history in European and Asian descriptions of agrarian adaptations in certain social orders. The plantation concept, although it is of later origin, goes back at least to the early days of the colonization of the New World and finally became restricted to a certain kind of productive enterprise producing certain kinds of social arrangements. The concept of pluralism, on the other hand, is of more recent origin and, in addition, also has a different frame of reference. Furnivall,[1] a political economist, used it in the early 1930s to characterize multiracial societies in southeast Asia, where Europeans, Chinese, Javanese, and Indians, among others, retained distinctive social characteristics. Social conditions in that part of the world had created and strengthened the internal social cohesion of nationality groups and, in turn, encouraged or facilitated, through their cultural orders, the relationships of conflict among outgroups. Furnivall used the concept of pluralism to explain the cultural and social heterogeneity of this part of the world.

Geographers, political scientists, historians, economists, and historical sociologists, among others, studied peasant and plantation societies long before anthropologists came to grips with the study of modern agrarian societies and their cultures. An important early contribution of interest to anthropologists is the work of Edgar Thompson, summarized in his cyclical theory of plantation systems. This theory provides a framework for an historical analysis of plantation societies, their structural components, and consequent social correlates.[2] Thompson's work has had cross-cultural applicability, as he has examined the cyclical development of plantation societies of the southern United States, Africa, Hawaii, and Asia.[2] Darkenwald and Jones,[3] among other geographers, have also used the concepts of peasants and plantations, although with a racial focus in addition to economic, social, and environmental foci. When used cautiously, their work still retains value for the study of social systems characterized by plantation or peasant economic adaptations. Ida Greaves' *Modern Production Among Backward Peoples*,[4] is perhaps the most important contribution of economics to anthropology in this area. This study has a typological emphasis, is comparative in scope, and examines an array of societies in a variety of qualitative and quantitative relationships to the market system. It is also important to us because this work was influenced by Bronislaw Malinowski and comes closer than others to the objectives of anthropological analyses of types.

In anthropology the first attempts at studying peasant societies in the field were those of the late Redfield in his study of a Tepoztecan Mexican village.[5]

In England, a few years later, Raymond Firth published a study of Malay fishermen whose economic and social system he characterized as peasant.[6] The fishing practices, the social relationships, and the ways of life of these fishermen were structurally so similar to those of peasant agriculturalists that Firth conceptualized them as being of a common type. The first efforts by anthropologists to link the concepts of peasants and plantations as well as subvariants of these types to a horizontal scheme or national society were those of Steward and his associates in Puerto Rico.[7] In this investigation a number of local communities were chosen, after a survey, as instances of cultural variations or types within the island and studied intensively. These communities were focused upon as part of the larger national whole, as well as examples of unique instances within that whole. Historical and institutional studies at the national level were to provide the linkages of the local communities to the total national scene. As a pilot study by anthropologists, the Puerto Rican project has raised many questions even among those who participated in it. Recently two of the communities studied at that time, Cañamelar and San José—the first a corporate-plantation subculture and the second a peasant subculture—were restudied, and I understand that a third one, Nocorá, is now being restudied.

The restudies of Cañamelar and San José by Theodore Brameld and his associates at the University of Puerto Rico are of importance in the context of this paper. Brameld is an educator; his book, *The Remaking of a Culture*,[8] is an attempt to provide a framework for a culturally oriented educational system for Puerto Rico. His study attempted to characterize the culture of Puerto Rico as a whole by studying the interrelationships within the whole and, by using Steward's concept of levels of organization, to relate the parts to the whole. He calls the study interdisciplinary, and so it is, because his concepts and methods are drawn from a variety of fields such as anthropology, sociology, and philosophy. Brameld presupposes the historical treatment of the development of subcultures in Puerto Rico and the study of the five subcultures done by the team of anthropologists in 1948 and 1949. He chose Cañamelar and San José for field studies and used questionnaires as a principal instrument. The plan of the project was presented and discussed in a series of meetings with the faculties of schools and parent-teacher associations of the town. Members of these groups were asked to nominate respondents, and an election of respondents was held through secret ballot. Of the five respondents who provided the data for San José, four were elected and one was chosen by the team because he had lived in the country all of his life and had been an informant in the earlier study. Similar procedures were followed in the selection of informants in Cañamelar. A number of national leaders were also selected as respondents on issues of the national society. These national leaders were nominated by a jury of eight national-level educators. The jurors in question were selected by the research staff. The average time spent with each informant was ten hours; each interview lasted for an average of one hour. Schoolteachers did most of the interviewing. This brief description of the methods used by Brameld gives the essentials of the difference between the methods and conceptual approaches of Brameld and those used by the Steward team. Participant observation and use of schedules and ques-

tionnaires, but mostly the administration of these in the atmosphere of con-
viviality and rapport in which the anthropologists lived in those communities,
added a dimension to acquiring social and cultural knowledge for which no
substitute technique has as yet been developed.

Brameld's conclusions about Puerto Rico do not prove or disprove the validity of the findings of the Steward project. In fact, Brameld's findings cannot even be interpreted as a study of social changes occurring from the time
the original field work was conducted to the time of the restudy. As one of
the participants in the Steward project, however, I do feel that a critical evaluation of the approaches and methods of that study is in order. Such an evaluation requires empirical retesting in addition to a re-examination of the theoretical framework. Another society in the Caribbean will be approached in a
manner similar to that of Steward in Puerto Rico, but in our present state of
knowledge we need not fall again into some of the theoretical inconsistencies
and difficulties that beset us when formulating, carrying out, and analyzing
the findings of the Puerto Rican project.

The Puerto Rican study was oriented to the cultural ecological hypothesis
that Steward formulated for the first time during the mid-1930s in his study
of primitive hunting bands.[7] Cultural ecology refers to the manner in which a
society adapts to environmental circumstances by function of its technology
and its culture (norms). Environment in this context is an active factor that
man can transform technologically. The system of social relationships necessary to such creative control of the environment is related to the norms and
cultural behavior prescribed by the society in question. In other words, the
hypothesis implies a conceptual difference between culture and society. In
one sense, its cross-cultural applicability refers to recurrent social structural
conditions within a variety of cultural circumstances. In another sense, it is
concerned with culture as a system, as an organized order, and as a form. If
we are interested in the patterns of a particular culture, in exhausting the
range of cultural phenomena within a society, the cultural ecological hypothesis is irrelevant, because this hypothesis is of an order of abstraction that permits us to select those characteristics of structure and of formal cultural content that we can generalize and compare. The generalizations that derive
from such a hypothesis are not statistical values; they are qualitative and
require a definition of conditions under which, whenever certain circumstances
appear, others will follow as a consequence. The next step is to examine other
possible circumstances and to seek their consequences; this approach will lead
us in turn to formulating additional types.

Steward's theoretical construct and particularly the cultural ecological hypotheses are convenient devices for investigating certain problems in culture,
but are far from representing a school of thought or a conclusion about society
and culture.

Peasants and plantations may be described and analyzed as social types
with reference to their formal economic characteristics. When a given crop
is selected as the basis for defining either type as a system one encounters conceptual misrepresentations. We know that, because of modern technology
and the elasticity of markets, both qualitative and quantitative, social and
economic changes, including political revolutions, have been taking place in

many colonial societies, with the result that the organization of production has changed.   For example, many crops that traditionally were grown only on plantations can now be grown by farmers or peasants on small land units, while other crops that were traditionally small farmers' and peasants' crops are now grown on large plantations or estates.   Shifts in the size and operation of units of production requiring changes in capital outlay and volume of credit have in turn inevitably followed changes in the social arrangements of production and the opportunities of those involved in such systems.   Many types of subculture other than those of peasants and plantations are found in traditionally typed peasant or plantation societies.   For this reason it is doubtful whether the constructs of plantation and peasant are meaningful frameworks for the modern Caribbean world.   As yet we have no estimate of the ways of life, the culture, and structural components of such segments as the intellectuals, professionals, businessmen, slum dwellers, and other groups who live independently of the processes of land production.   Such knowledge will not come from the study of the plantation system as, to some extent, it is incompatible with the rise of sociocultural groups independent of the land or of a peasantry, which also shrinks our focus to agrarian ways of life and its consequent agrarian-based social system.

A review of the recently published literature on the Caribbean shows little coordination of scientific aims and methodological approaches to this area. M. G. Smith's *Framework for Caribbean Studies*[9] is a unique attempt at delineating conceptual approaches for the study of Caribbean societies.   Smith is concerned primarily with social structures and with the variations within societies that result from the alignments of certain social groups.   In the Caribbean, as in Indonesia and Malaya, for example, these are separate ethnic groups, each with its social identification characterized by a subsystem of social arrangements.   With this focus in mind, the concept of the plural society is central to Smith's system of thought.   This concept is underlined by the recognition that modern societies cannot be described as uniform in culture and social form; it also implies that there are organized social segments within such societies, and that these are characterized by subcultural variants.

This concept is more fruitful than the terms "heterogeneous" and "complex," which in themselves are pregnant with plurality.   By definition, peasant and plantation systems in modern societies are not self-contained or self-definable wholes to themselves; hence, they are parts of a plural society.   This is true to the extent that they are involved in one way or another with other segments and within networks of institutional systems that are not local and integrated within the local situation, but are parts of a colonial or national system. Along the same lines of thought, it follows that plurality is a necessary condition of a society that has such economic arrangements as plantations and peasantries.

In societies whose social arrangements have been laid partly on racial grounds, as is the case for many societies of the Caribbean region, the crucial social criteria are still social rather than biological.   The social structure is predicated upon a distribution of statuses, life opportunities, and prestige allotments associated with racial ascriptions.   Consequently, one does not study in a sociological frame of reference the characteristics of a *racial* group, but the characteristics of a *social* group, the racial factor being in itself a residual category.   This is also the case when one uses the altogether unclear concept of ethnic group.   Studies of nationality, ethnic, or so-called racial groups as local communities or cultural groups have been a center of attention for anthropologists here and in England.   These studies naturally deal with social and cultural behavior, but the context of the universe studied and its field still remain unsettled.   In the study of Caribbean societies, even among those that are segmented along racial or ethnic lines, other segments derived from economic, political, religious, and educational alliances form part of the plurality of the societies.   In societies in which ethnic differences in social alignments do not determine segments within the society one must seek the sources of plurality in other types of analyses of the social system.   From the standpoint of cultural diversity it follows that, in societies with status distribution that creates racial groups as social units, the cultural attributes and ideologies that characterize such groups will be adapted to other cultural characteristics.   These are derived from other cross-cutting segments of the society not necessarily predicated upon national, ethnic, or racial origins.   In societies in which assimilation of racial and nationality groups has proceeded without castelike formation, the plurality of culture must be sought in terms of whatever system has been developed to allocate status distributions.   In both types of societies it is necessary to analyze social structures in terms of their units: status, role, and office.   For both types of societies it is necessary to distinguish culture from society and cultural plurality from social pluralism.

The concept of the plural society, on the other hand, is too limited to give us more than an assumption or postulate, for only when each so-called plural society is characterized in terms of its components and behavioral expectations or norms that accompany each component are we advancing beyond simply saying, "this society is plural."   Perhaps at present the answers to these problems are to be sought more productively in terms of microtheories than in the ambitious schema of totalities or wholes, as has been the trend in other behavioral sciences.

To summarize: societies of the contemporary Caribbean are plural at both the social and cultural levels.   Each society consists of many segments, each having certain subcultural characteristics.   Plantations and peasants are among these; it is possible and fruitful to study peasant and plantation communities as parts of the larger polysegmented context into which they fit, but plantation and peasant local communities, while representing aspects of the larger sociocultural system, do not necessarily increase our understanding of such a system.   We must study additional variant subgroups and their relationships to the whole, as well as undertake institutional and horizontal studies of wholes to reach the objective of understanding modern societies.

References

1. FURNIVALL, J. S. 1944. Netherlands India, a Study of Plural Economy. Cambridge Univ. Press. Cambridge, England.
2. THOMPSON, E. T. Cyclical Theory of Plantations.

3. DARKENWALD, G. G. & C. S. JONES. 1954. Economic Geography. Revised ed. Macmillan. New York, N. Y.
4. GREAVES, I. 1935. Modern Production Among Backward Peoples. School of Economics. London, England.
5. REDFIELD, R. 1930. Tepoztlan. Univ. Chicago Press. Chicago, Ill.
6. FIRTH, R. 1946. Malay Fishermen. K. Paul, Trench, Trubner. London, England.
7. STEWARD, J., et al. 1957. The People of Puerto Rico. Univ. Ill. Press. Urbana, Ill.
8. BRAMELD, T. 1959. The Remaking of a Culture. Harper. New York, N. Y.
9. SMITH, M. G. 1955. Framework for Caribbean Studies. Univ. Coll. West Indies. Mona, Jamaica.

THE ROLE OF THE INTELLECTUAL IN
HAITIAN PLURAL SOCIETY

Rémy Bastien

Program for Advanced Training in Applied Social Sciences, Pan American Union, Mexico, D.F., Mexico

Heir to Plato and his *Republic*, the intellectual dreams of changing or at least influencing the society in which he lives. Whether he seeks Truth for itself or is bent on seeing the triumph of some personal theory contrary to current ways of thought, the intellectual wishes to act, to manipulate and convert his fellow human beings to his ideas. He sees himself as the guide of public opinion, the educator, the master, but a master often incapable of foreseeing the corruption and debasement of his teachings at the hands of rebellious or willful disciples.

This discussion is restricted to the intellectual who, either through objective or passionate study of society, has proposed and at times succeeded, although often posthumously, in modifying that society. Let us consider the intellectual as a social scientist, and see him as the fomenter of cultural changes, the man who knows how to sum up a social situation, is endowed with the power both of analysis and synthesis, and is capable of pointing out a new direction. His influence may be world-wide or only local, he could be a Marx, a Locke, a Rousseau, a Machiavelli, a Madison, or a Durkheim. Less well known but highly influential in the transformation of his country, he could be a Gökalp, the theoretician behind Kemal Ataturk's political and social revolution in Turkey.

Whether or not we share their theories, these men point to success and fame. But what of the unsuccessful intellectual whose ideas are still ignored despite the fact that they promise a better life, peace, order, and human dignity to his countrymen? Why is it that the strong minds of Latin America, nurtured on liberalism and democracy, have not, through their writings, as yet achieved the social betterment they preach so convincingly? Why is it, when the patterns for just government have been carefully laid out, that the Latin American intellectual more often than not sees his country the prey of dictatorship? Is it due to immaturity, lack of realism, or the inadaptability of imported ideas to local conditions and economic factors? Is the answer in the pluralistic nature of most of these countries?

Undoubtedly, unbalanced pluralism affects the development of Latin America adversely. Languages, cultures, and races have not found the harmonious formula that allows for the equilibrium of Switzerland, for example. Therefore, the role of the intellectual is first to observe and learn objectively about his society and then to find the way of cooperation between the plural elements.

This is easily said. In practice, the difficulties are countless because, if the intellectual wishes, as Kallen puts it,[1] "union, which is the teamplay of the different" as opposed to "unity, which is liquidation of difference" (pp. 123, 124), then he must respect individual rights. In a word, he is bound to democratic ways, the very ways that are so difficult to follow in Latin America.

Let us illustrate the problem with an example. I choose Haiti for two reasons: it is my country and it is undergoing some deep social changes.

Generally called the Black Republic because the population is 95 per cent Negro, Haiti at least should not present a racial problem, yet it does, and a lively one. Since colonial times, a minority of mulattoes born from the French masters and the African slaves have been at odds with the black majority of the population. The two groups united briefly to achieve Haiti's independence in 1803 and then drifted apart again, the mulattoes taking advantage of their education to control the government machinery and becoming a bureaucratic group living in relative security and comfort as compared to the rural masses. This group has been variously described as an elite, an aristocracy, a caste and, since 1946, a bourgeoisie.

Language is a second plural trait. While the entire population speaks Créole, only a small group is able to speak and write French, the official language. In the past the mulatto group made up the majority of the French-speaking clique. We may observe, in passing, that Haiti's linguistic problem is not one of French and/or Créole, but rather one of literacy. At least 85 per cent of a population of 3,500,000 is completely illiterate.

In cultural matters there is another gap. The rural population, no less than 85 per cent of the population, lives on tiny plots of land, barely subsisting. The peasant cultivates his land with primitive implements, practices certain forms of cooperative labor, and believes both in Catholicism and in the popular religion called *Vodun*. African derivations are numerous in his folk culture, but they mix with Western practices of inheritance, land tenure, justice, and administration. In the town, proletariat and elite alike are subject to the same institutions and laws, but the elite despises the folk culture and does his best to separate himself from it (childhood associations with that folk culture, through contact with the servants, at times make adult separation psychologically difficult). The *bourgeoisie* considers its activities as basically French and has created an abundant literature, often highly original when inspired by national ways of life.

This is a very generalized sketch of pluralism in Haiti. Matters have been somewhat simplified by presenting the elite as composed entirely of mulattoes or by giving the impression that they are or have been in absolute control of government posts and the professions. Had this been the case, subsequent events that we shall discuss shortly would not have taken place.

Faced by such a social structure, what has been the traditional attitude of the Haitian intellectual? In spite of long periods when it was dangerous to criticize governmental acts, the intellectual, black or mulatto, has tried to find a solution to Haiti's problems. So far, he has had very little success. Efforts were mainly in the educational and economic fields. Political writers were always plentiful, but none has influenced the traditional play of politics.

In the social and cultural fields the picture varies. As the first Negro republic, Haiti was severely attacked all during the Nineteenth Century and part of the Twentieth. The intellectual, whatever his color and class, has always been prompt to answer his country's enemies in proud and effective terms. Anténor Firmin, Jacques-Nicolas Léger, Louis Joseph Janvier, and Dantès Bellegarde are good examples. Firmin, showing an extraordinary grasp of the anthropological concepts of his times, wrote *On the Equality of Human Races*,[2] an answer to Gobineau's attacks against the Negro.[3] Both Firmin and Janvier, in spite of their outstanding intellectual qualities, failed when they attempted to change the political mores of Haiti (both of these men were dark-skinned). The Haitian intellectual of sixty years ago, when he criticized *Vodun*, for instance, labeling it a superstition and denying its importance, was at the same time piously defending his country against pitiless attacks from European and American writers. Anthropology had not as yet taught tolerance, nor had the fashionableness of primitivism yet given titles of nobility to folkloric manifestations in underdeveloped countries.

It is worthy of mention that between 1890 and 1915 Haiti produced a remarkable crop of above-average men; brilliant lawyers, doctors, essayists, poets, and novelists. However, ironically enough, it was in that generation of intellectuals that the national collapse occurred. After a long series of senseless army coups ending in massacre and anarchy, Haiti, in 1915, was occupied by the armed forces of the United States. The intellectuals then set about, first, to defend national sovereignty against the invader and, second, to try to discover, through self-criticism, the causes of the national disaster. A group of young men and a solitary writer will illustrate these efforts.

The young men, belonging to the *Mouvement indigène* (Indigenous Movement) and headed by sons of elite families educated in Europe, adopted an iconoclastic attitude toward both the past and the present. According to them, the earlier Haitian writers had had no originality (the young rebels were interested chiefly in literature) and had never looked to their national culture for inspiration; instead, they had tried to be European and had failed. Socially, the Haitian upper class was considered stuffy, narrow-minded, and utterly ignorant of the real life of the country. Passing from theory to practice, the members of the Indigenous Movement (Jacques Roumain, Émile Roumer, Philippe Thoby-Marcelin, Antonio Vieux, Jean Brierre, and others) wrote and published short stories, novels, poetry, and essays embodying their social and literary ideas.

After taking a leading part in organizing the general strike against the American occupation, which hastened its end, the members of the Indigenous Movement came to blows because of political divergences. Individually, they continued to write, but it was as a group that they gave their best, recapturing the dignity of the intellectual and doing their utmost to help unite their divided country. Meanwhile, another writer was pondering the same problems, but in a different fashion.

Jean Price-Mars, a physician and civil servant, undertook the task of making known to the city-dweller the life of rural Haiti. In 1928 he published his classic *Ainsi Parla l'Oncle*[4] with the subtitle *Ethnographic Essays*, a collection of lectures on folklore. In his foreword Price-Mars criticized the Haitian elite for denying its African origins and, even worse, for trying to be something it is not; that is, European. That brief foreword was to serve later as the charter of the whole Haitian ethnological school. Price-Mars, whether describing courtship, marriage, or *Vodun* ceremonies, shows us a gentle, idyllic and happy peasant, a peasant always dressed up in his Sunday best. There is no way of determining whether or not his intention was to make the peasant and his culture acceptable to the city elite, but the ethnography of Price-Mars in this book is very one-sided, prudently ignoring the disastrous power of magic, the precarious economy, and diseases in Haitian communities.

In spite of its shortcomings, the book was a success and folklore became the password of anthropological research in Haiti. The *bourgeoisie* began openly to show some interest in popular songs and dances. The intellectual's effort to bridge the cultural gap between elite and masses was beginning to bear fruit, but the ripest fruit was yet to fall. A wise man living a quiet life, Price-Mars slowly became the head of a school, the leader of Haitian ethnology. Before 1942 his teaching consisted of lectures and occasional publications, but on that date he founded the Ethnological Institute in Port-au-Prince. Shortly before, Jacques Roumain had created the Haitian Bureau of Ethnology. Because of his political ideas, Roumain, whose prestige was great among the youth, had been forced into exile in the mid-1930s. In order to know his own people better, he studied anthropology in Paris under Paul Mauss and Marcel Rivet and worked at the Museum of Man in that city.

Roumain saw in the modest Bureau of Ethnology a tool for national unity. With the help of exhibits, lectures, and systematic visits by schoolchildren, he hoped to break down the obsolete prejudices of the upper class against the popular culture and also to destroy some of the superstitions the masses themselves held. Roumain was no blind devotee of folklore; he wanted objective studies and good descriptive monographs of Haitian culture. His view was that *Vodun* should not be persecuted, but that it was bound to disappear eventually in the face of medical and economic progress. Roumain died in 1944, before realizing most of his anthropological projects. A versatile and talented man, he left to his country, however, a posthumous novel, *Masters of the Dew*,[5] with the simple message: "Unite or perish!"

Anthropology as an intellectual pursuit was now more in vogue than ever, but with a definitely new orientation. Since for more than a century the Haitian elite had tried and failed to be European, the new black intellectual and folklorist undertook a "Return to Africa" attitude while praising unconditionally every aspect of Haitian culture that actually (or supposedly) had something to do with Africa. To support this attitude there sprang up an emotional ethnography, at times frankly mystical, written in a rococo style and showing little or no capacity to grasp the over-all problem of Haiti. One enthusiastic writer suggested national salvation through *Vodun* and proposed the construction of a *Vodun* temple in front of the cathedral of Port-au-Prince. Clearly, some of Price-Mars' followers were getting out of control, but this is the tragedy of any master; too often his ideas are inflated, twisted, and distorted by overenthusiastic disciples. For anyone acquainted with Haitian internal affairs, folklore had become a political activity; something new was in the offing.

For a better comprehension of what follows, let us leave the folklorists and review the social and political situation. The United States occupation was begun in 1915, and perhaps because of a need for an organized social group the occupation authorities favored the election of mulattoes to the presidency, thus bringing back the elite to power after an eclipse of seventy years. After some unnecessary killings of peasants order was restored, roads opened, clinics established, and schools reorganized at various levels. The elite rode high, although resenting the presence of foreigners who excluded Haitians (even the elite) from their social life.

After orderly elections in 1930 the United States troops withdrew in 1934, leaving the country in peace and with democratic institutions. The first things to go were the democratic institutions: one half the Senate was summarily discharged and intellectuals and journalists were jailed and killed. The price of coffee dropped as a result of World War II, and the Haitian economy became chaotic. The economy recovered after 1942 due to United States demand for strategic materials, but the production of these materials in Haiti required land, and many peasant holdings were expropriated. Discontent was at a high pitch. Also, the government ignored the black intellectuals and was bent on favoring the mulattoes regardless of their capacity. At a glance, such was the situation in 1945.

Many groups had begun working more or less underground. The principal ones were made up of some young leftists of all skin colors and the folklorists, most of whom were black. The latter had found an unexpected ally in the person of a United States scholar. In 1941 *The Haitian People* by James G. Leyburn[6] was published. This book was to play an important role in the coming years of Haitian social history. Leyburn, with faultless objectivity (he becomes subjective only when describing some Haitian landscapes) studied Haiti's institutions with, as he said, a "main objective to show what adjustments a group of ex-slaves in a tropical country made to their sudden independence" (p. 305). However, being a foreigner not subject to local influences and possible retaliation from powerful groups, Leyburn was free to apply to his analysis all the rigor of the sociological method. In order to make his findings clearer he used a terminology new to the Haitians. Thus the elite and masses are for Leyburn two castes. "They are as different as day from night. . ." he wrote; "all the professions, most governmental and military offices and the large business enterprises are effectively closed to young men of the masses" (p. 4). The elite is the aristocracy. Always in the same vein, Leyburn stated: "Theoretically, Haitian education is free and democratic; actually, no peasant child could be spared from labor long enough for schooling, or find money for proper clothes to go to school in" (p. 5). By 1941 these statements were no longer entirely correct, and some were already clichés.

Whatever its hasty generalizations, Leyburn's book was a great success, chiefly among the black intellectuals, who found in it new fuel for action against the existing political and social conditions. *The Haitian People* was studied almost in secret, partially translated for the benefit of those who knew no English. It strengthened one idea: the black intellectual must regain political power for the benefit of the country's majority.

Furthermore, Leyburn made one interpretative mistake that the local politicians were quick to observe; he thought that the small constabulary trained by the United States Marines was definitely cured of political fever. The Marines left in 1934, and, in 1937, the army was already involved in a plot to overthrow the government. The blow fell in January 1946 and, in a matter of days, the apparently strong government of Elie Lescot was swept away. The next president was elected under the banner of the Authentics (meaning blacks from the masses) and the slogan "A Black in Power." Their man was Dumarsais Estimé, the well-educated son of a peasant family who had shown great ability as minister of education.

Sociologically speaking, the work of Estimé is supposedly being continued in 1959 by the regime of Haiti under François Duvalier. For the sake of clarity and continuity, we shall first sum up the historical facts before analyzing the social consequences of the Revolution of 1946.

Taking advantage of the economic prosperity of the postwar years, Estimé had gained a great measure of popularity through his own personality and his program of public works which, unfortunately, embodied little of a productive character. The desire to gain absolute control over the Senate was the pretext for an army coup that sent Estimé into exile in May of 1950. Estimé was succeeded by Paul Magloire, the popular young army officer who had planned his downfall. Magloire organized a Government of National Unity, undertook a vast program of public works (again, with little planning), but soon condoned administrative corruption and dictatorial measures. A general strike and indifference from the army forced him to resign in December 1956. In the 6 months following, 4 civilian governments tried to rule, but all were toppled by the struggle between the mulatto's candidate, agronomist Louis Déjoie and Estimé's successor, François Duvalier, ardent folklorist and the black's candidate. The latter quickly won the support of the army and became president of Haiti in September 1957.

Let us now return to the year 1946. The traditional elite had been squarely beaten at the political game. Was the elite in decline? Personally, I think that it was in stagnancy rather than in decline; its relative weakness was due less to deterioration than to the growth of an opposing force. The presidential campaign of 1956–1957, during which the mulatto group showed great vitality, is sufficient proof of this. Consequently in 1946, contrary to appearances, there were, in addition to the *bourgeoisie*, two important forces: first, the army, and second, the black intellectuals and professionals, reinforced by influential rural dwellers of their own color.

Estimé's government endeavored further to break down the power of the mulatto group by depriving it, to a large extent, of civil service positions and hastily forming, through patronage, a new power elite, a black *bourgeoisie*. An important socioeconomic event took place. For more than thirty years the standard of living of the ruling class had hardly varied; the size and cost of villas were almost established by tradition; wealth was moderate and seldom overdisplayed. By 1949, however, what with the construction of the International Fair of Port-au-Prince, Haiti dropped her provincial frock and tried to appear cosmopolitan, with gambling, luxurious hotels, and very costly private residences. The purpose was to attract the tourist trade, since labeled a national industry.

Meanwhile, what about the rural masses and the proletariat? Fundamentally, Estimé had turned his back on them when he decided to satisfy the social ambitions of the politicians. Labor unions, at first encouraged, were quickly disrupted and kept under stifling control. Agricultural production such as that of bananas, was reorganized for export, but for the sole profit of hungry politicians who quickly bungled it. Economic planning and rural organization were of little interest to officials. The hope was tourism, and, to attract the tourist, there was folklore. The results were well below expectations.

Under Magloire's six-year regime class tension had been lessened, and the mulatto had been given a breathing spell. However, the elite's bid for power in 1957 may spell its doom for a long time to come. It is perhaps too early to judge the government of François Duvalier, but from all accounts it is carrying on the principles of 1946 to unexpected extremes. According to foreign press reports, political and human rights have been ruthlessly suppressed, thus deterring the cooperation of all social groups in the attainment of national union. The elimination of all forms of opposition is affecting all classes. The army has undergone drastic changes. In the spring of 1958 a foreign official, well acquainted with Haitian affairs, remarked in private after a visit to the local military academy: "Rather odd, I've not seen a single mulatto among the cadets."

We have come far from the social picture of Haiti generally accepted by scholars in the late 1930s, at least as far as the ruling class is concerned. No one can deny that Haiti is in transition, and that intensive research is needed to evaluate its social transformation. One aspect remains the same however: 85 per cent of the population, consisting of black peasants, is still undernourished and has not yet learned how to read and write. The peasants are waiting for *their* revolution.

This long summary of the Haitian sociological movement and political life was necessary to indicate the role the intellectual played in devising, so to speak, the philosophy of a partial change in a plural society. After 13 years the change has not yet benefited those in whose name it was undertaken. The peasant is still waiting for the means and the incentive to organize his productive capacity.

Will the intellectual, once more, take up the task and teach union instead of class hatred, tolerance instead of persecution, some measure of freedom against dictatorship, and the priority of the masses' needs over personal ambitions?

If Haiti wants a decent way of life for everyone, there must be a reorientation in the ethics and behavior of her rulers. The love of folklore is not enough: what is needed is love of the people.

References

1. KALLEN, H. M. 1957. Alain Locke and cultural pluralism. J. Philosophy. **54**(5): 119–127.
2. FIRMIN, A. 1885. De l'Égalité des Races Humaines. Paris, France.
3. GOBINEAU, J. A. DE. 1854. Essai sur l'Inégalité des Races Humaines. Paris, France.
4. PRICE-MARS, J. 1928. Ainsi Parla l'Oncle: Essais d'Ethnographie. Imprimerie de Compiegne.
5. ROUMAIN, J. 1944. Gouverneurs de la Rosée. Port-au-Prince, Haiti.
6. LEYBURN, J. G. 1941. The Haitian People. Yale Univ. Press. New Haven, Conn.

CULTURAL ASSIMILATION IN A MULTIRACIAL SOCIETY

Daniel J. Crowley

University of Notre Dame, Notre Dame, Ind.

When numbers of people from one culture move to another, they cannot help but alter their original culture. Even the most prolonged and powerful attempts to preserve intact a racial or cultural group in a new milieu have ended in failure. Since culture is both conservative and ever changing, we preserve bits and pieces of our ancestral cultures, but combine and recombine them with the forms and values of the one or more cultures in which we participate in the course of a lifetime.

Since the time of Columbus, West Indian societies have been both biologically and culturally mixed. European institutions adapted to new local circumstances by provincials were soon being used by Africans and their Creole children, who gave them a content never found in Europe. As other peoples from Asia, Europe, and Africa arrived, old traditions merged and new ones developed, and the Creole cultures of the islands are the result. These are local variants of Western culture, but with considerable retention of non-Western forms, attitudes, and values.

Racial purity is an infinitely more personal concept than cultural integrity, but every West Indian street corner attests to the fact that, for this area at least, it is a thing of the past. Except for a very few groups, the West Indians who are not yet mixed will be mixed in a few generations. The last handful of pure Caribs are dying, while their daughters "make babies for" Dominican Creoles. Every year a few more Windward Island whites emigrate permanently to Canada or Britain or marry their colored mistresses, so that the once-large local white populations of Dominica, Montserrat, Carriacou, or Grenada are dwindling. Although overlooked by the 1946 Census,[1] the so-called Blacks include a large number of people more precisely described as Coloured, if the presence of at least one known non-African ancestor is the criterion. In the same census, the Chinese in Trinidad were already nearly half mixed, and this figure is undoubtedly far too low for anyone who knows the population of the north coast, where every family is reputed to have "one Chinee chile."

East Indians, too, have more racial mixture than they sometimes care to admit, as well as ancestry from different castes and areas in India, which in traditional terms is almost as objectionable as race mixing. Most, but certainly not all, offspring of Indians and non-Indians in Trinidad are classed with the Creoles. On the other hand, both Creoles and Indians seem uncertain as to how to classify the many unmixed Indians who are leaders in typically Creole activities such as steel bands, acting, dancing, and carnival masquing.

However, cultural assimilation can take place even without race mixture, as in the American melting pot, where all but a few ethnic groups seem to be melting into three lumps based on religious affiliation.

In the United States much of the assimilation has been conscious on the part of emigrating Europeans desirous of adapting as quickly and as completely as possible to their new culture. In the contemporary Caribbean, conscious assimiliation can be found among culturally Europeanized upper-class local people who, in the throes of racial or other nationalisms, have decided to cast their lot, especially politically, with the local lower classes. They learn the local dialect, salt it well with Creolisms, cook local dishes, espouse local beliefs and prejudices, "jump up" in carnival, and play at being "real Creoles."

Unconscious assimilation is a much more subtle process and, like culture itself, not often perceived by its practitioners. Through this process West Indian-born whites are no longer Englishmen or Frenchmen and can never fully belong to their ancestral cultures. The same process works for the Chinese, Syrians, Portuguese, and other groups who preserve some aspects of their ancestral traditions in their homes, but otherwise belong to the local culture more than they realize.

The only group in the West Indies for which a case of cultural isolation can be made is the East Indian, particularly in Trinidad. Elsewhere their numbers are so small that almost complete Creolization has taken place, as in St. Lucia, St. Vincent, and Grenada, or East Indian customs may be preserved only within the family circle, as in Jamaica. In Trinidad, however, the nearly 30,000 East Indians make up one third of the population. Current politics in the island, although complex, is divided more and more sharply between Creole and East Indian. Diet, dress, and especially family patterns and economic attitudes are clearly distinguished by members of the two groups. Unquestionably, both Creoles and East Indians think they are culturally different; neither group intends to assimilate with the other, but what are the facts of their actual relationship?

Like the other groups, the Indians were forced to leave behind much of their culture when they emigrated. Hindu "indentures" broke a basic law of their religion by "crossing water." The great majority of the East Indians were low caste or casteless, poor, uneducated, rural, and drawn from far-flung and culturally diverse areas of the subcontinent. Undoubtedly, some upper-caste Hindus, even Brahmins, came as indentures, and a few of these knew the written language and some of the religious and secular traditions. In spite of half-hearted attempts to keep families and friends together, the barracks and, later, the rural villages were mixed in caste, class, religion, and language, so that East Indian cultural variations became generalized. Although neither group liked it, Creoles and East Indians were compelled to associate with each other in the fields, in the market and shops, and in village life and, because of the scarcity of Indian women, many men took Creole mates. By converting to Christianity, low caste could be left behind and opportunities for mobility increased. Some East Indians soon became wealthy but, instead of reorganizing their lives and surroundings on Indian principles, they seem to have become thoroughly Europeanized, although some did return to India to visit.

The less successful East Indians, or those less interested in adapting to the standards of the rest of the island community, became small landowners or day laborers in the sugar fields. They often work side by side with "small-island" Creoles, speak English or Creole with them, and drink and gamble together. Doubtless there are tensions and divisions between these two racial groups, but until recently these divergencies were hardly more serious than cleavages within each group on the basis of religion, class, caste, and color.

According to one estimate (Arthur Niehoff, personal communication) one fifth of the Trinidad East Indians live in St. George County, in and around Port of Spain, while many others live in the string of contiguous villages running east to Arima or in the populous San Fernando area. Even when these people work land they go in and out of town almost daily and, in my opinion, are best considered suburban. Even in the Caroni and Oropouche enclaves, where nearly all the people are East Indian agriculturalists, the amount of daily contact with the towns is tremendous. Schools, libraries, the motion pictures (both Western and Indian), sports such as cricket or the races, newspapers, and the omnipresent radio are all sources of unconscious assimiliation. While in town, East Indian men see the newest in clothes, cars, and gadgetry, watch the shipping and tourist activities of the port, and meet the demimonde on Green Corner, the Broadway of Port of Spain. Even in homes where they are relatively secluded, women must go out to market and to shop, to visit relatives, to attend socioreligious events, and to visit the doctor and the dressmaker. The East Indian community has never seriously attempted self-segregation from the Creole world around it, and most East Indians interact daily with their Creole neighbors.

There are East Indians in all social classes. Those at the top are culturally indistinguishable from white, colored, or black urban locals of the same class, except where Hinduism or Islam requires some variations in dietary patterns. These people are more Europeanized than Creole, like their non-Indian compatriots of the same class. Toward the middle of the social scale, urban and suburban Indians again tend to be quite similar to their neighbors. In communities such as Tunapuna, St. James, and San Fernando they share most of each other's popular culture, and have similar attitudes toward government, education, leisure, and the acquisition of wealth. Dietary patterns are frequently interchanged, as people of different origins share each other's foods at homes or at fetes. The Creole kiosk at a bazaar held on Government House lawn in September 1953 served *pelau* as the typically Creole dish, though it is East Indian in both name and origin. The East Indian kiosk served *roti* (wheat pancake) made in the "oil-bake" manner preferred by Creoles, rather than the *sada roti* of traditional Indian homes. Neither example of assimiliation was conscious, and doubtless considerable embarrassment, even disbelief, would have resulted had these facts been mentioned.

Since World War II, Trinidad Creole and East Indian intellectuals have been inspired by the success of India, Ghana, and other formerly colonial areas, and have developed greater race pride and political consciousness. The Indians grew concerned over the rapid attenuation of their ancestral culture. Hindi was dying with the last of the indentures, children attended Christian schools, few of the pandits could explain or defend Hinduism against the better-educated and more prestigeful Christian clergy and, most important of all, the younger people began to leave the land and parental domination, especially in choosing marriage partners, for the greater freedom, better pay, and higher prestige of town life. Local Indian nationalism was thus born in reaction to the extreme degree of assimilation that had already taken place. The usual devices of cultural separateness were then introduced: Hindu and Moslem schools where Hindi is taught, a study program in India for young pandits and other promising scholars, bigger and better mosques and shivalas (Siva temples) in more prestigeful locations, and the building up of social pressure against further Creolization and conversion. However, in the words of Kumari Santosh Chopra, the Punjabi headmistress of Gandhi Memorial High School in Penal, "This latter-day 'revival' of Indian culture is not Indian at all." In the typical competitive Creole way, East Indians are using Indian culture and often mythical caste for "making style" and as a club with which to beat contemptuous Creoles.

Except for the recent racially oriented political developments, the Hindu and Moslem schools seem to be the most effective means of creating and/or preserving a Trinidad East Indian subculture. However, it is difficult to find teachers, and they are among the most Europeanized of all Trinidadians. In the Moslem schools, teachers flatly refused to adopt the wearing of the *orhni* (head veil) in spite of the insistence of the religious leaders. Many of these schools are staffed by Christian East Indians and even by Creoles and, of course, the great majority of East Indian children continue to attend Christian denominational schools with their Creole age peers. Conversely, some Creoles attend Hindu and Moslem schools, learn Hindi and, in a few cases, are converted to Hinduism or Islam. Hindi is still a home language for some families and a religious language for a much larger number but, being largely unwritten, it has become virtually unintelligible to a non-Trinidadian Hindi speaker, since it has acquired vocabulary and pronunciation from English, Creole, and Spanish. A course in Hindi offered by the Extra-Mural Department of the University College of the West Indies had scores of students at the first meeting, but only a handful completed the six-week course. Since practically all of the East Indians already speak English, Hindi seems to have little chance in the future except in rote prayers, sermons, and rituals.

Informed Trinidad East Indians are likely to admit all of these facts and to have little hope for the success of their goals. Students of the Indian community such as M. Klass, M. Freilich, and A. Niehoff also make no claim of a present or future subculture in Trinidad that is like any in India, but both scholars and East Indians seem to feel that in economic and family matters there remains a clear line between Indian and Creole. Indians are said to be willing to save and plan and work toward a distant goal, while Creoles are supposed to spend their money in constant "fête" and not to give a thought to the morrow. Anyone who has met with a carnival band on Ash Wednesday morning to plan next year's masque knows that Creoles can and do plan ahead for distant goals, though their prestige forms may be different from those of some East Indians! The attitude of Creole families toward education and their willingness to make heroic sacrifices for their children can be validated in the lives of most prominent Creoles, although these characteristics may actually be more closely connected with middle-class status or the desire for it than with ethnic origin. Profligate, rum-drinking Indians, or thrifty, abstemious Creoles are definitely not unknown in any Trinidad community but, since they do not serve the stereotype, they tend to be dismissed as atypical. Indians seem to talk more about saving money, even when their actual performance is not unlike that of Creoles of their same class, and the Creoles, traditionally averse to "money-grubbing" business careers, see the growing economic power of upward-mobile Indian businessmen, with its concomitant political power, as a threat to their own social hierarchy, which is based on the Civil Service.

In family structure the ideal pattern for East Indians is an early, family-arranged, monogamous marriage but, like so many ideal patterns both in the Caribbean and elsewhere, it is often honored in the breach. "Under-the-bamboo" Indian marriages are similar in function to Creole consensual unions, and Hindu widows, forbidden by their religion to remarry, merely take a new mate in the Creole manner. Many Indian youths recognize early marriage as an effective means of parental domination, "to keep me in the rice field," and fiercely resist it. Girls, disliking the arranged union, sometimes give their husbands reason to wish for the reintroduction of *purdah* (seclusion). Both sexes show the strain of trying to approximate an ideal Indian value system in a real Creole world by a suicide rate phenomenally high in contrast to that of the Creoles. In the higher classes, where social pressures are more effective, Indian women are more likely to be monogamous, although the men are expected to experiment more widely, often with Creole girls. While more Indian men may be more faithful more often to their wives than some Creole men, their behavior is so similar that the habits of both in this respect are not readily distinguishable.

If the data have been correctly interpreted, both racial and cultural assimilation have proceeded far in Trinidad, although admittedly with a wider range of variations than in some other societies. The somewhat similar institutions of slavery and indenture produced parallel results, so that the East Indians have no more valid claim on an Indian culture in Trinidad than Negroes have on a fully African culture there. Most of Indian culture in Trinidad has been so drastically reinterpreted that even the most nationalistically minded East Indian is culturally a Creole, as he realizes if he has an opportunity to visit India. Real differences exist between the lives of some Indians and some Creoles, but these differences can be explained as readily in terms of class and of rural-urban variations as in terms of ancestral cultures.

Even the most assimilationistic Creoles do not expect the Indians to give up their attempts at racial endogamy and do not want them to abandon Hinduism or Islam, which provide so many popular magic practitioners for the Creole world. East Indians understandably want to better their position in the Trinidadian social structure and are using effective, typically Western techniques of capital accumulation, education, and the espousal of middle-class mores to gain these common goals just as are the upward-mobile Creoles. The permissive Creole culture has already made a place for Indian fêtes, foods, magic practices, and thousands of East Indians. The intelligent self-interest that West Indians of all ethnic origins have displayed in the past may still stave off serious disintegration while the necessary compromises are evolved.

Reference

1. WEST INDIAN CENSUS, 1946. 1950. Part H, Windward Islands. : xxiv–xxv. Government Printer. Kingston, Jamaica.

EAST AND WEST INDIAN: CULTURAL COMPLEXITY IN TRINIDAD*

Morton Klass

Columbia University, New York, N.Y.

No one disputes the fact that the island of Trinidad exhibits a marked degree of ethnic heterogeneity. Confusion and disagreement set in as soon as one attempts to go beyond that statement. What, for example, are the nature and number of significant groups and subgroups to be distinguished? For census purposes the government of Trinidad and Tobago recognizes six racial categories (Annual Statistical Digest). Braithwaite also lists six groups, but he calls them ethnic, and the two lists are not identical (p. 50). Crowley proposed thirteen "racial and national groups" for Trinidad (1957, pp. 817–819).

These differences reflect the use of local standards of evaluation and the apparent absence of any consistent set of criteria deriving from current anthropological or sociological theory. How else may one explain the use of a category—call it ethnic, racial, or national—such as "Syrian," under which heading are subsumed both Polish Jews and Lebanese Christians? Furthermore, before any attempt is made at a fine categorization of the island's population, it would certainly seem advisable to explore the nature of Trinidad's sociocultural complexity. In an effort to determine whether Trinidad contains one society with one culture or some form of sociocultural pluralism, primary attention will be given in this paper to social structure, to underlying values, and to the effect of rapid change over a short period.

In 1946 about 61 per cent of the population of Trinidad was composed of individuals of African or partly African ancestry. This entire group will be referred to hereafter as West Indians, although attention will be given when necessary to significantly different subgroups. Again in 1946, over 35 per cent of Trinidad's population was composed of the descendants of immigrants from India. This entire group, which also has its subgroups, will be referred to as East Indians. Little attention will be given here to the remaining elements in the Trinidad population; together they accounted for less than 4 per cent of the 1946 total.

Crowley (1957, p. 824 and elsewhere) has used the term "Creole" to designate the culture of Trinidad. The West Indian segment of the population unquestionably participates in this culture, but whether the same thing may be said of the East Indian segment is a matter of dispute. It becomes necessary, therefore, to understand something of the nature of this Creole culture. The following analysis derives from the writings of Braithwaite, Crowley, and others, as well as from my own observations in Trinidad.

* The data in this paper on present-day East Indian life in Trinidad derive from a one-year study conducted on that island during the period 1957–1958. This study was financed by a fellowship from the Social Science Research Council, New York, N. Y., to which I extend my sincere thanks. I am also grateful to the Research Institute for the Study of Man, New York, N.Y., for the Fellowship awarded me under its Research and Training Program during the summer of 1957.

In almost all aspects of the Creole culture high value is attached to that which is considered to be of European or predominantly European derivation, and a correspondingly low value is placed on that which is considered to be of African origin. This phenomenon may be observed most clearly in an examination of standards of physical attractiveness and in the relationship noted between physical appearance and stratification. This does not mean, however, that a simple value continuum exists, with "pure" European at one end and "pure" African at the other. There is a developing feeling, affecting all aspects of West Indian life, that the highest value should be given to that which is essentially European but exhibits also some additional quality that is West Indian or Creole or Trinidadian. Braithwaite writes (p. 97):

"By 'good hair' is not meant the aesthetically pleasing; or rather the aesthetically pleasing is identified as the 'straight hair' of the European, and only something which approximates to this can be classified as good. Similarly European features and the absence of thick lips are considered good. And the judgment of 'good-looking for a black man' expresses both the sentiment that the black man cannot in general be good-looking and that even within the category of black men there is a necessary differentiation between those who possess and those who do not possess European-like features."

One may observe, however, that the white European is in the process of being replaced as the symbol of physical attractiveness by the light-colored, West Indian-born Creole. It is no longer assumed by the majority of the island's population, for example, that the annual beauty contest winner, the Carnival Queen, need necessarily be white. However, it is likely to be a long time before she is black. That which is African is still undesirable.

According to Braithwaite, social stratification in Trinidad in the postslavery Nineteenth Century exhibited certain castelike qualities. In recent years this "caste idea" for the most part has been replaced by the elements of the full open-class system; that is, individual social and economic mobility is much easier today than in former years, and there is much more interpersonal association and even intermarriage between members of the three subgroups of West Indian society. The castelike appearance of Trinidad society derived from the presence of a color-class hierarchy and, although modified, this is still very much in evidence. The upper class is still predominantly white, the middle class predominantly colored, and the lower class predominantly black (pp. 46–48, 60–63, and elsewhere).

This prestige continuum from high-value European to low-value African, with a special value placed on that which is Creole, is reflected in other aspects of West Indian life. Thus, Roman Catholicism and Anglicanism enjoy the highest prestige, while religious sects considered to have large African elements in their composition find their following only within the lowest socioeconomic section of the population (Braithwaite, pp. 130–131). It is interesting that Carnival, the festival observed by many Roman Catholics in the period immediately preceding Lent, became associated with the lower class in the late Nineteenth Century, but recently has become respectable once more. Powrie writes: "The middle class are at last inclined to take pride in something which is Trinidadian" (p. 231; see also Pearse, p. 192).

In recent years considerable attention has been given to the prevalence of nonlegal or "keeper" unions among the West Indian lower class. There is a pattern of free choice of mates and a tacitly permitted premarital sexual experimentation that often results in the birth of a child to a girl still living with her parents. It must be emphasized that this is not a pattern of promiscuity. After a period of experimentation, a choice is made, and a couple will set up house together. The emphasis in the literature on illegitimacy and on matrifocality or mother-dominated families tends to obscure the fact that such unions are reasonably stable and about as unlikely to break up as are any other forms of marital union. It would appear, simply, that in the West Indian lower class, family formation is not necessarily regarded as a major life crisis. Whatever the reasons, be they historical, social, and/or economic, the setting up of a marital union in this group does not require the ceremonial *rite de passage* of a marriage ceremony. In the rural West Indian community, death is the most important life crisis, involving community participation in an extended ceremony requiring financial assistance (Hershovits and Hershovits, pp. 134–166).

The common-law union, according to Braithwaite, is rarely encountered in the Trinidad middle class, for it is "a direct violation of the middle-class code" (p. 108). However, while church marriage is the approved form of mating for upper- and middle-class West Indians and for socially mobile members of the lower class, there are indications of a developing admiration for what is considered to be a peculiarly West Indian propensity for the *affaire d'amour*. This was the subject of a recent paper by Crowley (1958), and Braithwaite devotes attention to the sharp change in middle-class attitudes toward sex and marriage (pp. 109–111).

To sum up, the West Indian Creole culture is a variant of European culture, and prestige is accorded to that which is considered to be of European origin. Highest prestige, however, is of late given to traits that are primarily of European origin but exhibit a West Indian quality and may therefore be termed Creole. This appears to reflect an emergent West Indian nationalism, and it might be argued that commercial and political interests consciously foster some of these tendencies. Nevertheless, it is significant that the majority of West Indians respond eagerly to the suggestion that a Creole society (that is, an integrated and assimilated one) with a Creole culture (that is, a West Indian variant of European) is developing in Trinidad. A very high value is placed on assimilation. The favorite description of Trinidad is a cosmopolitan melting pot within which many ethnic strains are blending, contributing the best elements of their various heritages to what might be termed the culture-trait pool shared by the total society, which is expected to remain distinctively West Indian and Trinidadian (*see* Crowley, 1957, pp. 823–824).

This consummation is so devoutly desired by West Indians that they frequently appear unaware of different attitudes among other elements of the population. This should not be taken to mean that all who are not West Indians oppose assimilation, but it should be obvious that such different groups as foreign-born whites, Trinidad-born whites, Chinese, and Portuguese must all respond very differently to the pressure for Creolization.

Within the East Indian group there are individuals who accept the values, and consider themselves part, of the West Indian society and its culture. Such

Creolized East Indians are usually Christians, although the group does contain a few Moslems and a very few Hindus (Crowley, 1957, p. 819). Nevertheless, as Crowley notes, barely 15 per cent of the East Indian population may be considered Christian (p. 817). Furthermore (and again as Crowley has noted, pp. 818–819) the greatest amount of acculturation has taken place among the urbanized East Indians, but from the census reports we may see that the overwhelming majority of Moslem and Hindu East Indians resided outside of the urban and even suburban areas (Annual Statistical Digest, p. 13). My own field work (1959) from which the following statements derive, was done in a village in County Caroni, populated almost exclusively by Hindu East Indian cane laborers.

Among rural Hindu East Indians the Creolized individual is rare to the point of nonexistence; traits and values deriving from India take precedence over those deriving from the non-Indian environment. It is necessary to note, however, that these people are for the most part East Indians of the West Indies; few still live who were born in India. Knowledge of what is Indian, therefore, does not derive from first-hand experience. Second, acculturation has taken place, and there is a value attached to being "modern"; however, to an East Indian, being modern does not always mean being West Indian.

Skin color plays almost no part in the East Indian group as internal stratification. The primary determinant of status among rural Hindus is caste membership. Education, occupation, and wealth are also important, but they all tend to cluster along with high-caste membership. Fairness of skin is one element in individual physical attractiveness, but a dark-skinned Brahman is socially superior to, and maritally more desirable than, a light-skinned Chamar, all else being equal. Individuals of low-caste origin who acquire wealth will often pretend to membership in one of the higher castes. The widespread East Indian tendency to deprecate caste obscures but does not change the fact of its importance in social stratification. In the rural village, leadership, wealth, and high-caste membership go hand in hand, and an examination of the caste affiliations of Hindu members, of whatever party, of the Trinidad Legislative Council reveals that almost all are of the two highest castes, Brahman and Kshatriya.

The rural East Indian might travel to Port of Spain to observe the Carnival festivities, but he would rarely participate in them. His own religious activities occupy much of his time, for the Trinidad Hindu is involved in a yearly cycle of public festivals and private prayers. The average West Indian knows nothing of this, and is rarely even aware that, every year, tens of thousands of Trinidad Hindus journey to the beaches of the island for a day of ceremonial bathing and picnicking. In Trinidad Hinduism, certain religious practices are rated as superior or inferior. Among the criteria are the caste of the officiating priest, the use of alcohol, the question of animal sacrifice, and certain other points of ritual. The problem of European versus African origins is, of course, completely irrelevant here. Ceremonies rated as superior are almost invariably sponsored by high-caste families (or socially mobile ones), with Brahman priests officiating.

While "modern" East Indian young people insist upon "free choice" in marriage, this means something very different from Trinidad West Indian free choice. The overwhelming majority of rural East Indian marriages are arranged by the respective fathers while the boy and girl are in their teens. The fathers make sure that the marriage is kin-and-village exogamous and caste endogamous. At some point in the proceedings, however, the two young people are allowed to meet each other, if only for a short while, and on the basis of this interview either may veto the match.

Marriage is the most important life crisis for the East Indians. It involves community participation and often requires financial assistance. The East Indian bride must begin her married life as an alien in her husband's father's household and village, for marriages are normally virilocal as well as village exogamous. Her experiences, obviously, will be very different from those of her West Indian counterpart. Indeed, in family structure and life cycle there are few points of similarity between East and West Indian.

To sum up, Indian forms and values underlie Trinidad East Indian culture. Modifications have occurred, but they do not necessarily make the East Indian any more of a West Indian. The West Indian may be said to be striving to become more European, or at least more Creole, and less African. The East Indian might like his circumstances to be bettered, but he has no desire to be anything else and, least of all, a West Indian.

Since Trinidad unquestionably exhibits only one socioeconomic system, within which both groups participate, it may be said to have most of the important characteristics of a plural society as they are given by Furnivall. Here, as in his examples, "different sections of the community [are] living side by side, but separately, within the same political unit" (p. 304). However, Trinidad society exhibits at least one additional characteristic not provided for in Furnivall's scheme. It would seem likely, from Furnivall's description (pp. 303–312), that members of the culturally distinct groups making up the populations of Burma or Java are aware of, and appear to accept, the pluralistic nature of their respective societies. In Trinidad, on the other hand, this would be true only of the East Indian. From the Trinidad West Indian point of view, the island contains an essentially homogeneous society; if it did not it should and soon would.

Crowley (1957) writes: "A Trinidadian feels no inconsistency in being a British citizen, a Negro in appearance, a Spaniard in name, a Roman Catholic at church, an obeah (magic) practitioner in private, a Hindu at lunch, a Chinese at dinner, a Portuguese at work, and a Colored at the polls" (p. 823).

To the West Indian, moreover, this process of assimilation and integration, what Crowley has termed plural acculturation, is worthy of unquestioned approbation. The merger of different ethnic strains and the emergence of one Creole physical type are also viewed as highly desirable. Braithwaite notes: "people will proudly proclaim that they have 'English', 'Spanish', 'French', blood in their veins. They can even be heard boasting that they are a 'mix-up'" (p. 102).

It is the universal Trinidad West Indian contention that within twenty to fifty years the East Indian ethnic group will have merged indistinguishably into the West Indian Creole society.

This view is subscribed to by only a very small segment of the East Indian population; for the most part only by those who have become Creolized to the extent of having married out of their ethnic group. Even for most Moslem and Christian East Indians the idea of the East Indian group losing its ethnic identity and disappearing into the West Indian population is not acceptable. An East Indian who changes his religion is still considered an East Indian by the members of his ethnic group. Among the Hindus, a child of parents of two different castes will be accepted as a member of his father's caste, but a child of an East Indian and any non-Indian is called a *doogla* (bastard) and is considered to have no caste at all.

Thus integration and assimilation, whether cultural or biological, are processes the East Indian tends both to fear and to resist. Although it is customary for East Indians to deny the importance of caste in their social structure, it is very much present, and the values underlying the Indian caste system may well affect present East Indian attitudes toward assimilation. It might even be said that, from the East Indian point of view, Trinidad appears to be composed of permanently separate endogamous groups. These may be ranked relative to one another, and the East Indian's abiding interest in the rise of his entire ethnic group well may be compared with attitudes in India toward caste mobility (Cohn, 1955).

The conflict in attitude and viewpoint between the East and West Indians of Trinidad has recently found expression in politics. Two parties dominate the Trinidad political scene. Although both deny racial orientation, one is for all practical purposes a West Indian party and the other an East Indian party. West Indians, unable to ignore this manifestation of the conflict, frequently are heard to complain that the conflict between the two ethnic groups came into existence with the arrival of party politics. They see the development as a highly unfortunate one, but hope that the emergence of an East Indian party is a temporary phenomenon and that, when East Indians have become West Indians, in time and through education ethnically oriented parties will have no reason to exist. East Indians, on the other hand, appear to see the emergence of such parties as natural and inevitable. They believe that in time they will elect their own leaders to office, and the primary concern of any political leader, many of them seem to feel, is the well-being of his particular ethnic group.

A partial explanation for the divergent views as to the nature of present Trinidadian society may be found in an examination of the rapid changes that have taken place over a comparatively short period of time. From the first arrival of indentured laborers from India in 1845 until fifteen to twenty years ago, the East Indians constituted a cultural enclave* within the Trinidad socioeconomic system. The group had clustered within the lowest economic stratum of the society, that of the rural agricultural laborer. Even the limited amount of education available to the group could be had only in schools run by Presbyterian missionaries. Social and economic advancement was possible for an individual only if he were willing to leave his ethnic group and accept the

---

* The term "cultural enclave" is used here to contrast the phenomenon described in this paper with that of subculture. By subculture I understand an offshoot of a parent culture that is distinct but not separate from it, although it may become so. Using the terms in this manner, New Englanders exhibit a subculture of the total culture of the United States, but the Navajo represent a cultural enclave.

conditions of life in the Christian West Indian society. Despite these circumstances, while there was considerable acculturation, the majority of East Indians resisted significant Creolization.

Today, there is a Hindu East Indian middle class and even an upper class. There are wealthy East Indian businessmen, educated professionals, and powerful politicians. An East Indian youth today may acquire an education and rise both socially and economically without ever venturing outside his ethnic group or questioning its values. The recent independence of India and Pakistan has affected both Hindu and Moslem East Indians. There is both a pride in origin that was lacking before and a strong religiocultural revival.

If East Indians have successfully resisted Creolization thus far, is it likely to occur now that the ethnic group has changed from a cultural enclave to what is effectively a parallel sociocultural system within the total Trinidadian society? Moreover, it is well known among Trinidadian East Indians that within about twenty years they will form the largest single ethnic group on the island. What will happen then if there is at that time no change in either the East Indian desire for a separate and equal status within the Trinidad society, or in the West Indian desire for complete integration?

References

ANNUAL STATISTICAL DIGEST. 1956. Government of Trinidad and Tobago. Central Statistical Office. Port of Spain, Trinidad.

BRAITHWAITE, L. 1953. Social stratification in Trinidad. Social & Economic Studies. **2:** 5–175.

COHN, B. S. 1955. The changing status of a depressed caste. *In* Village India: Studies in the Little Community. M. Marriott, Ed. Amer. Anthropol. Assoc. Mem. No. **83:** 53–77.

CROWLEY, D. 1957. Plural and differential acculturation in Trinidad. Amer. Anthropologist. **59:** 817–824.

CROWLEY, D. 1958. Polygyny and class in the West Indies. Unpublished paper read at Ann. Meeting Amer. Anthropol. Assoc.

FURNIVALL, J. S. 1948. Colonial Policy and Practice. Cambridge Univ. Press. Cambridge, England.

HERSHOVITS, M. J. & S. F. HERSHOVITS. 1947. Trinidad Village. Knopf. New York, N. Y.

KLASS, M. 1959. Cultural Persistence in a Trinidad East Indian Community. Unpublished doctoral dissertation, Columbia University, New York, N. Y.

PEARSE, A. 1956. Carnival in nineteenth century Trinidad. Caribbean Quart. **4:** 175–193.

POWRIE, B. E. 1956. The changing attitude of the coloured middle class toward carnival. Caribbean Quart. **4:** 224-234.

ATTITUDES OF JAMAICAN ELITES TOWARD THE WEST INDIES FEDERATION*

Wendell Bell

Center for Latin American Studies, University of California, Los Angeles, Calif.

Introduction

The emergence of new and self-governing nations out of a past of economic deprivation and political dependence is one of the most momentous social developments of modern times but, in spite of some excellent recent studies, we still understand little about the underlying processes of these changes, about the consequences of the changes for traditional culture and social structure, about the shifts in the distribution of power and prestige that occur, and about the factors that set the course of the new nation and determine its character during its initial period of growth.

Among the factors that influence the character of a new nation, indeed that may result in its success or failure as an independent state, are the elites: those persons who occupy the positions of power and authority and who make the decisions. Their numbers, their social backgrounds, their technical training, and their attitudes and values can have far-reaching effects.

This paper represents a modest attempt to discover how the attitudes of the elites in a new and developing nation are affected by their differentiation as viewed in relation to the course of political, economic, and social change. The new nation under consideration is The West Indies, and the elites studied comprise business, political, religious, educational, and other leaders in Jamaica, the largest unit of the federation.

On January 3, 1958 The West Indies, comprising the ten island territories of Antigua, Barbados, Dominica, Grenada, Jamaica, Montserrat, St. Kitts-Nevis-Anguilla, St. Lucia, St. Vincent, and Trinidad, was formally established with the swearing in of Lord Hailes as first Governor-General of the West Indies. On March 25 the first federal elections were held, and on April 22 the first West Indies parliament was opened by Princess Margaret Rose. Thus, after more than ten years of conferences, plans, and reports initiated at the Montego Bay conference in 1947, a new nation was brought into being.[1,2]

The West Indies is a new country of about 3 million people who live on relatively small islands separated by the vastness of the Caribbean Sea. It has an average population density in excess of 360 per square mile and, in one of its territories, Barbados, this density is as high as 1380.[3] It embraces considerable social and cultural diversity, its predominantly Negro population being augmented by East Indians, Europeans, Chinese, mixed and others. Its elites are relatively remote from the culture of the mass of West Indians, and its English is peppered with Africanisms as well as the styles and vocabularies

* The work reported in this paper was performed during the tenure of a Faculty Research Fellowship from the Social Science Research Council, New York, N. Y. I also thank the Graduate School, Northwestern University, Evanston, Ill.; the Research Committee of the University of California, Los Angeles; the Penrose Fund, American Philosophical Society, Philadelphia, Pa.; and the Research Institute for the Study of Man, New York, N. Y., for grants-in-aid for the larger study of which this report is a part.

of other languages. For example, in Trinidad, the most cosmopolitan island, the language is said to be "Spanish in origin, French by tradition, English by adoption, and not without traces of the languages of India, Pakistan, China, Syria, and Palestine."[4] However, the unifying features should not be dismissed. The majority of the population has African ancestry, the people share the common cultural background characteristics of plantation America and have had somewhat similar experiences with the dominant metropolitan country.

The West Indian economy is largely dependent on agricultural production for the world market, with all the vulnerability to fluctuation that this can entail, and it is still dependent to some extent on grants from the United Kingdom, especially for support of some of the smaller islands. Per capita productivity is low, the level of living is low, and the opportunities for capital formation are poor, but there is oil in Trinidad, bauxite in Jamaica, and some evidence of the success of efforts, especially in Jamaica, to develop a more diversified economy and to increase per capita income.

The West Indies federation is almost completely self-governing and looks forward to full dominion status in the near future, but it is still to some extent under British political control. In addition to problems flowing from the relations of the federal government to the British government, there are difficulties deriving from the relations of the federal government to the various unit governments that compose the federation. British Guiana and British Honduras have chosen to stay out of the federation altogether, at least for the time being. The power of the federal government may prove insufficient to bring about the free movement of goods and people within the federated islands or to plan for the nation as a whole with a regional perspective in the face of the strong insular interests of some of the unit governments.

There were rumblings as early as November 1958. By then the pro-federation Jamaican government already had threatened to withdraw over the issue of federal taxation. Whether or not Jamaica will stay in the federation, whether or not there will be a strong federal government if she does, and whether or not federation will collapse altogether depend on many things, but the beliefs and attitudes of the Jamaican elites are important in influencing the course of developments.[5,6]

Basic Data

The data reported in this paper were collected during 1958. A total of 810 persons were sent questionnaires. These persons constituted a random sample selected from *Who's Who, Jamaica, 1957*[7] and represented, in addition, a series of smaller, special samples selected from the King's House Invitation List, the Civil Service Seniority List, and other sources. Insofar as I was able to determine, 7 persons of the total of 810 had died, were critically ill, or had left the island permanently, leaving 803 qualified potential respondents. Of these, 238 returned questionnaires that were properly filled out for a response rate of 30 per cent.*

* Bell, W. "Jamaican Elites: A Study of Political Change, Leadership and Social Mobility." To be published.

The questionnaires were mailed to the potential respondents between May 27 and June 1, 1958. The first returns began coming in by May 31 and, after one follow-up letter, a second mailing of questionnaires, and a final follow-up of personal telegrams, the last questionnaire to be returned was in by December 22. However, all but 5 of the 238 returned questionnaires had been sent back before October 25, 1958.

The response rate is lower than one would desire; the reader is cautioned therefore to accept the findings as tentative. However, the major types of elites are each represented, and the attempt at systematic sampling was at least a partial success. Thus, the findings are important and useful supplements to the information concerning the West Indies federation now available from experts and in newspapers, magazines, government documents, and elsewhere.

TABLE 1
ATTITUDES TOWARD FEDERATION IN THE TOTAL SAMPLE

Does Jamaica have more to gain or lose as a result of being part of the federation?	Percentages
Jamaica has more to gain	41
Federation makes no difference	4
Jamaica has more to lose	51
Gain in some ways, lose in others	4
Total	100
Number of cases	232
No answers	6
Total number of cases	238

The Findings

Attitudes toward federation in the total sample. The results of this questionnaire survey hardly show a leadership clamoring for federation for Jamaica and the advantages that it is supposed to bring. Over one half of the Jamaican leaders feel that Jamaica has more to lose than to gain by federating with the other West Indian territories. This can be seen from their responses to the question: Does *Jamaica* have more to gain or lose as a result of being part of the federation? (TABLE 1).

There is somewhat less disagreement, however, in the perception of the situation than might be inferred from the division of opinion shown. This is revealed by an analysis of the open-ended responses that were given when the respondents were asked to explain their answers. One hundred per cent of the respondents who say Jamaica has more to lose than to gain from federation say that Jamaica would suffer an economic loss. The two most frequently mentioned sources of the loss are: first, the cost of the federal government, from which few benefits of an economic nature are expected to come (Jamaica has about 38 per cent of the seats in the Federal Parliament and 53 per cent of the federation's population, and provides 43 per cent of the federation's general revenue), and second, the economic liability of the smaller, less developed islands, which will be felt through taxation and eventual customs union within the area.   In a few cases (13 per cent of those elites who feel Jamaica will lose) these comments were accompanied by the remark that Jamaica may gain in the long run, but that the losses will be immediate and sure.

Somewhat over one third of those who see Jamaica gaining by federation say the same thing as does this latter group.   They agree that Jamaica will lose economically and cite the same economic losses given above, but argue that Jamaica's losses will be only in the short run, and that the future holds more gains than losses for Jamaica as a result of being part of the federation. The difference between the two groups is in part a difference in their evaluation of short-run losses in the face of long-range gains rather than a difference in perception concerning the time and nature of the gains and losses involved.

If the Jamaican elites generally think that Jamaica will suffer economic losses by being part of the federation, what do they think will be the nature of the gains?   The answer is that they believe that Jamaica will gain political power and prestige by being part of a larger nation-state.   Sixty-four per cent of the respondents who say that Jamaica has more to gain than to lose from federation explain their answers in this way: they say that the West Indian nation will be better able than Jamaica alone to take her place in the community of nations, that her impact will be greater, and that she will command more respect.   Five per cent of those persons who say Jamaica will lose say the same thing.   It should be noted that such political power and prestige are often viewed as a necessary condition for the achievement of greater economic benefits in the future through increased bargaining strength in their associations and negotiations with other countries.

However, some of the elites disagree more directly with the judgment of economic loss, and they say that Jamaica will benefit economically by being a part of the federation.   Specifically, they point to the development of West Indian markets for Jamaica's expanding economy, the development of a West Indian Bank, and the greater ease of using experts to greater advantage on a regional basis, among other things.   Forty-one per cent of the elites who think that federation will benefit Jamaica make these statements.

Among the miscellaneous comments were these: 18 per cent of the elites who say that Jamaica will lose by federation support their answer by saying that Jamaica is geographically too isolated from the other islands to allow federation to succeed.   Eight per cent say that they would change their answer and admit that Jamaica has more to gain from federation if, at least, British Guiana, if not British Honduras, were also part of the federation.

Before leaving a discussion of the open-ended responses concerning the advantages or disadvantages of federation for Jamaica, two additional comments should be made.   One concerns the role of social and cultural diversity in relation to federation.   Several writers have pointed out that the East Indian population may have been partially responsible for keeping British Guiana out of the federation and, in Trinidad, may account in part for the initial reluctance to join.[8]   Others have suggested that social and cultural heterogeneity in the West Indies, although not as great as in many other countries, may present a problem for the success of the federation.[4]   Also, it has been said that, given this diversity, democracy is best served by unity through federation rather than through complete integration and unification. However, this concern about social and cultural diversity is not reflected in the attitudes of the Jamaican elites. Only one respondent mentioned it, and he suggested that Jamaica would gain culturally by increased contact with and awareness of the other islands.   Thus, whatever political, economic, and social problems exist due to the pluralistic nature of West Indian society, it is apparently not a factor in the Jamaican elites' attitudes toward federation.

A second point is the extent to which self government and federation are linked in the minds of the respondents.   Thirteen respondents, persons who feel that Jamaica will gain, believe that Jamaica will attain dominion status and complete self-government more quickly by being part of federation, but 21 others, among those who say Jamaica will lose, point out that by being part of the federation Jamaica has taken a step backward on the road to self-government.   It is, of course, a fact that the federation, in its relations with the United Kingdom, is somewhat less autonomous than was Jamaica at the time the

TABLE 2
ATTITUDES TOWARD SELF-GOVERNMENT

Does Jamaica have more to gain or lose as a result of political independence from the United Kingdom?	Percentages
Jamaica has more to gain	66
Political independence makes no difference	7
Jamaica has more to lose	26
Gain in some ways, lose in others	1
Total	100
Number of cases	234
No answers	4
Total number of cases	238

federation was formed.   These positions are not, theoretically, irreconcilable if one considers that Jamaica is now tied to a larger West Indian governmental unit that is less self-governing than she already was and that Jamaica may not have received rapid advancement to full self-government in the face of a pro-federation British government that may have been reluctant to let Jamaica abdicate from any economic responsibility for the poorer islands.[9]

In addition, 12 respondents feel that Jamaica has also lost some political independence to the federation because Jamaica's 17 members of the Federal Parliament are less than she should have if representation was proportionate to population size.

Attitudes toward self-government. Although 41 per cent of the Jamaican elites feel that Jamaica has more to gain than to lose from federation, considerably more (66 per cent) say that Jamaica has more to gain than to lose as a result of political independence from the United Kingdom.   These findings are shown in TABLE 2.

It is clear from the figures cited in this table that political independence is viewed as beneficial for Jamaica by more leaders than is federation.

The attitudes toward federation by attitudes toward political independence are shown in TABLE 3. In general, TABLE 3 reveals a positive correlation between these two attitudes, those persons saying "gain" in response to the political independence question being most likely to say "gain" in response to the other question, and those elites saying "lose" to it most likely saying "lose" to the federation question.

However, there are deviant cases, and the largest number of them in TABLE 3 is among the elites who say that Jamaica will gain by political independence, but will lose by joining the federation. A sizable minority, 39 per cent of the

TABLE 3

JAMAICAN ELITES' ATTITUDES TOWARD FEDERATION BY THEIR ATTITUDES
TOWARD POLITICAL INDEPENDENCE

Does Jamaica have more to gain or lose as a result of being part of federation?	Does Jamaica have more to gain or lose as a result of political independence from the U.K.?		
	More to gain (Percentages)	No difference (Percentages)	More to lose (Percentages)
Jamaica has more to gain	53	19	19
Federation makes no difference	4	19	2
Jamaica has more to lose	39	62	76
Gain in some ways, lose in others	4	0	3
Total	100	100	100
Number of cases	150	16	62
No answers	4	—	—
Total number of cases	154	16	62

TABLE 4

PERCENTAGES OF JAMAICAN ELITES WHO SAY THAT THEY ARE VERY INTERESTED IN WORLD,
WEST INDIAN, AND JAMAICAN AFFAIRS

Very interested in:	Percentages	Number of cases on which the percentages are based
World affairs	82	237
West Indian (federation) affairs	71	233
Jamaican affairs	97	236

elites who say that Jamaica has more to gain from political independence (one fourth of all Jamaican elites), are in this deviant class. They want Jamaica to be a nation in her own right, apart from the other West Indian islands.

Interest in world, West Indian, and Jamaican affairs. Turning to TABLE 4, one can see the percentage of elites who say that they are very interested in world, West Indian (federation), and Jamaican affairs, respectively. Bearing on the viability of the new West Indian nation is the fact that practically all (97 per cent) of the Jamaican elites are very interested in Jamaican affairs, 82 per cent are very interested in world affairs, and 71 per cent are very interested in West Indian affairs. As expected among the leaders of a country, these are relatively high percentages, and the fact that as many as 71 per cent of Jamaican elites are very interested in things that happen within the West Indies federation perhaps bodes well for the development of West Indian, as opposed to Jamaican, nationalism.   However, 26 per cent fewer elites are more interested in federation affairs than in Jamaican affairs, and 11 per cent fewer are more interested in federation affairs than in world affairs outside the Caribbean, and this perhaps bodes ill.

That this may not be simply idle speculation may be seen from TABLE 5, in which interest in West Indian affairs is related to attitudes toward federation. Forty-nine per cent of the elites who say that they are very interested in West Indian affairs think that Jamaica has more to gain than to lose from federation, but only 22 per cent of the elites who are only fairly interested or not interested in West Indian affairs think so.

Selected social characteristics.   The Jamaican elites are not a completely homogeneous group.   They represent a variety of social and cultural segments and are differentiated further into various functional roles.   The relationships between attitudes toward federation and various social characteristics of the elites are given in TABLE 6.

TABLE 5

PERCENTAGES OF JAMAICAN ELITES WHO THINK THAT JAMAICA WILL GAIN BY BEING PART OF THE FEDERATION BY AMOUNT OF INTEREST IN WEST INDIAN AFFAIRS

Amount of interest in West Indian (federation) affairs	Percentages who think that Jamaica will gain	Number of cases on which the percentages are based
Very interested	49	165
Fairly and not interested	22	64

There are small differences by age.   Older elites are somewhat less likely to believe that Jamaica will gain by being part of federation than are the younger ones.   This may represent a tendency of the younger elites to be generally more receptive to change and more favorable to modernization than the older ones, but data are insufficient to establish this explanation as a fact.

Since the wives of Jamaican elites are not included in the operational specification of elites per se, the only women included in the sample are those whose names appeared in *Who's Who* or on one of the other lists used to define elites. Thus, relatively few women are among the elites as defined here.   TABLE 6 shows that there is little difference between the attitudes of men and women leaders toward federation, women being somewhat more likely than men to think that Jamaica will gain.

For the purposes of this study, Jamaican elites are defined with respect to their performance of elite functions and with respect to the consequences of the performance of these functions for Jamaican society.   Thus, it is not necessary for an elite to be born in Jamaica to be considered a "Jamaican" elite. A British born director of a Jamaican government department, an American-born engineer employed by a sugar estate in Jamaica, and a Trinidadian-born professor at the University College of the West Indies, for example, are considered to be Jamaican elites.   From TABLE 6 one may see that country of birth is a differentiating factor in attitudes toward federation.

The largest percentage of respondents who think that Jamaica will gain by federation are not Jamaican-born, but are Caribbean-born (in practically all cases West Indian-born). Elites born in the United Kingdom or in Jamaica

TABLE 6

PERCENTAGES OF JAMAICAN ELITES WHO THINK THAT JAMAICA WILL GAIN BY BEING PART OF THE FEDERATION BY SELECTED SOCIAL CHARACTERISTICS

Selected characteristics	Percentages who think that Jamaica will gain	Number of cases on which the percentages are based
Age (years)		
55 and over	34	70
40 to 54	42	113
25 to 39	47	49
Sex		
Men	40	215
Women	53	17
Country of birth		
Jamaica	40	168
Caribbean other than Jamaica	67	15
United Kingdom	43	30
Canada and the United States	31	13
Income		
£3000 and over	28	50
£2000 to 2999	37	49
£ 0 to 1999	49	111
Education		
Graduate school	49	49
Completed college	51	43
Some college	31	35
Secondary or training school	34	88
Elementary only	44	16
Occupational rating		
1 (highest)	41	135
2	35	82
3 and 4 (lowest)	67	15
Respondent's perception of his financial mobility		
Better off than his father	45	166
The same as his father	21	33
Worse off than his father	44	25
Religious preference		
None	36	11
Catholic	40	25
Jewish	14	14
Protestant	43	173
Number of foreign countries lived in for at least 1 year		
2 or more	43	97
1	38	64
None	42	69

are next, and Canadians and citizens of the United States are least likely to believe that Jamaica has more to gain than to lose by federation. It is of considerable interest to see that non-Jamaican West Indians are most likely to say that Jamaica will gain by federation, especially in view of the fact that many experts agree that, whatever Jamaica has to gain from federation, the smaller islands should expect considerably more.

TABLE 6 also shows that lower-income elites are more likely to favor federation than are upper-income elites, as are the elites of the lowest occupational ratings when compared to those of higher occupational ratings.

The respondents were asked to compare their present financial status with the financial status of their fathers during their youth. Those persons who say that their financial situations are the same as were those of their fathers are least likely to say that Jamaica will gain as a result of federation. There is no significant difference between those who say they are financially better or worse off than their fathers were. The financially stable individuals are generally elites who are now fairly well off economically and who come from well-to-do families. They are more upper-class than the upwardly mobile elites in that their family background is more prestigious, and they are more upper-class than the downwardly mobile elites in that they have lost little, if any, of their families' economic and social positions, although the sources of their incomes may have changed. This is fairly well borne out by data on career and generational mobility not given here.

The relationships between attitudes toward federation on the one hand and income, occupational rating, and financial mobility on the other, suggest that elites who are economically dominant and traditionally most entrenched, economically speaking, are overrepresented among those who oppose federation for Jamaica.

The relationship between education and attitudes toward federation is another matter. Elites who have completed college or postgraduate work have the largest percentages saying that they believe Jamaica will benefit from federation when compared to persons having lower educational attainments. Elites with some college and secondary or training school education only have the lowest percentages, and elites with only an elementary school education have an intermediate position. However, this does not necessarily negate the conclusion drawn from the data on income, occupational rating, and financial mobility, because higher education has been a means of achieving elite status for many persons with relatively low socioeconomic backgrounds. Among the more highly educated persons are many elites who have been financially mobile and who have relatively low incomes for elites, and a few elites who have (for elites in general) relatively low occupational ratings.

Religious preference (TABLE 6) appears to make no difference in attitudes toward federation except in the case of the Jews, who are much less likely than any other religious group to think that Jamaica will gain as a result of federation. The small number of Jews who are in this sample are practically all business elites and prefer the Jamaica Labour Party (JLP). An examination of the cross-tabulations shows that these facts may explain the attitudes of the Jews on this question. That is, Jews have about the same attitudes toward federation as do non-Jewish business elites who prefer the JLP.

The amount of foreign residence as measured by the number of foreign countries lived in for at least one year appears to account for no appreciable variation in attitudes toward federation (TABLE 6).

Type of elite position. The percentage of Jamaican leaders by type of elite position who think that Jamaica will gain by being part of the federation is given in TABLE 7. Although many of the leaders occupy more than one type of position, as shown, they are classified for the purposes of this paper only once, either on the basis of their dominant position or, if that is not clear, with respect to a set of priorities arbitrarily established.   For example, a member of the House of Representatives who also owns and operates a business is classified only once, as an elected politician; he is not classified as a business elite.

Nominated officials (that is, members of the Legislative Council and the *custodes* of the parishes) and teachers are most likely to believe that Jamaica will gain.   Civil servants are more likely to think so than are the elites as a whole.   However, the elected politicians (including eight members of the Federal Parliament), doctors, businessmen (the economic dominants), ministers of religion, and barristers and solicitors, in that order, are less likely to think so than are the other three types of elites.

A general explanation of these findings may be found in the differential impact of political changes, that is, self-government and federation, on the various segments of the Jamaican leadership structure.   The differentiation of

TABLE 7

PERCENTAGES OF JAMAICAN ELITES WHO THINK THAT JAMAICA WILL GAIN BY BEING PART OF THE FEDERATION BY TYPE OF ELITE POSITION

Type of elite position	Percentages who think that Jamaica will gain	Number of cases on which the percentages are based
All political elites	48	97
Elected politicians	39	18
Nominated officials	62	13
Civil servants	48	66
Business elites	33	70
Ministers	30	10
Teachers	60	15
Doctors	35	23
Barristers and solicitors	13	8

functions reflected in the classification of types of elites may delineate one group of leaders as more vulnerable to the deleterious aspects of federation, to economic uncertainty, and perhaps economic burdens from taxation, now Jamaican and later federal, and customs union.   At the same time it may delineate another group of leaders whose positions are benefited by, and in some cases dependent upon, the proliferation of governmental functions.

Since the riots and disturbances in 1938 the move toward self-government in Jamaica has received general support.   World War II interfered with immediate implementation of governmental reforms, but by 1944 a new constitution permitted universal adult suffrage for the first time, and since then additional advances toward political independence have been made.   The trend toward self-government has been accompanied by an extension of governmental services in social welfare, in economic development, and in other activities.   A form of government best described as democratic socialism now exists.   This has meant an increase in governmental and quasi-governmental offices, which in turn has meant the opening of new job opportunities.   Although grossly underestimating the new positions that developed, the increase in higher civil servants alone from 1939 to 1954 was 191 per cent.[10]

At the same time that new positions were being created as a result of the increase in governmental services, national self-consciousness resulted in efforts to fill governmental and quasi-governmental posts in Jamaica with Jamaicans, or at least with West Indians, rather than with Englishmen and others. Thus, not only were there new opportunities for Jamaicans created by new positions, but new opportunities for Jamaicans were also created by assigning them to old posts formerly held by British civil servants. With expanding governmental functions and with self-government has come a set of governmental and quasi-governmental positions that have been the stepping-stones to middle- and upper-middle-class status for many Jamaicans. It should be noted that an increase in amount and stability of income has accompanied this rise in social class, but equally important, and perhaps more important, has been the increase in prestige that has resulted. Of the types of elites shown in TABLE 7, civil servants and teachers have benefited most by these trends, and they may view federation as offering additional positions that will have still higher pay and still higher prestige.

On the other hand, the economic dominants, the business elites, may have most to lose by these political changes. However, it should be pointed out that they may not lose in any absolute sense; in fact, they may gain financially in the long run as a result of general economic advancement. However, they have most to lose in property, power, and prestige relative to the emergent elites within the Jamaican social structure. By taxation of one form or another, income is redistributed from the economic dominants to other sectors of the economy, including the governmental functionaries who perform many of the planning, coordinating, and control functions associated with governmental projects. Because of lack of space a more complete statement of the relationships between political changes and the social class system is precluded, but it should be added that the same processes mentioned above have resulted in the reduction of power of many of the business elites or, more accurately, have forced many of the economic dominants to seek indirect access to power that in times past they have held directly. This may explain why only a third of the business elites, as shown in TABLE 7, feel that Jamaica will gain rather than lose as a result of federation. Since all but one of the elites classified as barristers and solicitors in TABLE 7 are associated with commercial interests, it may explain their lack of enthusiasm for federation as well.

If the above analysis is accurate, then one may wonder why nominated officials, who largely represent the economic dominants, are so favorable to federation, and why elected politicians and civil servants are not more favorable. In the case of nominated officials I can only suggest that they may be more inclined than are other elites to present the official line with respect to federation. With respect to elected politicians and civil servants, one must differentiate between self-government and federation. Although self-government has favored these groups with more power and prestige, federation was still (in the summer of 1958) a somewhat unknown quantity. Potentially, it might extend the amount of their power and prestige, but there were also dangers stemming from the uncertainties of new competition from other elite groups in the wider arena of the federal territories. Fears and insecurities resulting from unknown outcomes of new situations undoubtedly entered into the formation of their attitudes.

The general explanation concerning the differential effects of political changes on the career patterns of various types of elites may explain some of the responses to the federation question on the part of ministers and doctors. By the nature of their professions they are perhaps least affected by federation or self-government, and to the extent to which non-West Indians are over-represented in this group, as they are, nationalism, self-government, and federation may be seen as having no particular advantage for them.

Political party preference. Another variation in attitudes toward federation is found when comparing the political party preferences of the respondents (TABLE 8). As anticipated, elites who prefer the People's National Party (PNP) are most likely to say that Jamaica will gain by joining the federation. Sixty-one per cent of them say so. This is compared to 29 per cent of those who say they have no political party preference and to only 19 per cent of those elites who prefer the Jamaica Labour Party (JLP).

TABLE 8

PERCENTAGES OF JAMAICAN ELITES WHO THINK THAT JAMAICA WILL GAIN BY BEING PART
OF THE FEDERATION BY POLITICAL PARTY PREFERENCE

Political party preference	Percentages who think that Jamaica will gain	Number of cases on which the percentages are based
None	29	62
People's National Party	61	102
Jamaica Labour Party	19	63

Of course, these differences may simply reflect a growing dissatisfaction with Jamaica's prospects with federation, dissatisfaction that was held at bay for supporters of the PNP by the great prestige of the determined, pro-federation head of the PNP, Norman Washington Manley, present chief minister of Jamaica. This source of support for federation, it should be added, apparently has been reduced considerably since November of last year. However, a more satisfactory answer may be found in the source of elite differentiation reflected in political party preferences and the variant effect of political changes on careers as discussed above and as tested below.

Perception of the career effect of political changes. TABLE 9 shows the percentage of Jamaican elites who perceive that federation or self-government within Jamaica has or has not affected their careers. Twenty-four per cent report that these political changes have been beneficial to their careers in every way; 2 per cent say that their business or professional career was deleteriously affected, but that new opportunities were opened for them in politics; 8 per cent believe that their careers have been adversely affected; and 5 per cent say that their careers were affected, but do not say how. Three per cent report that the political changes have not yet affected their careers, but that they will, and 58 per cent think that political changes have not affected their careers at all. However, this is not of primary concern here. We are interested in the possible interrelationships between type of elite position, political party preference, perceived consequences of political changes on careers, and attitudes toward federation.

That the perception of federation affecting one's career is related to attitudes toward federation may be seen from TABLE 10. The association is about as anticipated: those who see that federation or self-government is helping their

TABLE 9

PERCENTAGES OF JAMAICAN ELITES WHO PERCEIVE THAT POLITICAL CHANGES HAVE OR HAVE NOT AFFECTED THEIR CAREERS

Has federation or self-government within Jamaica affected your career in any way?	Percentages	
Yes		39
Beneficially	24	
Deleteriously for business career, but opened new opportunities in politics	2	
Deleteriously in every way	8	
Unspecified	5	
Not yet, but will		3
Beneficially	1	
Deleteriously (1 respondent)	0	
Unspecified	2	
No		58
Total		100
Number of cases		233
No answers		5
Total number of cases		238

TABLE 10

PERCENTAGES OF JAMAICAN ELITES WHO THINK THAT JAMAICA WILL GAIN BY BEING PART OF THE FEDERATION BY WHETHER OR NOT THEY THINK THAT POLITICAL CHANGES HAVE AFFECTED THEIR CAREERS

Has federation or self-government within Jamaica affected your career in any way?	Percentages who think that Jamaica will gain	Number of cases on which the percentages are based
Yes, beneficially	58	59
Yes, unspecified	56	9
Yes, deleteriously in every way	33	18
Not yet, but it will	11	9
No	37	132

careers are most likely to say that Jamaica will gain by it; elites who say that it has affected their careers but do not specify in what way are next (we can assume that they perceive benefits); next are elites who report that these political changes have not affected their careers; they are followed by elites who indicate that their careers have been affected deleteriously; and last are elites who say that their careers have not yet been affected, but will be.

In tables not presented here I have attempted to separate the effects of type of elite position, political party preference, and perceived consequences of political changes for one's career.

Political party preference and perception of career effect. Perceiving that political changes affects one's career does not explain the relationship between political party and attitudes toward federation. However, the difference between the political parties is somewhat reduced for those elites who say that their careers have not been affected, and it is somewhat increased among elites who think that their careers have been affected beneficially. The career question still differentiates attitudes toward federation, but much less so when political affiliation is considered. Also, career is clearly a less important determinant than is political party. PNP adherents are more likely than JLP adherents to say that their careers have been beneficially affected by federation or self-government. The group most favorable to federation comprises the PNP supporters who have been helped in their careers.

Political party preference and type of elite position. Although teachers are generally favorable to federation, and ministers and doctors unfavorable regardless of political party differences, within most of the other types of elites the differences between supporters of the different political parties are increased from what they are in TABLE 8. For example, in this sample of business elites as among business elites generally in Jamaica, there are fewer supporters of PNP than there are of the JLP, but 85 per cent of the PNP business elites believe that Jamaica will gain by federation compared to only 14 per cent of the JLP business leaders.

Most of the civil servants are supporters of the PNP. Sixty-three per cent of them favor federation, compared to none of the JLP civil servants. The same is true of the elected politicians. Sixty-three per cent of the PNP-elected politicians think Jamaica will gain, compared to only 11 per cent of the JLP politicians.

Persons with no political party preference generally have attitudes intermediate between the PNP and the JLP supporters, but they tend to be closer to the JLP point of view than the PNP point of view.

Differences in attitudes toward federation by type of elite position are reduced, in some cases reversed, after political party preference is introduced into the analysis. This striking effect of political party preference will be the subject of detailed discussion in a forthcoming publication.

Conclusion

This paper represents a preliminary attempt to understand the attitudes of the Jamaican elites toward their new country, the West Indies, within the context of the social, economic, and political positions that they hold; the nature of the social structure of Jamaica; and the recent political changes that have affected Jamaican social structure. The data were collected in connection with a mail questionnaire survey of the attitudes of Jamaican elites conducted in 1958.

In a paper of this length it seems unnecessary to review the findings, but some comment seems in order regarding the implications of the results for the future of the federated West Indies. The question asked the Jamaican elites was, "Does Jamaica have more to gain or lose as a result of being part of federation?" This may not be the same as asking them, "Do you believe that Jamaica should be part of the federation or should she seek independence in her own right?" That is, it is possible for a person to feel that Jamaica may have more to lose than to gain from federation, but to feel simultaneously that Jamaica should become part of the federation despite that belief. A few of the respondents indicated that this was their view, saying that even though it had more to lose, Jamaica should pursue federation because the smaller islands had little hope for independence on their own. That is, they expressed an altruistic course for Jamaica based on what the island had to offer to federation. However, from an analysis of their open-ended responses, the vast majority of elites did not distinguish between these two questions, and their answers to the one reflect what their answers to the other would have been. Thus, there is a considerable amount of antifederation feeling among the Jamaican elites.

A great deal may depend on the next election in Jamaica. Throughout much of the data presented the importance of political party preference in influencing attitudes toward federation was shown. If the PNP is returned to office, then the chances of an increased Jamaican commitment (ideological, if not economic) to federation, and the development of a strong federal government may be enhanced; if the JLP is elected, this seems unlikely. This, of course, is not news to anyone familiar with the Jamaican political scene.*

However, even if the PNP is returned to power, Jamaica's continued participation in federation may be uncertain. In view of the fairly general feeling that Jamaica is losing economically and the suspicion that advancement toward full self-government may be impeded by federation, the British government, if it is as pro-federation as some writers say, may be forced to come out into the open in "selling" federation to Jamaica by contributing considerably more financial support to federation than it does now. Cricket, the Crown, and British culture may not be sufficient to keep Jamaica in the federation.

Acknowledgments

I gratefully acknowledge the assistance of the staff of the Institute for Social and Economic Research, University College of the West Indies, Mona, Jamaica, West Indies; the use of the facilities of the Western Data Processing Center, University of California, Los Angeles; and the research assistance of Lora-Lee Bell in the coding and tabulating of the questionnaire responses.

References

1. BRAITHWAITE, L. 1957. Progress toward federation, 1938–1956. Social and Economic Studies. 6: 133–184.
2. LEWIS, G. K. 1957. West Indian federation: the constitutional aspects. Social and Economic Studies. 6: 215–246.
3. ROBERTS, G. W. 1957. Some demographic considerations of West Indian federation. Social and Economic Studies. 6: 270.
4. MOOSAI-MAHARAJ, S. 1957. Problems of race and language in the British Caribbean. In Canada and the West Indies Federation. : 79. P. A. Lockwood, Ed. Mt. Allison Univ. Publ. No. 2. Sakville, N. B., Canada.
5. BRAITHWAITE, L. 1953. Social stratification in Trinidad. Social and Economic Studies. 2: 5–175.
6. BROOM, L. 1954. The social differentiation of Jamaica. Am. Soc. Rev. 19: 115–125.

* Since this paper was written, elections have been held in Jamaica, and the PNP was returned to power.

WHO'S WHO, JAMAICA. 1957. C. Neita, Ed. Who's Who (Jamaica) Ltd. Kingston, Jamaica.
8. SMITH, M. G. 1957. Ethnic and cultural pluralism in the British Caribbean. 30th Study Session of the Intern. Inst. Differing Civilizations. Lisbon, Portugal.
9. PROCTOR, JR., J. H. 1956. Britain's pro-federation policy in the Caribbean: an inquiry into motivation. Can. J. Economics and Political Sci. **22:** 319–331.
10. BELL, W. & E. R. SMITH. 1957. Social characteristics of Jamaican political elites. Paper presented at Ann. Meeting Amer. Anthropol. Assoc. Chicago, Ill.

DISCUSSION: POLITICS, POWER, AND
THE PLURAL SOCIETY*

Chairman: Hugh Smythe

Brooklyn College, Brooklyn, N. Y.

Rapporteur: Paul Bradley

Flint College, University of Michigan, Flint, Mich.

WENDELL BELL (*University of California, Los Angeles, Calif.*): The exposure of the Jamaican elites to various sources of information on the West Indies federation before our interrogation has not been included in this study, but I assume that there is relatively little variation in exposure to mass media among the elite.   Attitudes toward political independence or self-government were not set in an exclusively West Indian federation frame of reference.   The questionnaires for Jamaican elites had been circulated before November 1958; thus, changes in elite attitudes toward federation stimulated by the retroactive tax discussions would not be reflected in this study.   Even so, many of the elites indicated that they did not favor federation.

COMMENT: The opinions of the civil servant category might be subject to rapid change.   Such an event as their regrading might swing statistical enumeration of their attitudes toward federation one way or another to a significant degree.

BELL: The female respondents in the questionnaires were elites in their own right (headmistresses, chief nurses, and the like), and were not the wives of the male elites studied; otherwise, a greater variation in the responses of this category might have been recorded.

[Considerable discussion centered on the "teacher" category in the study. Bell pointed out that it comprised more headmasters and other administrators than classroom teachers.   It also included members of the faculty of the University College of the West Indies, Mona, Jamaica.]

BELL: Regarding the category of nonrespondents in the study, further evaluation is being made.   This group includes about 70 per cent of the total recipients of the questionnaires.   Some nonrespondents had indicated concern over possible lack of anonymity due to the very detailed personal data they had been asked to include.   The question asking for the names of ten persons with whom the respondent had discussed federation and other important issues and problems had in particular aroused anxiety.

Similar questionnaires might be utilized for the elites of other islands of the federation.   I should prefer interviewing to the mailed-questionnaire method

* Statements have been paraphrased and condensed.

if such an extension of the study proved possible. This would require considerably more resources, however, than I had available for the Jamaican study.

COMMENT: I have used the questionnaire method on a different subject in Jamaica, and found that journalistic publicity stating that our respondents would not be identified by our study greatly facilitated the flow of returns.

COMMENT: The number of favorable responses of Jamaican elites to federation would have significantly increased, I believe, if by federation they had understood the ultimate inclusion of British Guiana.

[Considerable discussion followed, centered on the element of self-interest stimulating favorable responses on federation by elite groups, especially among the bureaucratic elites.]

COMMENT: Federation is one way in which new bureaucratic functions would proliferate, as in defense and foreign affairs.

COMMENT: Insular bureaucracies might find their governmental roles reduced as the federal bureaucracy expanded its functions.

[Discussion centered on attitudes toward federation in relation to the different segments of a pluralistic society.]

COMMENT: In a recent study we found that a surprising number of East Indian secondary school students reported favorable opinions on federation.

COMMENT: In a study in an East Indian village in Trinidad we encountered no favorable opinion regarding federation. Incidentally, the fear of the consequences of unlimited integration, presumably Negro, was very widespread among these villagers.

[The discussion returned to the matter of self-interest in explaining attitudes toward federation.]

BELL: In our study there was a considerable number of respondents who, recognizing that Jamaica would suffer immediate economic losses by federation, felt that intrinsic gains would materialize by the emergence of a West Indian nation.

COMMENT: Insular nationalism in the West Indies, especially in Jamaica, has in part sprung from the competition of members of the local middle class for government posts held by Englishmen. Thus, the value of independence was judged partially by an increase in the number of employment opportunities for the natives. The smaller islands in the South Caribbean much more frequently conceived of themselves as members of a federation whereas, in more isolated Jamaica, the first national self-consciousness was experienced as Jamaicans rather than as future federationists.

[A discussion of the conception of elite used in the Bell study followed.]

BELL: In general we used a Lasswellian[1] conception of elites as those holding positions of power, the decision-makers. We surveyed primarily the national leaders occupying different elite positions, although some parish and local community leaders were included. The elite categories were separated by differential functions within Jamaican society, but some overlapping membership among different elites was observed.

QUESTION: What is the structure of modern plural societies?

SMYTHE: Practically all of the emergent nations today are plural societies, made up of a complex of peoples and cultures.

Modern world developments have seen the rise of new classes of people who have taken over the authority structures long held by traditional elite families and ruling cliques.   Whereas in most of the current plural societies power and politics were the province of a traditional and well-established landed aristocracy, postwar changes have resulted in shifts in relationships and altered social and economic patterns of the societies.   Those who now move into the roles of power, the new elite who wield political authority, are caught up in a situation that poses real problems for them.   The societies in which they exercise leadership are composed of numerous subcultural, racial, ethnic, and religious segments, each a part of a possibly new whole, yet each striving to preserve its own individuality.

The federation of The West Indies represents pluralism of another sort, the basic problems of which stem mainly from economic factors.   Although there are underlying animosities among the people in the various islands that form the now semicolonial entity, major antagonisms apparently center around differences involving Jamaica and its economic relation to the federation; while in Trinidad, with its numerous East Indian segments and ethnic minorities, there seems to be a note of racial discord.

There is also the problem of communication and distance between the islands. Also interisland migration barriers still prevail, and an acceptable customs union is not in effect.

The problem of the day involving power, politics, and plural societies is generated out of the conflict between the ideal of the homogeneous national state and the reality of ethnic and racial heterogeneity.

Reference

1. LASSWELL, H. D., D. LERNER, & C. E. ROTHWELL.   1952.   The Comparative Study of Elites.   Stanford Univ. Press.   Stanford, Calif.

URBANIZATION AND THE PLURAL SOCIETY

Leonard Broom

University of Texas, Austin, Texas

The Caribbean may be the ideal locale for the comparative study of differentiation, an extreme manifestation of which is the plural society, but it is less than ideal for investigating the bearing of urbanization on plural societies, because the cities of the Caribbean are for the most part not highly developed urban centers. On the other hand, the fact that the ethnic minorities are concentrated in the cities, where they specialize in distinctively urban occupations, lends a significance to these populations far out of proportion to their numbers, and their urban concentration makes feasible relatively economical and efficient research.

The Plural Society

The preoccupation with conceptual matters in the papers of this monograph suggests some terminological insecurity, and this paper is no exception. At the risk of retracing ground that has already been covered and creating some fresh complications, I want to be as clear as possible about my terminology. If a plural society is nothing more than a condition involving a multiplicity of populations with diverse identities or cultural backgrounds, economy dictates that we dispense with the additional term. The burden of proof always rests on those who propose terminological propagation, and it is the responsibility of the contributors to this monograph to show that it is entitled to its title, however interesting its substance may be.

In the comment that immediately follows, my debt to M. G. Smith as well as some divergences from his thinking are apparent.[1,2] The distinctive feature of pluralism is that it evokes questions about social order, as Smith has put it, "... preoccupation with structural relations between the principal social sections"[1] (p. 79). However, I desire to place a limitation on the concept. A society is not a plural society just because it contains populations from more than one racial or cultural origin. Diversity is a necessary, but not a sufficient, condition for the plural society. Not all, and perhaps not most, nations made up of differing populations are plural societies.

Perhaps the problem may be clarified with examples drawn from outside the Caribbean. The United States affords both positive and negative illustrations. In one respect, the most durable and institutionalized cleavage between Negroes and whites, it is a plural (or dual) society. Terms of limited association are being worked out and, although no social system is ever fixed, the United States will remain a plural, that is a biracial, society for a long time. This is the case despite the fact that the culture of American Negroes deviates less from the modal American types than do some immigrant cultures. (The question of the reality of American Negro culture is moot and requires an extensive and straightforward empirical investigation. Discussions centering on African survivals and syncretism probably obscure rather than clarify the problem.)

Some of the American ethnic minorities are numerous and culturally more differentiated from the dominant population than are the Negroes, but for them the mechanisms of isolation and social control, both internal and external, are much weaker and less elaborate. Areas of primary immigrant settlement in great cities and the enclaves of nationality-religious populations satisfy some of the preliminary conditions of pluralism, but one can not foresee the development of well-differentiated and stable segments of the social order. Some encysted elements of ethnic minorities in the United States may survive indefinitely, but most of the nationality-religious populations will probably endure only for a few decades or a few generations.

Perhaps the characteristics of the plural society may be clarified with a negative case: Australia before the recent flood of immigration. It had minimal cultural variability, little differentiation between country and city beyond characteristics related to their respective functions (surely no folk-urban dichotomy), and a community of identity. I do not mean to imply that Australia was an absolutely homogeneous and coherent society. Australia had important internal differences based on regional interests and class distinctions, but it was not a plural social order.

Canada, by contrast, is a good case of a plural society because it is so exactly the converse of the ideal-typical nation state.[3] The two major populations are distinguished by almost everything but race: language, religion, territory, and culture. As a consequence, constitutional adjustments have been made to accommodate government to reality, and political adjustments are continuously made to strengthen the agencies of accommodation. A political order that explicitly recognizes pluralism is the capstone of a plural society, but plural societies may solve their problems in other ways.

To summarize, the idea of a plural society does not merely refer to a condition in which a diversity of populations is present. It presupposes that the populations severally have valued identities, interests, and a degree of internal cohesion that tend to separate them from each other. In order to maintain the society as a going concern, the several populations are taken into account as such. In the extreme case this takes explicit political form, the ideal type of which is probably federalism. In other words, in a plural society the problem of diversity has been resolved by adjustments that presume the continued separate identity of significant population elements and a specification of limited spheres of contact, especially in the market place and in politics.

Variability and Urbanization in the Caribbean

By this circuitous route we arrive in the Caribbean, which is a region of great diversity in cultural origins and of considerable diversity in racial composition. Viewed as a whole, it is a patchwork of cultures that have been Creolized and acculturated in settings remote from the ancestral sources. The tendencies of color slavery and its elimination, colonialism and its decline, and urbanization based on trade have created some thematic parallels among the islands, but heterogeneity remains a striking feature. Authentic cultural variability may be observed within any of the larger islands, and even in the smaller ones the Creolized rural and lower-class town populations are marked off from the middle and upper classes, which take the metropolitan nation as their reference culture. (Probably the folk-urban dichotomy does not faithfully reflect this distinction. I suggest it is more accurate to speak of Creole versus metropolitan orientations.)

Apart from the Creole-metropolitan division, two kinds of situations attract our attention. In one, small racially or culturally distinct populations are concentrated in urban areas, usually the primate city, and perform specialized tasks (the other situation of the East Indians in Trinidad and British Guiana is reserved for later comment). These differentiated populations, which may be called ethnic minorities in distinction to the Creoles, are not only relatively urban in location but also more highly urbanized in function than the majority of urban Creoles. Were they not urban, the ethnic minorities would be almost lost in contemporary Caribbean society. These populations often compete with each other in trade, but there is a tendency for them to specialize so that direct competition is reduced. This segmentation of commerce according to ethnic specialization and its consequences for maintaining ethnic communities deserve increased research.

The Chinese in Jamaica, numbering about 19,000, are a case in point.[4] Arriving in the island with commercial skills that were in short supply, the Chinese remained in agricultural labor for only a brief time. By the turn of the century they had made a place for themselves in the retail grocery trade that extended by vertical development to wholesale groceries and in time to the food products industry. Their concentration in the grocery trade is remarkable (Lind's hypothesized relationship of alien status and trade is suggestive but undemonstrated). As far as I know, there is nothing in the qualifications of the Chinese population that should have led them to this particular line of commerce. The underlying causes are to be found in the Jamaican economic situation. The grocery trade had been poorly developed, and the archaic system of plantation stores was ill adapted to independent purchases by urban populations. It is also possible that the Chinese embarked on enterprise at a strategic point in the rehabilitation of the Jamaican economy. The Chinese extended their activity through a network of communal and kinship bonds, first in the oft-repeated pattern of the recruitment of immigrants and subsequently through sponsoring and training them. In this fashion the network of kinship was integrated with reciprocal economic obligations. Under these conditions it is to be expected that voluntary associations would further strengthen ethnic solidarity. To recapitulate, the Chinese cut a niche for themselves in the Jamaican economy and enlarged it into a social nest.

The Syrians, numbering about 1000, a much smaller population than the Chinese, are also highly concentrated in commercial activities and are highly urbanized. Because of their small numbers and the type of enterprise in which they engage, they are far less conspicuous than the Chinese. Probably most Jamaican peasants and agricultural workers have had dealings with Chinese, but few have knowingly encountered Syrians. Strong kin and commercial ties affect the operation of Syrian enterprises, and their association with other Syrian communities in the Western hemisphere and beyond tends to mute their commitment to Jamaican society.

Unlike the Chinese and Syrians, the 1000 or so Jews in Jamaica are in the late stages of assimilation. Although they are occupationally differentiated and show some persistence of religious identification, it appears that consider-able numbers have been lost to the community over the past decades.   Their high concentration in a few urban areas may be a survival of earlier segregative tendencies and an impediment to final assimilation.

In any close investigation of the differential statuses of the ethnics, the primate city in each island or constellation of islands is the chief unit of analysis.   Only the leading urban centers are sufficiently differentiated from the countryside and contain significant numbers of distinct populations.   In Jamaica, for example, the Kingston-St. Andrew metropolitan area, with a population of about 290,000, makes up less than 20 per cent of the island total (no other city in the island exceeds 25,000).   However, whereas about 19 per cent of the Coloured and Blacks (combined) live in the metropolitan area, fully 65 per cent of whites, 59 per cent of Chinese and Chinese Coloured, and 56 per cent of "others" (including Syrians) reside in Jamaica's primate city.   Of all the populations separately treated in the 1953 sample census, only the East Indians with 22 per cent in the Kingston-St. Andrew area resemble the Creole population in their low metropolitan concentration.

Unpublished data from the 1943 Jamaican census permit additional com-ment.   This census separately reports Coloured and Blacks, and an important distinction masked in the 1953 census may be discerned.   In 1943 the metro-politan area made up about 16 per cent of the island total, but only 12 per cent of Blacks compared with 28 per cent of the Coloured lived in the major city. Looked at another way, Blacks made up 78 per cent of the island population, but 60 per cent of the Kingston-St. Andrew metropolitan population.   The Coloured comprised 18 per cent of the island, but 31 per cent of the metropolitan total.

Syrians and Jews, who were not separately reported in 1953, were highly urban.   One half of the Syrians and 86 per cent of the Jews lived in urban Kingston-St. Andrew.   Another white population, the Spanish-Portuguese, showed the highest urban concentration of all (95 per cent in the city and 78 per cent in one census district).   To the best of my knowledge, they have not been the subject of close study, and some special attention would seem indi-cated.   It is not possible to report in this paper details on the relative con-centration of the several populations within the metropolitan area.   Although it should cause no surprise, it may be mentioned in passing that other minor ethnics are highly concentrated.   One half of the Jews, one third of the Syrians, and one third of the "British-Isles" whites live in two of the census dis-tricts.

The whites, Chinese, and "others" are by all criteria the most highly dif-ferentiated populations.   In the skills they carry, in their life styles, in their occupations, they are distinctively urban.   They make up less than one tenth of the city's total, but they perform a large part of the properly urban functions. Although these ethnic populations are numerically and proportionally small, in some cases they come close to satisfying the conditions for true pluralism. This is not merely because of their cultural distinctiveness; rather, the func-tions they perform place them in special niches in the economy and, in varying degrees, they utilize segregated institutions instead of common ones.   The network of associations stemming from economic activities and ingroup ties tends to fill a large part of their lives, minimizing opportunities for contact that might impair ethnic unity. It may be mentioned in passing that the ethnic minorities perform typically *gesellschaft* activities in the large society but, paradoxically, kinship and communal arrangements characterize the internal organization of their enterprises.

From the standpoint of the African Creoles the presence of skilled and experienced ethnics in commerce has two effects: first, the Creoles gain some preparatory training and socialization for business, but this is usually limited by the fact that the enterprises are ethnically circumscribed. Second, the movement of Creoles into business is retarded and even forestalled by cartel-like domination of large parts of the economy.

A study of the extent of ecological segregation of ethnic populations is indicated. Such a study should attempt to separate voluntary from imposed segregation, but one may guess that it is chiefly voluntary and a reflection of functional concentration and socioeconomic status. At the same time additional work should be done on occupational specialization. It could take as its point of departure studies of the relative share of various populations in the more differentiated occupations.[5] After this necessary first step, it would proceed to a determination of the extent to which the network of ethnic associations influences the organization of various enterprises, the amount of monopoly by ethnics, and the extent to which competition is interethnic rather than ethnic versus Creole.

Are the urban minorities participants in a plural society, or are they transitional and specialized appendages to it? I feel that in Jamaica they are the latter. The conspicuously privileged condition of the ethnic minorities in Jamaica is an accident of history that is not likely to be translated into stable arrangements. These populations can fight a delaying action, as they have been doing for many decades, but they cannot win the war. In the long run they have three alternatives: first, to leave the field, as Creole whites have done for more than two centuries; second, to assimilate with the Creole Africans (probably the Coloured); or, third, to defend a vulnerable and conspicuous if privileged status as long as it will last.

The East Indian Case

The East Indians, totaling 35,000, are a peculiar case in Jamaica. We have already observed that they are the most numerous of the minorities, resembling the Blacks and Coloured in their low urban concentration. The rural part of the population may tend to be absorbed in the rural Creoles but, unless the urban segment succeeds in recruiting substantial numbers from rural areas, it will share the predicament of the other urban ethnics.

The East Indians have an additional theoretical alternative. Because of the large numbers of East Indians in British Guiana and Trinidad and because of their strategic political status in those two colonies, it is just possible that effective and continuous communication could be achieved on a pan-Caribbean basis. In this case the smaller ethnic population would be sustained by the larger ones. This still might not make a plural society in Jamaica, but it would give Jamaican East Indians another solution at a large price.

If a pan-Caribbean movement of East Indians is doubtful beyond British Guiana and Trinidad, it may be close to realization for the Syrians and perhaps for the Chinese. Although numerically small, the Syrians in the federation of The West Indies maintain effective ties with each other and with Syrians in independent islands, as well as with Syrian communities in New York and in the Levant. This does not make for pluralism in the sense in which I prefer to use the term, but it may have a greater significance for Caribbean societies than the size of the population involved. Comparative study of the modes of communication and the devices of solidarity that minorities use to bridge the gaps of space may be efficiently undertaken in the Caribbean, and the yield should be of theoretical as well as empirical interest. It might even throw some sidelight on the problems of federation in an archipelago.

At least in British Guiana and Trinidad the conditions of a plural society obtain, for there are two cultures, two races, separate urban foci of activity (although the East Indians are again the less urban), two hinterland populations and, to a considerable extent, separate institutions. The major populations in the two colonies are too nearly equal to produce a domination of one by the other. There are two more likely alternatives: either a kind of federalism in which the separate identities would be protected or a secessionism. The latter would verify Klass's hypothesis, presented elsewhere in this monograph, that the strains between the East Indians and the Creoles in Trinidad preclude a plural society, but it is too early to presume that a viable plural order may not mature along federalist lines.

Conclusion

In retrospect, I have said little directly about urbanization, although a good deal by implication. I am not prepared to make any strong assertions about pluralism and Caribbean cities because there are unanswered problems about their classification. Tentatively, I surmise that most Caribbean cities would be designated by Sjoberg[6] and others as preindustrial. Havana, Cuba, and San Juan, Puerto Rico, may be exceptions. It would be worthwhile to explore the relevance of the Sjoberg classification to the problem of pluralism.

In a sense, urbanism and pluralism are redundant. Throughout history the city has been the stage on which diverse peoples encountered each other, where conflicting values and differing social orders met. The city is the proper focus for the study of pluralism because it is able to sustain alternative types of social order whereas, until recently, the countryside was sharply limited in the kind of society it could bear. Of course, the countryside can sustain an infinite variety of cultures, but only of minor differentiation; in any place and time it can carry some diversity, but not nearly so much as the city. However, it would be erroneous to equate the diversity of urban cultures with true social pluralism unless there were more than one substantial population capable of affecting, in a fundamental way, the distribution of political power and the utilization of institutional forms. If segregation, specialization of function, significant size, reproductive potential, and a degree of autonomy are not all present, there is no plural society; there is merely a congeries of minorities. Most of the situations in the Caribbean are of the latter variety.

Whether or not there is a consensus on this conclusion, there should be a consensus about the importance of the research task. It is hoped that this paper has indicated some necessary steps, and that the identification of some cases as negative ones will encourage rather than deter comparative analysis.

References

1. Smith, M. G. 1953. Social structure in the British Caribbean about 1820. Social and Economic Studies. 1(4): 55–79.
2. Smith, M. G. 1957. Ethnic and cultural pluralism in the British Caribbean. Working paper for the 30th study session of the International Institute of Differing Civilizations. Lisbon, Portugal.
3. Hughes, E. C. 1943. French Canada in Transition. : iii. Univ. Chicago Press. Chicago, Ill.
4. Lind, A. W. 1958. Adjustment patterns among the Jamaican Chinese. Social and Economic Studies. 7(2): 144–164.
5. Broom, L. 1954. The social differentiation of Jamaica. Am. Sociological Rev. 19: 115–125.
6. Sjoberg, G. 1955. The preindustrial city. Am. J. Sociology. 60: 438–445.

DISCUSSION: URBANIZATION, COMMUNICATION, AND THE PLURAL SOCIETY*

Chairman: Robert Manners

Brandeis University, Waltham, Mass.

Rapporteur: Alexander Lesser

Brandeis University, Waltham, Mass.

Manners: Broom has not clarified pluralism definitively, but he has clarified the problem of pluralism in urban centers.

[Discussion centered on pluralism in relation to preindustrial versus industrial cities.]

Question: Historically, the city brings together diverse societies and cultures but, at the same time, is it not true that urbanization is the strongest force for the merging of cultures?

Broom: I am confident that is correct, but preindustrial and industrial cities have different effects. The rapid acculturation of the so-called melting pot refers to the great industrial cities of the Nineteenth and Twentieth Centuries. Most Caribbean cities, with the possible exception of Havana and San Juan, are predominantly preindustrial, with economy based on trade, the city tied to the countryside, and most urban children socialized in the countryside. While the hypothesis that the city tends to merge ethnic groups is probably correct, we must distinguish between preindustrial and industrial cities. Ethnic subgroups may survive longer in preindustrial cities than in industrial ones. The duration of such groups involves the extent to which they have identity, and their own institutions. In Jamaica the Chinese began by invading the retail grocery trade, expanded to embrace the wholesale grocery trade as well, and are now predominant in the food-producing industry. The Chinese also have an exclusive club and an exclusive school. A small Chinese population has built a packaged life, encysted for a long time.

[Discussion turned to pluralism as a concept.]

* Statements have been paraphrased and condensed.

QUESTION: Can pluralism include differences based on ecology?

BROOM: The concept may be stretched, but it becomes less useful.

COMMENT: The stability of ethnic groups over a period of time is used as one criterion of pluralism, but usually a smaller community within a larger nation—a minority, not a plural segment—maintains itself for not more than several generations. Defining plural entities by what happens in the future is not good operational definition.

BROOM: It is not part of the definition. The definition emphasizes the underlying structural conditions rather than the time aspect. There is a prediction about the future, and that becomes a test.

[Discussion returned to city types.]

QUESTION: What is a preindustrial city?

BROOM: I would follow Sjoberg,[1] who defines it by its economic base, by its social organization (with a tendency toward feudal type of control and domination), and by its ecological features.

COMMENT: By definition, all Caribbean cities are preindustrial, and the distinction between preindustrial and industrial cities is exhaustive.

QUESTION: Is the city of New York postindustrial?

BROOM: In Sjoberg's terms, New York is an industrial city. Manufacturing is moving out, but the controls of industry remain in New York.

COMMENT: Nevertheless, a new urban form is emerging. The city is handling the paper work, but losing industrial production.

BROOM: That would be a faulty truncation of the character of industry. New York is an elaborated development of the industrial structure.

COMMENT: Still, the distinction amounts to this: as the United States is an industrial society, its cities are industrial cities. The Caribbean is agrarian, hence its cities are preindustrial. Is this the most fruitful dichotomy, the most fruitful way to understand Caribbean cities?

BROOM: The classification alone cannot take us far. Most Caribbean cities are of the same kind. Additional factors should be considered. For example, there is the problem of scale. Compare the magnitude of Havana or San Juan with that of Kingston, Jamaica; a different kind of social order is the result of the smaller size of a city. There is the question, do additional aggregations of the same thing mean that a different kind of thing results?

MANNERS: The question is getting at the problem of concomitants of the urban, whether preindustrial or industrial. From this viewpoint, is the distinction important?

COMMENT: What I have in mind is: What kinds of cities do we find in the Caribbean? They are not all of the same kind. There are differences related to cities of the parent country. The Puerto Rican city, for example, differs in form from the French West Indian city.

BROOM: True, but what is significant for society? Are different original arrangements merely historical, or do they modify life today? Is ethnic segregation different in Caribbean cities of French, Spanish, or English Creole origin? Social orders may be deflected by differences in historical city forms, but are they determined by them?

COMMENT: Do not overlook the fact that Caribbean cities precede the ethnic diversity.

BROOM: If we are to illuminate pluralism, the question is, even if cities antedate their present plural character, what is the relation involved? If ethnic minorities are found to be localized differently in Spanish, French, and English cities, then we know something about urban environments. [In reply to a comment on the uselessness of negative findings] I do not agree; negative findings are valuable and publishable. What is probably determinate (in urban pluralism) is not the shape of the urban community, but the discrete functions of the different ethnic groups.

[Pluralism as a concept is again considered.]

QUESTION: Pluralism and urbanism both seem to have a multiplicity of meanings. Are these concepts too elastic? Do we not need more specific terminology, a more specific model?

BROOM: I also dislike elasticity, but the core of pluralism has to do with social order, boundaries, identities, and functions that separate ethnic groups. I prefer the test of definite research projects on critical problems to exercises in definition. Is there the same kind of Chinese and Syrian distribution in the primate cities of different islands? What are the discrete functions of different ethnic groups in exchange? What are the characteristics of ethnic enclaves? What are the political forms and powers of a given minority? What is the influence of a minority and the nature of its political activity?

COMMENT: We create concepts to help in research. The distinction between industrial versus preindustrial cities is useless for understanding the variation of Caribbean cities. Although pluralism may help in some discussions, it is not helpful in the Caribbean: it occurs throughout the Caribbean. We can go on discussing the concept of pluralism and how it helps in research or we can consider the Caribbean itself and decide what concepts are needed to deal with it.

COMMENT: We still seem to be on the taxonomic level. Beyond that, there are questions of our purpose in inquiry, involving social values. Are we interested in the rights of people, and especially children, caught in the pluralistic situation in the Caribbean? How are they affected by conditions described? How are we to understand the effects of industrialization on different levels?

BROOM: Nomenclature is not important. We control the words, they do not control us. Pluralism and heterogeneity do not do anything; they cannot. Our inquiry is directed to the question of social order; we wish to isolate diverse conditions within which we can see different social arrangements. As to the moral or ethical question, however much I may care about these matters personally, from the viewpoint of the inquiry I mention, I consider them quite irrelevant.

COMMENT: There is another question about the usefulness of the concept of the plural society. As Smith used it in his presentation, it refers to segments, distinct in basic institutions, except political and possibly economic ones, bound together by the common political and possibly economic institutions of a larger society. In this sense a plural society is always a state, although there may be states that are not plural societies. The problem of pluralism thus viewed is therefore always a part of the problem of the analysis of modern states with plural segments. Such a state is not a society in the sense of commonly understood sociological and anthropological usage. Why should it be termed a society, even if the reference is qualified by the word plural?   It is in fact a state of a certain kind and can be defined in terms of an analysis of states and their forms and structures.   Moreover, as Wagley has suggested in his discussion of Smith's paper elsewhere in this monograph, the plural society may be merely a transitional form of the state, arising from the amalgamation of diverse ethnic groups but becoming, in time, heterogeneous rather than pluralistic, as Smith defined this difference.

QUESTION: If the concept of pluralism is useful, the test must be empirical. Is this a set of concepts that help to distinguish different kinds of diversity or different situations encountered, or not?   To test the concept, we need a definition of institution; we need operations for deciding what are basic institutions and what are not.   Have we a checklist of institutions in this sense?   Do we say, for example, that kinship is a basic institution in one type of society, but not in another?

COMMENT: If we adopt Smith's usage and definition it is not merely a question of defining cultural pluralism.   If we accept them, there follows an essential independence of society and culture, as Smith pointed out.   We are not merely taking on a new term, but we are buying new concepts of society and culture.

MANNERS: Does not the general question with which we are dealing concern diversity in all modern societies and our wish to analyze what elements link diverse groups together in complex societies?

QUESTION: How much does pluralism add to older concepts?   We seem to be setting limits on the nature of political and economic institutions.

BROOM: In this connection I propose to distinguish between nation and state. A nation is the antithesis of plural order.   A nation implies common ancestry and cultural homogeneity; a state refers to a dominant political unit, regardless of the variability of its components.   A state may contain a plural society.

COMMENT: That fits Smith's distinctions, but it still leaves the question of the plural society and the problem of analysis of the modern state.

MANNERS: I suggest we get back to the subject of ethnic minority communities in the urban setting.

QUESTION: There are still two themes: the Caribbean and its problems, or ethnic diversity and its problems.   Which shall we discuss?

MANNERS: As chairman, I will not arbitrate.

[Discussion turns to urbanization and stratification.]

QUESTION: What is the relation of urbanization and stratification?   Stratification can increase in an urban setting.   Is an ethnic group in a Caribbean city based on class or ethnic difference?   Does not class blur the distinction?

BROOM: In the United States, with its social stratification, class locations blur ethnic lines and vice versa.   Is the same tendency true of the Caribbean? It probably occurs to a much smaller extent, because Caribbean stratification is flatter.   I think the difference in the Caribbean is mostly ethnic.   Analysis of stratification should include more than horizontal cuts.   The specific location of function is important.   Caribbean ethnic groups are narrowly located in the range of functions in society.   We need empirical studies of strata plus situs.

QUESTION: Are not class differences more important than ethnic diversity in any city?

MANNERS: For example, does the Chinese club in Jamaica cross class lines?

BROOM: I have no direct information about some features of Chinese voluntary associations in Jamaica. The distribution of the Chinese in Jamaican society is narrower than for the population as a whole. The Chinese occupy a segment that is well up in the socioeconomic scale and not highly stratified; none is probably below the upper lower class or perhaps even below the lower middle class. Ethnicity versus social rank is not as clear as it would be with a full hierarchy of classes. There is only limited stratum variability. The voluntary associations are entirely metropolitan and are not found in outlying areas. In the city, as you go up the strata, a larger proportion of the ethnically eligible are found to belong to the associations; at the top everyone participates; at the bottom, fewer participate.

COMMENT: In Trinidad the upper-class Chinese are now colored as a result of intermarriage and racial mixture. Those on the lower social scale do not fit into the club. New arrivals are technically welcome, but few in the club can now speak Chinese. The Portuguese also have married out a great deal, and the richest of them are black. New Portuguese arrivals are definitely lower in the social scale.

QUESTION: The basic problem in actual study is to clarify differentiation and stratification. Within stratification, for example, what are the different styles of life? At what point is it analytically convenient to distinguish groups as distinct? The groups are changing and achieving national identification. They differ in ways of life. In one sense the United States is ethnically heterogeneous. Is this a difference of basic institutions, or a difference of life style?

COMMENT: There is also the question of adhesion of the rural population to the urban group and center. Even where there are no cultural differences, the recent rural migrants remain a distinct social group for a decade.

MANNERS: Should the component parts of a society be distinguished for life style?

QUESTION: The question is, when is a difference not a difference?

BROOM: We distinguish those that are significant by empirical analysis; that is, the differences that affect social relations and structure. Minor differences can and should be recorded, but identified as such. [After further comment.] Differences are important that affect statuses and situses, that involve functional roles and significant locations in the social order.

COMMENT: The migrant group that comes into the city is not dissimilar in culture from the lower class of the city, but is nevertheless distinct from it.

BROOM: When we deal with urban migrants from rural areas who have the same culture base, there is the question of degree of adaptation to urban forms. For example, Jamaican culture is cut horizontally into the metropolitan-oriented and the Creole. There is a continuum of Creole from the isolated but emancipated modes of the peasantry to the lower-class urban workers already absorbed. Latecomers to the city occupy an intermediate position. There is no direct shift from rural to urban in the metropolitan ethnic minority groups. The shift takes place by way of an absorption first of all of the rural migrants into the lower-class Creole of the city. The rural Creoles can get into the metropolitan upper class only by way of urban participation, not directly from their rural status.

[Several questions were raised on this point. Manners spoke of rural migrants as a proletarian segment of an urban population.   A speaker from the floor discussed the urban proletariat and an appendage.   Another asked where distinctions in cultural patterns are meaningful, how people live, and how they are related to other groups.]

QUESTION: Urbanization, the transition from rural to urban, is a contemporary world process.   Sociologists have tended to use the American and European city as a model.   World phenomena are different, and sometimes there are ethnic differences between urban and rural populations as, for example, in Southeast Asia.   Does urbanization throughout the world follow the same course as in Europe and America?   Can the sociologist's hypothesis be expanded to include all these areas into a wider theory of urbanization?

COMMENT: There are certain regularities as a result of economic forces.

BROOM: There are regularities, but variations in form should take our attention.

QUESTION: How do we use the distinction between urban and rural when rural people may live in town?   What are they?   For example, it would be hard to find a rural person in Trinidad.

MANNERS: Are we interested only in local adaptations or in the basic fact that people come into town to work for wages?   Is there not an over-all pattern that is the effect of a cash economy?

BROOM: Not necessarily for wages only, but to make money.   For example, as by trade.

COMMENT: There is a new urbanization in America.   People live in towns, but work rurally.

COMMENT: In some countries, on the other hand, people work in factories and come home to farm.

COMMENT: When people migrate, there are men who leave their families behind and some who bring their families with them.   Differences in the kinds of institutions would be related to these patterns.

References

1. SJOBERG, G.   1955.   The preindustrial city.   Am. J. Sociol. **60**: 438–445.

THE WRITER IN THE CARIBBEAN

Wilfred G. O. Cartey

Columbia University, New York, N. Y.

It is perhaps a truism to say that the artist, be he sculptor, musician, painter, or poet, is a product of his moment and milieu. The moment enters into his bloodstream, sullying or purifying it and, whether the artist speaks with his heart or his head, the blood mutation of the moment still remains. Then, ever so imperceptibly or ever so evidently, the moment absorbing the milieu becomes the creation and the art.

The milieu is the Caribbean, the Antilles, Middle America, the West Indies —call it what you will—but place it as a group of islands and lands sun-blown and moon-bound, girt by the blue seas and by legend, where there is tropic luxuriance and growth of indolence, music, and pleasure intertwined with the vines of economic instability, political immaturity, and grinning, stark-smiling insouciance and poverty.

The word thus comes to us charged and saturated from these regions: "The word comes to us damp from the forests,"* sings Nicolás Guillén in *Llegada*.[1]

The tropics offer the writer rhythm, color, odors, and tastes, the descriptions of which delight artists as dissimilar as the Haitians Duraciné Vaval and Emile Roumer, the Venezuelan Antonio Arraiz, and the Puerto Rican Luis Palés Matos. It gives the writer his words:

> "the lovely words
> alas the lovely words!"†

sings Carlos Pellicer.[2]

For Samuel Selvon words are everywhere:[3] "I move around in a world of words. Everything that happens is words. But pure expression is nothing. One must build on things that happen . . . So now I weave."

The pattern and the threads can be woven from a feeling of mystery that floats in this milieu. Colombia's Gérman Arciniegas finds magic there, magic that moves in and through the poetry. The deepest impression that the poetry of the Caribbean makes is one of a magic spell.

In the midst of this picturesqueness and exoticism, which writers and journalists too often depict in superficial and exaggerated tones, reside many other forces at work in this region. This milieu has a common heritage of colonialism that still permeates its society. In all of the islands there has been and is the desire to shrug off the cramping clutch of the colonial powers: France, Britain, Spain, and now the United States. Its consequent background of antiquated European modes and the superimposition of still other patterns from Africa, China, and India, make it possible to call this region, with a great degree of accuracy, the clinical cauldron of the continents, where a cosmic people is simmering.

---

* *"La palabra nos viene humeda de los bosques."*
† *". . . las hermosas palabras*
"¡ ay las hermosas palabras !"

These islands and other Caribbean countries are all comparatively new and young, and all are searching for a spiritual and cultural identity that is rapidly evolving. Also young are the archipelago's economy and political machinery. As is common to youth, there are instability and flights of imperfection; consequently a certain poverty, a lack of self-sufficiency, and a necessary (and I hope temporary) alignment with and dependence on the larger powers and nations and their fluctuating affairs result. However, the islands have not by any means reached the wasteland where pleasure is corrupt and the spirit is dead, or where the society is rotten at heart.

Given these common denominators, and despite certain historical differences in development, the artistic and literary motifs used in the Spanish-, French-, or English-speaking Caribbean are basically the same, even if the treatment of these motifs differs in emphasis. The vision of the Caribbean may be one of anguish: Nicolás Guillén of Cuba says:[1]

> "My country is sweet on the outside,
> And very bitter within."*

Luis Palés Matos cries out:[4]

> "And Puerto Rico? My passionate island
> You have your final end
> Within the wasteland of a continent.
> Puerto Rico bleats
> Sadly like a gilded goat."†

The vision may be a smiling one, however: Wilson Harris exalts the savannah lands of British Guiana, his country:[5]

> "Lands open
> To sunshine and sky
> And to the endless winds
> Passing their eternal rounds.
> Lands that hold in their bosom
> Space like a benediction.
> Lands smoky with their dreams
> That drift across the world
> Like memories of ancient beauty dimly recalled;
> Lands full of the music of birds
> Crying softly a vague and formless meditation."

Carl Brouard, a Haitian, sings of the Antilles:[6]

---

* "Mi patria es dulce por fuera,
  Y muy amarga por dentro."
† "Y Puerto Rico? Mi isla ardiente
  Para ti todo ha terminado
  En el yermo de un continente,
  Puerto Rico, lugubremente
  Bala como cabro estofado."

"Charming lands, the sapphire Antilles
Martinique, the Turks, the Grenadines, Haiti—
Singing names that sound like golden bells,
That cradle sweetly like a hammock.
Antilles! Golden Antilles:
Scented bouquets!"*

However, these four quotations, although containing poetic emotion, lack poetic fervor and depth. Their writers seem to have been lulled into a facile, not too deep effort of composition by the abundance of poetic motifs existing in the area. This is a very tangible danger facing the writer in the Caribbean: it is too easy for him to steep himself and emerge clothed in exotic novelty and color, which he could export like goods for tourists.

Why had these sprouts remained dormant for so many years in my islands? Why this sudden sun-crested outburst of bloom? Does Granpa in *Black Midas* have the solution to the riddle?[7]

"Boy, the white man does write down all they story in black and white, but we does keep we own lock up in we belly. Time will come when we got to write down we story too, cause if we don't write it down it going to get lost. Now all the young people going away from the land. In long time past days we used to tell we story with drum, but soon even the drum won't talk no more."

In Haiti the United States occupation (1915 to 1934) is said to have given birth to the New Generation of writers, a group sunk in deep concern for the soul of Haiti. In Cuba, the War of Independence (1895 to 1898) brought forth José Marti.

Can I or should I then point to the closer approach of federation as at least one of the motivating forces? The sunlight of freedom that has budded the closed leaves of our literary creation has given us a group of exciting, fresh, and industrious writers: Samuel Selvon, Derek Walcott, V. S. Naipaul, George Campbell, John Hearne, Jan Carew, George Lamming, and others.

These writers are faced with many problems, many exciting alternatives, and many exciting possibilities. In countries where there has been little or no literature of long standing the writer is fortunate, since the search for new themes and new subjects is very profitable. However, the greater the possibility of profit the deeper is the writer's responsibility to himself and to his island world, and the more sensitive he must be to his people and his islands. He is caught in the web of circumstance.

I have allotted a responsibility to these writers: that of revealing the shining morning dew to a newly awakened person. Not only must the writer reveal the beauty of the dew that has kissed the tender grass or the damp earth for a whole long slumbering night, but he must give spirit to the night, body to the

---

* *"Pays charmeurs, Antilles de saphir*
  Martinique, Îles Turques, les Grenadines
  Haiti
  Noms chantants et qui sonnez
  Comme des grelots d'or,
  Et qui bercez doucement comme un hamac
  Antilles: Antilles d'or:
  Vous êtes d'odorantes bouquets."

earth, and life to the grass. George Lamming, in *The Emigrants*, speaks of the writer's moral responsibility:[8]

"You're a public victim. You're articulate not only for yourself, but thousands who will never see you in person, but who will know you because the printed page is public property. And if you betray yourself, you can betray thousands too. To be trivial, dishonest or irresponsible is to be criminal."

However, all of these young writers must have their freedom, their skepticism or cynicism. Nevertheless, these qualities must lead to a new and deeper understanding of the soul of the people. The soul of a people is the most communicable element, an element most difficult to obtain. This should be the ultimate aim.

How have these writers attempted to confront their position?

Much poetry has been written, but there are few poets. Much of the poetry is commendable merely because a West Indian or West Indians were sufficiently sensitive to devote their free time to writing verse, even bad verse. The same can be said for the short story. Perhaps I could charge myself with being overcritical. Should I adopt the colonel's position in the following conversation from E. Mittelholzer's *Of Trees and the Sea*,[9] and apply the stereotyping process to the literary output of the islands?

"Oh, a book," said Roger,

"Hmf! Book on Barbados!"

"What kind of book?"

"On Barbados."

"Ah,—yes, I know, but I mean, what form does it take?"

"Don't be a fool! What other form could a book on Barbados take but poetical comedy-fantasy?"

"Oh."

"With marine, botanical and religious overtones as a matter of course."

I here judge some of these pieces as art, not as of a particular region, but as pure art.

The novelistic output in the Caribbean warms me with a touch of pride. In this genre the writers are, with a large measure of success, consciously experimenting with language and form and technique.

In language, the novelists have incorporated quite successfully the rhythm of the speech of the islands with all its cadences and wonderful flexibility of imagery. Occasionally the imagery of the natural speech is humorous, sometimes it is lyrical and musical, and sometimes it is argumentative and "fatiguing" (in the West Indian sense of bantering).

In *Black Midas*[7] Bullah Daniels says that "he had he share of woman—though me never marry, if me and Solomon take count me won't come off bad" and, going on to describe the personal attributes of women he wisely sums up: "Some of them had two faces and some of them three; some of them had birdseed in they mouth and talk more sweeter than tinamoon can sing."

Selvon in *Ways of Sunlight*[8] uses a technique based on the common, everyday things the West Indians call "fatigue" or "tone". The story "Waiting for Auntie to Cough" is a fatigue related with all the gusto of naturalness.

Mittelholzer in *A Morning at the Office*[9] which I consider a well-worked-out social novel, achieves a wonderful blend of class, language, and speech. Each social class and its peculiar social pattern is fitted into a speech niche. Elsewhere Mittelholzer's style could be termed imaginative stylized prose in which, as in Edgar Allen Poe and at times in Ernest Hemingway, the images are urgent symbols of inner reality.

George Lamming's style is heavy and charged with emotion, yet at times he achieves remarkable delicacy of imagery and lyricism.

V. S. Naipaul seems to be the comic eye of the West Indian novelistic storm. He tells the story of Ganesh[10] with a tongue-in-cheek attitude, with a mordant, laughable, yet corrosive satire that at times captures the travesty of the West Indian scene. Captures it, yes! but like most writers twisting, exaggerating, and distorting the distorted to highlight their effectiveness abroad. This is their privilege, their right even when the result is false to the reality that they are depicting.

John Hearne explains in the following words his technique of mingling the lived reality, the present circumstance, and the future:[11] "The words became things, almost beings, in which were carried what happened, what was and what would be. They were the only form of life he knew of which existed in so many worlds and were used by so many worlds simultaneously."

V. Reid in *The Leopard*[12] has transcended his West Indian limits, creating a novel of great lyric beauty combined with the tautness and tension of Ernest Hemingway in *The Old Man and the Sea*.[13] Here are the rains falling in Kenya: "Outside the window, the earth was in a joyous uproar beneath the rape of the long rains. The rain found all its hollows and embraced the hillocks. It soaked the trees to the roots."

In Biblical tones Reid sets the plot of his novel poetically. Here is his picture of Kenya:[12] "It is a land of immense folds and rolling parks; of water and forest and game; of hinged valleys so vast that you could lose the world's sins in them. . . . It is a rich land; rich in humus and equally rich in hate, for all men crave it. Know, therefore, that it is a land of feud: for the white challenger wants to conquer it and the black man to keep it.

"But none of the white and few of the blacks understand it, or cope with it. Nor do any of the noble beasts, the lion or the rhino or the bull buffalo. Only the leopard understands it, for he avoids the strong and eats the wounded and the weak."

Reid's prose in *The Leopard* is poetic prose, but some of the poetry written in the Caribbean is not even poetic prose. However, the sincerity of the creative intent, even when shrouded in English poetry of past centuries, is admirable. The novelists seem to have captured much more sharply the rhythm of the people. All peoples have their own powerful imagery; it is for the poet to capture it. The West Indies have their wealth of natural imagery waiting to be blown upon and heated and shaped into forms of beauty, but thus far this has not been done. In this sense there is not yet one true West Indian poet—true in the sense that the early Lorca is true of Spain.

Federico García Lorca suffuses the Andalusian reality with his creative imagination, infusing the real with the symbolic, bringing home the realities, or call it the folk soul, of their life to the Spanish people, yet migrating, through this symbolic imaginative sensual depiction, beyond the boundaries of Spain to the outer world.   As yet the West Indian poets do not sense that they will be most truly universal only when they are most truly West Indian.   In profusion, West Indian poets are photographing the visual reality of the islands, but their cameras are, with few exceptions, old single-lens instruments; you look through the viewer and you press the button.   The West Indian poet must experiment with speeds and openings, times and exposures, black-and-white and color; he must try to capture the native rhythm.

For instance, the poem *The Day before Ash Wednesday*, by A. N. Forde[14] tells of Carnival Tuesday in Trinidad, but has no native rhythm, no emotion, no sensuous life.   On hearing it our feet seem to be slushing through the cold snow of old England, not the black, hot pitch of the islands.   Here are a few verses:

> "There is a bee
> this morning
> feeding on the pollen
> of my breast
> as the sun
> with professional touch
> brings color to the limbs,
> a warm flood to the warm blood.
>
> "Pain is
> impanelled
> in the clenched heart;
> for this day is gay
> and warm with music-weather
> and air-rhyme.
>
> "There is a heat
> in my temples
> and in the stream
> of mad pounding
> my pulse leaps
> with its message
> to the waiting lips.
>
> The limbs take
> power and triumph
> from the beating hands
> and the bands
> of trivial maids
> tie their modesty in a fling."

Now listen to a few lines of *Steel-Band Clash*,[15] a calypso that in its very native simplicity is more effective than the preceding poem:

> "When two bands clash
> Mama-yo if you see cutlass!
> Never me again
> To jump up in a steel band
> In Port of Spain."

These poets write verses such as *Villanelle of the Living Pan*,[16] with the tender refrain of "Ah flute to him," or in *Homestead*[17] reincarnate the dead and buried Michael of Wordsworth. *Pocomania*[18] becomes a cold, lifeless English dance with its "Long mountain rise."

Give us rather the rhythm of the calypso or of the folk songs and music of the different islands; toil, and clothe the rhythm with creative imagination. The result would be a West Indian poetry that would apprehend the point of time at the intersection of the timeless.

There are good poets in the islands; poets who are born in the islands but who, if judged by their writings, are not of the islands, just as the light-skinned or fair-skinned person in the Caribbean is of no race or allegiance.

George Campbell, in his poem *Holy*,[19] achieves poetic stature. Errol Hill's *Beggarman*,[20] although somewhat weak in the middle, is a fine poem.

Derek Walcott is a poet by many standards. Ezra Pound was the poet who exercised the greatest influence on his earlier works. Walcott's ability to adapt Pound to his own emotion is commendable. Even more so are his patternings after Dylan Thomas and T. S. Eliot. I do not mean to be patronizing; all poets have been influenced by someone or other; Walcott is a poet in his own right. However, we still have no true West Indian poet. As T. S. Eliot pointed out:[21]

> "Words move, Music moves
> Only in time; but that which is only living
> Can only die. Words, after speech, reach
> Into the silence. Only by the form, the pattern
> Can words or music reach
> The stillness, as a chinese jar still
> Moves perpetually in its stillness."

Eliot has said:[21] "Whether poetry is accentual or syllabic, rhymed or rhymeless, formal or free, it cannot afford to lose its contact with the changing language of common intercourse."

I should like the poets of my islands, these poets who are striving so hard to master and mold our sensibility into poetry, to bear that quotation in mind. After these writers have bathed their senses, imagination must clothe clean as a whistle and produce a sweet, haunting, unheard melody.

The drama can apprehend the point of time at the intersection of the timeless; it is the genre essential to the Caribbean writer and to Caribbean literature. Unlike the West Indian novelist who, in trying to reach the outer public, explains and defines,* the dramatist can depict and define more naturally by his staging. He can present the outer visual reality, which the poets are mir-

* George Lamming explains how to make "Cuckoo," a Barbadian dish, in *In the Castle of My Skin*[22] and defines high school and how to dance the calypso in *The Emigrants*;[8] V. S. Naipaul depicts the nature of an East Indian wedding in *The Mystic Masseur*.[10]

·roring, by his setting and scenery. He can recapture or recreate the movement of the West Indian scene by the acting. He can use the fresh, fast, rhythmical dialogue and speech of the region without fear of incoherence in language.

Thus the West Indian dramatists, of whom there are several with potential, including Derek Walcott, Barry Reckord, Errol Hill, and Errol John, might have the key to the problem of how to enter the stream of world writing and yet have, below the surface, the depth of the Caribbean.

To conclude, the writer in the British Caribbean, indeed, in the entire Caribbean, stands in a most precarious and exciting position: precarious because of his limited public, and exciting because his huge nonreading public pinnacles him, thereby thrusting an inescapable responsibility upon him. Will he, too, join the band of emigrants, leaving his native shores to seek fame and fortune abroad, hearkening back, like Claude McKay, with nostalgia (but with facile, poetic nostalgia) to his homeland? Or will his travels abroad (again like Claude McKay) give him a frightened intensity and artistic tension?

Does this society that the Caribbean writer presents as fragmenting and changing and evolving with all its new, awakening consciences and consciousness of social and political patterns and problems of the pigment of skins and of ethnic substrata—does this society have a hold on him? Can he, like James Joyce, in silence, exile, and cunning, propose to purge the conscience of his land? Will the bonds of the islands hold him fast only for a time? In Selvon's *The Cane is Bitter*[3] a young man "kept telling himself he would go away and never return, but the bonds he had refused to think about surrounded him. The smell of burnt cane was strong on the wind."

The situation of the West Indian writer is exciting, for he must create a new, fresh, and vital literature, rejecting in the process the facile, jaded, stilted, literary criteria of his colonial heritage. However, he must heat it and pound it out, shaping it not into a tourist literature of picturesque realism, but into a dynamic, vibrant new literature. If only he can do this, the Caribbean writer, I shall be bold enough to say, could provide a nutriment for the universal literature of our times, a literature that is so out of joint. In Carew's words,[7] "The secret rhythms which reach from the earth on which a village child is born to his heart, had jangled themselves out of harmony."

The writer in the Caribbean must absorb, analyze, and reproduce the full tones of these secret rhythms, not in a jangled reportorial fashion but, through fruitful, reflective observation, must arrive at the essence, the very core and soul of the Caribbean.

References

1. GUILLÉN, N. 1951. El Son Entero. : 27–28, 129. Pleamar. Buenos Aires, Argentina.
2. PORTUONDO, J. A. 1951. The Caribbean at Mid-Century. : 260–261. Univ. Florida Press. Gainesville, Fla.
3. SELVON, S. 1957. The Ways of Sunlight. St. Martin's Press. New York, N.Y.
4. PALÉS MATOS, L. 1950. Tuntún de Pasa y Grifería. Bibl. de Autores Puertoriqueños. : 42. San Juan, Puerto Rico.
5. HARRIS, W. 1954. Kyk-Over-Al, an Anthology of Guianese Poetry. : 76. Seymour. Georgetown, British Guiana.
6. BROUARD, C. 1950. Panorama de la Poésie Haitienne. : 336. Henri Deschamps. Port-au-Prince, Haiti.
7. CAREW, J. 1958. Black Midas. : 22, 126–127, 132–142. Secker. London, England.
8. LAMMING, G. 1956. The Emigrants. : 101–102. M. Joseph. London, England.

9. MITTELHOLZER, E. 1957. Of Trees and the Sea. : 256. Secker & Warburg. London, England.
10. NAIPAUL, V. S. 1957. The Mystic Masseur. Deutsch. London, England.
11. HEARNE, J. 1958. Voices Under the Window. : 59. Faber & Faber. London, England.
12. REID, V. S. 1958. The Leopard. : 21, 15–16. Viking Press. New York, N. Y.
13. HEMINGWAY, E. 1952. The Old Man and the Sea. Scribners. New York, N. Y.
14. FORDE, A. N. 1957. The Day Before Ash Wednesday. In Anthology of West Indian Poetry. A. J. Seymour, Ed. Georgetown, British Guina.
15. KITCHENER, LORD. 1956. Steel Band Clash. Ságomes. Port of Spain, Trinidad.
16. ROBERTS, W. A. 1949. Villanelle of the Living Pan. In A Treasury of Jamaican Poetry. : 125. J. E. C. McFarlane, Ed. Univ. London Press. London, England.
17. ROACH, E. M. 1957. Homestead. In Anthology of West Indian Poetry. : 52. A. J. Seymour, Ed. Georgetown, British Guiana.
18. SHERLOCK, P. M. 1949. Pocomania. In A Treasury of Jamaican Poetry. : 103, 104. J. E. C. McFarlane. Ed. Univ. London Press. London, England.
19. CAMPBELL, G. 1957. Holy. In Anthology of West Indian Poetry. : 5. A. J. Seymour, Ed. Georgetown, British Guiana.
20. HILL, E. 1958. Beggarman. In Caribbean Quarterly: An Anthology of West Indian Verse. April. : 166–167. Univ. Coll. West Indies. Mona, Jamaica.
21. ELIOT, T. S. 1943. Four Quartets. : 17. Harcourt, Brace. New York, N. Y.
22. LAMMING, G. 1953. In the Castle of My Skin. McGraw-Hill. New York, N. Y.

DISCUSSION: THE INTELLECTUAL AND THE PLURAL SOCIETY*

Chairman: Rémy Bastien

Program for Advanced Training in Applied Social Sciences, Pan American Union, Mexico, D.F., Mexico

Rapporteur: John Murra

Vassar College, Poughkeepsie, N. Y.

[The discussion centered around the role of the intellectual in the Caribbean, the extent of his influence, his audience, and the sources of his material. It was questioned whether the essentials for a Caribbean poet are to be found in the work of the calypsonians.]

WILFRED CARTEY (*Columbia University, New York, N. Y.*): The writer should begin with the insular and then go to the universal, but using and weaving the known into the new. He faces a poor market and the problem of how to reach the people; calypso does reach them. The test of poetry is, can you repeat a line; does it have immortality? Calypso has the rhythm of the people, it can be sensed, known. The poet would create an enduring imagery by casting it in this rhythm, with greater possibilities of success.

QUESTION: I wonder if the best Spanish poetry is derived from the *cancionero* (folk singer) or the best Mexican poetry from the *corrido* (ballad). Cannot an intellectual create poetry?

CARTEY: Federico Garcia Lorca was one of the best Twentieth Century poets; his reach is so great that he is moving in many languages. Lorca used the rhythm of romance and beautiful imagery, "And the wind offers me dahlias from the sleeping moon.[1]" He was creative across a rhythm that the Spanish people knew.

QUESTION: What about the influence of non-West Indian writers who write about the West Indies? For example, Alec Waugh?[2]

* Statements have been paraphrased and condensed.

CARTEY: I feel that they present the sociological situation of 1935 as if it were the current reality.

QUESTION: What is the nature of the audience of the Caribbean writers; what is their influence?

CARTEY: Both are limited. There are three or four magazines that publish poetry and short stories, but not novels. The audience is limited to literary circles. Many writers migrate to England, where they are currently fashionable. As reviewers have emphasized the exotic qualities of the literature, there is a growing audience in the United Kingdom and the United States, particularly for novelists. Poetry has fewer opportunities, but drama does well. Since the literary public in the islands is limited, and the influence of the novelists is limited to people of a similar sensibility, it does not go very deep. Novels such as *An Island is a World*[3] and *The Mystic Masseur*,[4] which have a folk quality and are humorous, reach a somewhat wider audience.

QUESTION: For an intellectual to have an authentic identity, he must react to the life of his own society. In the West Indies the elite emulates its European counterparts. In such circumstances, are they not precluded from achieving leadership? Are genuine writers not more likely to come from marginal groups, uncommitted to the thought styles of dominant metropolitan communities?

CARTEY: If the elites emulate the Europeans, they are still part of the local society; even if their outlook is distorted, they nevertheless are transforming that which they have learned. They are a necessary complement to the marginal group you have mentioned.

COMMENT: The authentic artistic production of the lower classes was also affected by the metropolis in the Twentieth Century, since the mass media, in their never-ending search for themes, force the folk artist to react to the new markets opened for his work.

CARTEY: The local consumer of this literature knows what the novelist knows, and the novelist can rely on this knowledge. However, the writer also has the task of making understandable a way of life to a wider public, by presenting in the novel things that are widely familiar locally, such as a recipe for food, for example. In a colonial society one faces the problem of maintaining authenticity while reaching out to a wider public and market. The material sent outside may be unauthentic, like the newer calypsos, but locally the forms remain pure.

[The discussion moved to new trends in political and economic philosophy.]

QUESTION: Is there a school developing that is thinking of insular political and economic problems?

BASTIEN: There has been some attempt to formulate insular policies. Intellectuals must formulate their political and economic thoughts in relation to the problems of the Caribbean. However, who plays for them the role that John Locke played for Thomas Jefferson?

COMMENT: The various social science research institutes in the Caribbean are trying to train local people for research and eventual formulation of programs. The present meeting is another example of growing interest and possible contributions.

BASTIEN: Let us consider the matter of the independence of the intellectual. Can he really be active as an intellectual if he is part of a government staff?

COMMENT: In various parts of the world and in various epochs, for example, in economics and higher levels of government, there has been as much philosophizing as by the people in the universities. We should not downgrade the government intellectual.

COMMENT: The bureaucrat must sustain the established order. If the American Revolution serves any example for our discussion, as has been suggested, then we must look for independent areas of thought.

QUESTION: Let us consider economic development. If you wish to achieve it, you need certain kinds of trained personnel. It is often very difficult to find people who understand modern economics. Where are they?

CARTEY: Eric Williams, the present Premier of Trinidad, is to my mind an example of an intellectual who is trying to apply his principles to the betterment of the islands. On the other hand, the intellectual may prefer to be an adviser without being involved in administration, as in the case of Arthur Lewis.

COMMENT: The local supply of talent for planning and policy making is related to the local philosophies. The impetus for planning frequently comes from the outside, the implementation alone being local. The philosophy of economic development has thus far been European, from such agencies as the Fabian Colonial Bureau in England.

COMMENT: Such plans are now very widespread, but the problem is now that there are so few people who understand them.

COMMENT: The trends toward local political autonomy are paralleled by growing economic dependency, so that formerly dependent areas may be even more committed colonially. As economic development is a new need, based on alien skills, it was bound to be copied from outside models.

CARTEY: Some of the impetus came from the outside, but we must keep in mind the local needs. There is no necessity to reject everything from outside just because the outside master has been rejected. Local people must be trained to lead.

COMMENT: Many local leaders were abroad for a long time, and were probably selected for this very ability to act as a bridge. They are then influential in economic development which, by the way, benefits and is necessary for the West as well as for the underdeveloped countries, since there is a need for investment as well as capital. Investment is not so much asked for as pushed, with the alliance of certain local strata.

COMMENT: The changes and planning now taking place in the Caribbean are concentrated on economic developments and therefore cannot be easily grasped by the population, since they cannot see any effects of the planning as yet.

COMMENT: Outsiders cannot manage economic planning, in my opinion. It must be done by the local people, even if it runs counter to their previous training and habits.

CARTEY: There now are among young people those who study new skills, not only law.

COMMENT: As an historian, I should like to ask whether there are now intellectuals who actually influence trends, even if we allow for lag?   For example, what is the situation in Haiti?

BASTIEN: There are none now, although there have been several in the past and there will undoubtedly be others in the future.   There is no freedom of intellectual expression now in Haiti.

CARTEY: The West Indian novels now published in England are part of an important new trend, emigration, which is a drain of both skilled and unskilled manpower from the islands.

COMMENT: We are all heirs of Western European culture, which is universal in its nature and ideals.   The universal must be brought to the human equation, since world problems are basically the same.   Even emigration is a universal problem and should be viewed as such.

QUESTION: We should remember that small countries are like small towns to some extent: people of talent tend to leave them.   Would you stop them from "moving to the city?"

COMMENT: The other side of the coin is that there is local resistance to having suitably trained men return to the islands, for various bureaucratic and power reasons.   It is made difficult for the returnees.

COMMENT: I am from the Caribbean and I feel that nine of ten young men are ready to return there.

COMMENT: It is difficult to generalize about the Caribbean.   In the French islands there is no such rejection; such a man comes and goes freely as a government employee because there is a policy of assimilation.

COMMENT: We need philosophers to think about these matters, to coordinate economics, sociology, and political science, as none of these disciplines has a global view.   It is a mistake to think that any country has solved the problem. Even the United States has successfully managed only certain aspects of it, such as a high standard of living.   Many other things here remain to be understood.

References

1. LORCA, F. G.   1934.   Yerma.   Losada.   Buenos Aires, Argentina.
2. WAUGH, A.   1951.   Island in the Sun.   Kassell.   London, England.
3. SELVON, S.   1955.   An Island Is a World.   MacGibbon & Kee.   London, England.
4. NAIPAUL,   1957.   The Mystic Masseur.   Deutsch.   London, England.

GROUP DYNAMICS AND SOCIAL STRATIFICATION IN BRITISH GUIANA

Elliott P. Skinner

Department of Anthropology, Columbia University, New York, N. Y.

Group dynamics and social stratification in British Guiana must be studied against the background of an historical period during which many cultural, national, and racial groups were brought into that colony to serve European economic interests, subjected to European sociopolitical systems, and influenced by various European cultures. Today, out of a population of 478,310 inhabitants, East Indians number 239,250; Negroes 175,260; persons of mixed descent 57,240; Portuguese 7830; a category called Other Europeans 4390; and Chinese 3340. The Negroes (or Blacks or Africans) are the descendants of African slaves who were first brought to the colony in 1626 and continued to 1807, even though the country changed from Dutch hands to British in 1814. Slavery was abolished in British Guiana in 1834, but by this time the slaves at the bottom of the social ladder and the middle group of free black and mulatto people had acquired much of the culture of the dominant European planter class.

With the end of slavery, the Negroes bought up abandoned plantations and refused to work exclusively on the sugar estates. The planters were then forced to introduce labor, in the form of indentured servants, from the Madeira Islands, India, and China. The Negroes fought the entry of these laborers with all the weapons at their disposal. They terrorized the East Indians, ridiculed the Portuguese with the appellation of "white niggar," and appealed to the abolitionists and missionaries to save them from "the introduction of masses of sensual and idolatrous Asiatics . . ., [who] will render nugatory the effort of the emancipated labourers . . . who are endeavoring to inculcate upon their rising families a practical respect for the claims of chastity and other Christian virtues."[1] Their efforts failed. However, as soon as most of the Chinese and Portuguese finished their indentures they took to commerce and moved to the larger towns. Here they adopted the culture of the dominant group and, together with the mulattoes who had left the countryside after slavery, became members of the middle class.

Today in British Guiana the Negroes are mainly small-scale farmers, although numbers of them are skilled tradesmen, white-collar workers, and members of the liberal professions. Relatively few Negroes are engaged in commerce. Most of the East Indians have remained on the plantations but, like the Blacks, a number of them are now rice and vegetable farmers, white-collar workers, members of the liberal professions, and merchants. The Negroes felt secure in the fact that their Western culture and their landholdings gave them cultural and economic superiority over the East Indians. However, they find that they are now being outnumbered by the East Indians, and that this group's growing economic power and acquisition of Western cultural traits makes it a force to be reckoned with in the colony's future. The competition between the two groups for status is taking place against the background of a growing

Westernization of their country and a drive for political independence.   These two groups united against the British colonial regime in the early 1950s but, with self-government now assured, their relations with each other, rather than with the other groups in the country, create one of the major problems for British Guianese society.

Despite the presence of many ethnic groups, British Guianese society is not a plural society in Furnivallian terms.*   It is rather a society in flux with traditional group lines giving way at several points.   The groups involved are not only trying to gain as much as they can from the economic system, but one is trying to monopolize those traits in Western culture that make for high status, while the other through the process of acculturation is trying to acquire them.   It seems to me that the East Indians and Negroes in British Guiana are best seen as power-seeking ethnic groups.   Cox has defined an ethnic group "as a people living competitively in relationship of superordination or subordination with respect to some other people or peoples within one state, country, or economic area.   Two or more ethnics [groups] constitute an ethnic system or regime; and, naturally, one ethnic [group] must always imply another.   In other words, we may think of one ethnic [group] as always forming part of a system."[3]   He further refines his definition by referring to the relations of ethnic groups of the same race as minority-group relations and those between those of different races as race-relations.   Cox has made this distinction for methodological reasons because he feels that the opportunity for resolving the problem by assimilation may be, but is not necessarily, greater in one case than in another.   He feels that the "status relationship of both cultural and racial ethnics may persist with great rigidity for long periods of time or it may be short-lived," and insists that the degree of interethnic conflict can be explained better by the social history of the given relationship than by either race or culture.[3]

Harris, who has been dealing with the problem of group relations, eschews the designation of "ethnic relations" for that of "minority-majority relations." He sees minorities and majorities as "subgroups which depend largely upon descent for affiliation, are largely endogamous by choice or necessity, and actively contest their position in the hierarchy."[4]   Harris's definition encompasses most of what is present in Cox, but emphasizes the descent and endogamous aspects of these subgroups and their active contest for power.   His emphasis on descent and endogamy also leads him to the conclusion that regardless of the relative position of minority groups in the power struggle, the "formidable acculturative and assimilative pressures" that they encounter, and the "large percentage of defectors" from their ranks, one should not be

* According to Furnivall,[2] one of the principal features of South Asian societies that accounts for their being plural in character is that ". . . the races did not mix.   Each race and group had its own club or other meeting ground for social functions, its own liquor shops and so on, its own forms and places of entertainment and recreation.   They did not meet in these places, only in the market place—and possibly the race course—to make money out of one another or perhaps, not so often, with one another.   They had no common link except in business.   What was not so obvious was that each race and group had its own special economic function.   There was a plural society with its own distinctive and characteristic plural economy. . . . Social life was reduced to its economic content, and society was converted into a business concern, and only the foreign army of occupation preserved it from disruption."

blinded to the "existence of a permanent membership core which is lingering across generations, remaining constant or even increasing in absolute numbers."[4]   Cox, on the other hand, is not as certain about the fate of ethnic groups.   He believes that some of them are intransigent, others seek or oppose assimilation, and still others struggle for positions as ruling peoples.   He finds also that in some cases minorities may split to take sides on the basis of their economic rather than their ethnic interests or status positions while, in other cases, ethnic antagonism may so suffuse other interests that political or economic class differences are constantly held in abeyance.[3]

Instead of seeing ethnic minorities as monolithic groups competing, cooperating, or maintaining an equilibrium system although competing, that is, the "peace within the feud" sort of thing,[5] I want to show how groups relate to each other and point out how the activities of individuals within their own groups or with the members of other groups relate to the general interactions of the groups and individuals in question.   When we examine any human group we discover that it is made up of individuals in determined relationships.   Furthermore, we note that these individuals share whole patterns of behavior and expectations with each other.   When groups interact with others within the framework of a constantly changing cultural system, there is invariably a change in the nature of each group involved.   The patterns of behavior and expectations that formerly held the group together are modified, and new patterns of behavior are constructed.   When, as in the case of British Guiana, the groups are interacting against the background of a dominant Western culture, those groups that would successfully compete with each other must adopt many of the aspects of the dominant cultural group.   By so doing, however, the sentiments, loyalties and interests that held the original group together and regulated its interaction with other groups within the society are undermined, since the individuals in the groups adopt the "alien" standards at different rates. The highly mobile individuals are even forced to adopt sentiments and loyalties in keeping with their newer interests.   In many instances these interests unite them with individuals of many of the groups in the society, but invariably this conflicts with their group's values.   It seems to me that whether groups remain monolithic or break up into structures that cut across all the groups in the society is determined by the specific sociocultural system in which these groups find themselves.   As the total structure of the societies changes, so change the patterns of interaction between the various groups in it.   I shall now try to examine from this point of view the intergroup, as well as intragroup relations of the population of Canalville, a small village in Demerara, B.G.   I hope that this analysis will throw some light on the problem of group dynamics and social stratification in British Guiana.

Despite the self-images of the two groups in Canalville, it is difficult to rank them against each other.   For example, the wealthiest man in the village is an East Indian, but there are more poor East Indians in the village than poor Negroes.   Thus, with regard to wealth as a criterion, the status of the East Indian group qua group is lower than that of the Blacks.   Similarly, the Black group includes more educated people than the East Indian group; yet this circumstance, from the villager's point of view, is colored by the fact that the only illiterate young person in the community is Negro.   The Black group has had exclusive control of the political apparatus of the village since its inception, but today this control is at the sufferance of the East Indians, who are now sufficiently numerous to obtain at least one seat on the village council.

When we try to evaluate the relative rank of a person within the community, we must gauge, not only his own status, but that of his group. It is much easier to rank individuals within their own groups; a person's rank is then determined by his possession of few or many of those strategic traits on which the status position of his group is based. For example, most of the Blacks are farmers, but some are "big" farmers possessing as much as 10 acres of land, while others own only an acre or less. The differential income of these farmers determines, in part, their capacity to participate in the style of life ideally associated with their status group. For example, only those farmers with large incomes send their children to school in Georgetown, the capital, run for office in village elections, and provide for their families adequate food, clothing, and shelter. They are respected by the rest of the population and reciprocate by serving in the churches, being sponsors for children at baptism, and helping poorer families by giving them the use of farm land.

The more prosperous farmers are the only ones who are concerned with ranking within their group, and a status feud is still going on between two of the more important Negro families in the village, even though one of the main protagonists is dead.

Wealth and level of education rather than caste or religion are the most important factors that affect the interaction of those persons within the East Indian group. The wealthy East Indian shopowners in the village have little in common with the poorer village East Indians or with the East Indians who live and work on the nearby plantations. The relations between them are limited to commercial affairs and to activities that demand ethnic solidarity. For example, an East Indian shopkeeper who attends the wedding of an East Indian of lower rank does so in the name of patronage, and he does not reciprocate by inviting low-status East Indians to his house. The children of wealthy East Indians in the village go to school in Georgetown, while the children of poorer ones either attend the village school or go to schools on the plantations. It is taken for granted that these educated East Indians, regardless of caste or religion (for there is no correlation between caste, religion, and wealth among them) will marry people of their own rank or even marry outside of their ethnic group.

Both of the two main groups in the community are internally ranked, and in style of life some East Indians and Negroes are more like each other than they are like members of their own ethnic groups. However, in most cases the Black group, which until now has been superior, refuses to concede the fact that there are East Indians who now possess those traits that the Blacks consider necessary for high status. Thus the Negroes in Canalville, when informed, in answer to their inquiry, that I was served an "English" dinner (with the proper use of silver and crystal) at the home of a wealthy East Indian, reacted first with disbelief and later attempted to prove that my hostess had lived among Blacks all her life and had learned their ways. I did not check this fact, but it is revealing to note that the Negroes completely overlooked the East Indians and discounted my hostess when I asked them to identify the best-dressed women in the community. Incidentally, my hostess wore more expensive "English" dresses than almost everyone else in the village. Both of these facts illustrate the unwillingness of the Negroes to reward East Indians for acquiring "English" ways, while at the same time basing status on the acquisition of these cultural patterns.

The Negroes' stereotype of the East Indians is that these people would do anything for money, and that this money is hoarded rather than used to improve their style of life. Every attempt is made to show that, although an East Indian may have money, he is indeed a lowly "coolie." Once when an East Indian had just purchased a plot of land for $2000 from a Negro and approached another Negro to ask him whether a full quart of rum or a half quart would be adequate to seal the bargain, the Black man replied: "Man, if you too cheap to buy a bottle of rum, tell the people that." It appeared to me that a quest for knowledge, rather than niggardliness, prompted the East Indian man's query, but his behavior, much to his embarrassment, was seen in terms of the prevailing stereotype. One has the distinct impression that, if the Blacks had the power to do so, they would prevent the East Indians from obtaining any prestigeful traits.

Some of the wealthier Negroes in the community make it a point to see that no East Indian "let his eye pass" them, meaning by this that they would allow no East Indian to do them a favor that might be construed as denoting equality, or worse yet, superior status. When Mr. N., an East Indian, insisted on paying for a piece of mutton that Mr. P., a Negro, had sent to him as a present, Mr. P. thought that this was a slight and, from then on, never drank rum with him. Most of the Negroes in Canalville do not approve of Black girls working as domestics in the homes of the wealthier East Indians, even though Negroes employ East Indian females to weed their farms. The Blacks feel that when girls work for East Indians this tends to "lowdown" the status of the in-group, for as one man said to me: "Me won't let my relative work for no coolie, for me believe a Black man better than coolie anytime." However, this same man raised no objection when an East Indian man of comparable status borrowed his cart without asking permission, but objected violently when either Negroes or East Indians of lower status did the same thing. Moreover, when this man became ill and thought he might die, he called on an East Indian of comparable status to look after his wife and children.

The East Indians, too, hold stereotypes of the Negroes. They believe that the Negroes are spendthrifts who would rather spend money on entertainment than on food or clothing. In addition, they believe that the Blacks are uncooperative and ungrateful. Finally, they believe that Blacks are sexually superior to them and can easily seduce East Indian women. I once overheard an East Indian telling a Negro: "Me can't invite your nation to my house, because you na know how to act."

Despite the fact that there is little sexual hostility or rivalry between the two groups in the community, there is little intermarriage between them. An East Indian looks for a husband for his marriageable daughter from among the members of his own ethnic group. Only those young girls who run off to Georgetown marry outside of their group. One Hindu "nationalist" told me that he did not believe in intermarriage, and felt that each "nation" should marry its own women.   He felt that if he had married a Black woman he would be robbing his own group.   When a Black man enumerated the traits he looked for in a wife, I asked him whether he might not sooner find them in an East Indian woman than in a Black one.   He admitted to this possibility, but said that he would never marry an East Indian girl because they were ordinarily too shy.   On reflection, he qualified his statement by saying that he would only marry an "Englishified" (Westernized) East Indian girl, because only a person of her type would know how to conduct herself among Blacks.   What he carefully failed to mention, however, was the fact that at that very time he was having an affair with a not very "Englishified" East Indian married woman.

One interesting fact about Canalville is that, although there is not a great deal of intermarriage between the two groups there is a significant amount of sexual relation between them.   When asked to indicate the number of mixed marriages in the community, a man listed several, but laughingly added, "There is more mixing than that," meaning, of course, that surreptitious sexual relations existed between the groups.   The Black man mentioned above was not alone in his sexual peregrinations.   East Indian men, too, cross the ethnic boundary in search of sexual partners, and there are at least three East Indian men in the village who have children by Black women.

Most mixed marriages in the community are between Negro males and East Indian widows.   These women are forbidden to remarry according to Hindu rites and seldom establish households with East Indian men.   They normally start living with Negroes, and frequently legalize the union and gain respectability by marrying in Christian churches.   Except for the man who considers himself a nationalist, most of the villagers accept such marriages, and East Indian women have been known to flaunt their wedding rings in the faces of unmarried Negro women, or even of East Indian women "who were simply married under the bamboo."   The nationalist says that some East Indian women like to marry Negro men because such men perform such unmanly tasks as carrying water for them.   A Negro commenting on this statement said that, while he did not care whether people intermarried or not, he was gratified to see that nowadays, unlike a few decades ago, the Black men are marrying East Indian women rather than vice versa.   These attitudes show that marriage and sex are peripheral, and are not the focal point of competition between the two groups.

While a great deal of the interaction between East Indians and Negroes is circumscribed by ethnic affiliation, not all the relations between members of both groups are based on group membership.   The village people shift quite easily from regarding an individual as a member of a given group to regarding him according to his "real worth" as a man.

An East Indian stranger who owns a rum shop in the village often would not give rum on credit to local East Indians unless they brought testimonials from a certain wealthy villager who was a Negro.   A Negro informant bragged to me that his credit was so good that he could walk up to any East Indian man and receive monetary or nonmonetary assistance.   The truth of this statement was brought home when, after trying in vain to raise money among the Blacks to bail out one of his relatives from jail, he was able to borrow money from an East Indian. This Negro, in turn, often lends money to East Indians without interest and gives them fruits and vegetables from his farms.

In many cases the personal relations between East Indians and Negroes modify or take precedence over group relations. I once heard a Negro vilifying an East Indian stranger: "Me don't eat your coolie dahl [a sauce made from peas] and rice. You good-for-nothing coolie!" only to have him stop suddenly and say to me, "Me can't talk over much cause this boy here [referring to another East Indian] is me neighbor and it go hurt he."

In another case an East Indian man, on giving a Negro woman a donation for the anti-East Indian Jordanite cult group, said, "Neighb(or), I am supporting you, but not those ——— Jordanites." One of the East Indian shopkeepers in the village openly ridiculed the "Negro uplift" messages of the cult group as nonsense because he said he gave more credit to the Blacks in the village than did the Black shopkeeper. He showed his contempt for the movement and his fearlessness of the economic boycott advocated by the Jordanite elder; he even lent them his Primus lamp for their meetings.

Group loyalty does not transcend all factors in the evaluation of disputes between members of the two groups. It is not uncommon for an individual to be denied support simply because he is thought to be in the wrong. A case in point was the attitude of the Blacks in the community towards a Black shopkeeper who foolhardily became involved in a boundary dispute with an East Indian and lost the case. For days afterward the man raved at his inability to obtain some redress from the village officials and aid from fellow Negroes. He finally said in despair: "Black man is going down, because Black man is for coolie, and coolie is for coolie." What this man did not know and, what is more, could not discover, was that although many East Indians and Negroes sympathized with him as the underdog in the fight, his history of poor relations with both groups effectively cut off all support.

The picture of group dynamics and social stratification that emerges from a study of East Indians and Negroes in Canalville and that may have implications for British Guiana, since the majority of the Guianese are still rural, is that, while the East Indians are acquiring those traits that make for high status, their upward mobility is seen as a challenge by the Black group. The Negroes boast that they have taught the East Indians everything—how to read, write, sew, and build—but they refuse to reward the East Indians for the acquisition of desirable cultural traits.

Yet, despite these attitudes, there is a growing awareness by the people of Canalville of the similarity of individuals based, not on ethnic affiliations, but on such criteria as wealth, education, style of life, and life goals. As one East Indian said to me: "When me was a child, Indian and African children na want to see each other 'tall [at all]. Now me can be a koker-keeper [watchman for the dikes] and me no have nothing to do with an African who is a farmer. If me son become a hunter and the African son become a hunter, they go together and forget all about we old people and we ideas." Social scientists should be cautious in accepting local people's views about the social and cultural transformation of their society. However, probably the most positive and dramatic demonstration of the breaking down of actions along group lines took place during the national elections in 1953. The National Democratic Party appealed to the East Indians mainly along ethnic lines, the People's National Movement appealed to the Negroes to save themselves from East Indian domination, the Independents appealed to special interests or to no interests, while the People's Progressive Party phrased their appeal to all the groups in terms of racial tolerance, social equality, and economic betterment. When the votes were counted, the multiracial PPP won an absolute majority of 18 seats out of 24, the Independents won 4, and the NDP won 2. In Canalville the PPP received about 87 per cent of the votes in the village. The interesting thing about this local election result is that this predominantly Negro community voted for an East Indian member of the PPP. Much to the amusement of the villagers, the Negro village chairman who ran as an independent was beaten so badly that he even lost his deposit, a penalty imposed on those who receive less than one-eighth of the votes cast in their constituencies.

This impressive show of political solidarity, with all it augured for improving group relations, came to naught when on a charge of communism and activities "detrimental to the economic well-being of the country" the constitution was suspended by the colonial office in London and the PPP government deposed. This was not the first time that reactionary colonial forces defeated the progressive elements in dependent countries. As was expected, the PPP split into two parties under Cheddi and Janet Jagan and L. S. F. Burnham. I do not know whether the split is along ethnic lines, but in 1957 when constitutional government was restored to the colony, the PPP of the Jagans won 9 seats, the PPP of Burnham won 1 seat, while the racialist parties won only 1 seat each.

Since the main points made in this paper are based on field work carried out in 1954,[6] I am not certain that the processes described are continuing. However, writing about British Guiana in 1958, R. T. Smith states:[7]

" ... British Guiana is often referred to as a 'plural' society. This term, no matter what the degree of sophistication used in its definition, tends to be misleading because it concentrates attention upon differences in race and custom, and upon group conflict, while at the same time directing attention away from the processes making for unity and integration in the society.

"A more serviceable view is that Guianese society does constitute a unitary whole capable of containing such social and cultural diversity as exists within it and that it is still in the process of developing new forms for the expression of that unity."

Smith adds that among the different groups introduced into the colony were Chinese and Portuguese,[7]

" ... but they and their descendants have become much more fully assimilated into the main structures of the society, adopting almost completely the cultural standards of the particular social strata in which they are located. ... It would be a gross misrepresentation of the fact to regard the Indians as an organised community group within Guianese society. On the contrary, there is every indication that they are becoming even more rapidly assimilated into the main framework of the society and it is this very fact which often gives the appearance of group conflict.

"As Indians cease to be solely resident plantation laborers or peasant rice farmers and come to be more proportionately represented in the professions, in the Civil Service and in white collar occupations generally, there is an almost inevitable tendency for members of the other ethnic groups to misconstrue this as a threat to their own position, and to fall back upon stereotyped images of the group as a whole."

Smith analyzes the claims that different religious affiliations would create strife and disunity in the country, but feels that the Guianese are accepting the existence of different religions. He concludes:[7]

"Along with this growing recognition of the feasibility of a level of religious and cultural diversity, there is a quite explicit recognition of the impropriety of allowing religious or cultural differences to assume overt political significance.

"No political party in British Guiana professes to represent any particular ethnic or religious group."

It thus appears that group relations in British Guiana have not deteriorated. Furthermore, the vector of change seems to be toward a society in which common interests are cutting across ethnic group boundaries.

References

1. PARLIAMENTARY PAPERS, Great Britain. 1846. **XXX**(32): 166.
2. FURNIVALL, J. S. 1950. *In* South Asia in the World Today. : 63–85. Phillips Talbot, Ed. Univ. Chicago Press. Chicago, Ill.
3. COX, O. C. 1948. Caste, Class and Race. : 317; 318; 319. Doubleday. New York, N.Y.
4. HARRIS, M. 1959. Caste, class and minority. Social Forces. **37**: 248; 254.
5. GLUCKMAN, M. 1955. Custom and Conflict in Africa. Blackwell. Oxford, England.
6. SKINNER, E. P. 1955. Ethnic Interaction in a British Guiana Rural Community. Dissertation, Columbia Univ. New York, N. Y. Unpublished.
7. SMITH, R. T. 1958. British Guiana. *In* Sunday Guardian of Trinidad, The West Indies Federation Supplement (April 20). : 25–59.

DISCUSSION: MULTIRACIALISM AND THE PLURAL SOCIETY*

Chairman: M. G. Smith
Nigerian Institute of Social and Economic Research, University College, Ibadan, Nigeria

Rapporteur: Dennison Nash
University of Connecticut, Storrs, Conn.

[M. G. Smith opened the discussion by questioning the use of the term "minority group" to refer to such numerically large groups as the East Indians and Negroes in British Guiana.]

SKINNER: I am not using the term to represent a numerically smaller group, but rather a subordinate group.

COMMENT: However, neither of these groups is clearly subordinate to the other.

SKINNER: That is true. Also, with the imminent retirement of the British, two groups, the Negroes and the East Indians, are the important groups to consider. They will dominate the future of the country.

---

* Statements are paraphrased and condensed.

QUESTION: Is association between the two groups greater than dissociation? Is it on the increase or decrease?

COMMENT: There are divisions within these two groups (East Indians and Negroes) in some political action. There is cross-group voting.

COMMENT: It is the professed political ideal in British Guiana not to appeal to race, but actually such an appeal is used in some political situations.

COMMENT: The concept of race has many dimensions. Possibly it has been considered too simply.

SMITH: British Guiana is a plural society, but Skinner seems to have de-emphasized pluralism in his paper.

SKINNER: Groups that are being acculturated contain individuals who are acquiring traits at different speeds. These minority groups are interacting with each other. They are acquiring common characteristics against the background of a dominant British culture.

COMMENT: Do the two groups have different institutions? To what extent do they overlap, and to what extent are they different?

SKINNER: Both groups are monogamous. The Negro family is matrifocal, the East Indian patriarchal. They have different religions, but there is a degree of overlapping here. It is important to see the two groups as made up of individuals who are in interaction. Both groups are undergoing acculturation at different rates, and in this process they are being modified.

QUESTION: What will be the ultimate end of the acculturative process? Will the groups merge or remain separate? Skinner does not appear to have the data to make predictions.

QUESTION: Considering the Caribbean flux, should not the concept of race be abandoned in the analysis of societies there? Would it not be better to define these groups culturally and not racially?

SKINNER: The groups may be designated in at least two ways, that is, genotypically or sociologically. However, it does not seem possible to substitute rural-urban distinctions for racial ones in this situation. The concept of race is necessary.

SMITH: Skinner has not shown the differences or similarities in institutions between the two groups. His paper points up the problem of the relative utility of the racially or culturally pluralistic type of analysis.

SKINNER: The concept "minority group" helps us to understand the relationship between the groups better.

SMITH: Does the term "minority group" presuppose a homogeneity in the society and culture being analyzed?

SKINNER: Yes it does.

COMMENT: In the United States the term race has been replaced by ethnic group. This seems to be because the term race is in ill-repute. In British Guiana, on the other hand, people do not seem to be afraid to use racial terms such as Chinee. Such terms are current and usable.

QUESTION: Could not heredity be the criterion of race, and would not the lack of intermarriage be a clear indication of it? Is this not the case in British Guiana?

SKINNER: I quite agree in each instance.

COMMENT: We should limit our remarks to specific societies. It is not always correct to speak of Trinidad and British Guiana as though they were identical. Also, is it not more important to turn our discussion to problems rather than definitions? The important problem here is the power struggle, and it is important to find out what construct is being manipulated in this struggle. In this regard the British should be considered. Although they are not in the village studied by Skinner, they may create dynamics in the society as a whole that are different from those in the village and that may affect the village.

SKINNER: The British are leaving British Guiana. The reality now consists of the East Indian and Negro groups.

QUESTION: Are not both of these groups moving toward a supragroup (British) standard? Is this not pluralism?

SKINNER: This is true.

COMMENT: Is it not possible that group conflict will occur where there are few institutional differences? Indeed, social conflict would seem to require similarities. This is the case in the United States.

QUESTION: Is race, as such, an important factor in British Guiana?

COMMENT: If descent is used as a criterion, then it certainly is at present.

COMMENT: I feel it depends on how racial tags are used. In the United States the use of racial tags has been cut down through the power of the mass media.

COMMENT: The diagnostic criterion of race should be within the family. Do the children fall in the same or different groups, as in Brazil. If they fall in different groups, the concept of race does not apply.

COMMENT: From the East Indian point of view any mixture makes you Creole, not East Indian. A person who is half East Indian and half Negro is a *doogla*, or bastard.

COMMENT: The importance of racial criteria in the over-all culture and as a factor in the power struggle is demonstrated by a minimization of Hindu-Moslem differences within the East Indian group.

COMMENT: I do not think racial differences are important here. I feel that the reason for conflict between the groups is cultural. Also, group hostility can occur without institutional differences.

COMMENT: Political parties in British Guiana are not uniracial; there is cross-race political action.

COMMENT: Despite shifting allegiances, due to endogamy the racial factor is always present. It is important to discover why this is true, because it provides a basis for political power.

SMITH: Are the kinship systems of the two groups similar or different?

SKINNER: The triadic husband-wife-child relationship is similar in content in both groups.

COMMENT: The important questions are: first, what causes the endogamy, and, second what kind of functional relationship exists between the groups; that is, what do they do for each other?

SMITH: What we have been trying to do is to isolate the significant variable that is correlated with the cleavage between these two groups. Is it race, economic specialization, rural-urban dichotomy, cultural separateness, or institutional variation? There appears to be a cleavage extending far back into history. Our problem is to discover what is the basis of this cleavage.

COMMENT: Is there economic specialization between the two groups?

SKINNER: There is now no occupational exclusiveness. However, the groups originally were occupationally specialized. The fact that there is no specialization now is an indication of both acculturation and homogeneity.

COMMENT: I feel that self-esteem might be the major explanatory factor in analyzing the situation in British Guiana. The category that is important to self-esteem would be important as an explanatory device. I also feel that differences between groups can be talked about more comfortably in the Caribbean. In British Guiana Negroes and East Indians talk easily about race relations. This is not the case in the United States.

COMMENT: Are the sectional differences horizontal or vertical? In British Guiana it appears that they are horizontal. There probably would be more emotion and less frankness where the situation is vertical.

COMMENT: There appear to be differences between the two groups. What is the cause? What are the consequences? These are the major questions.

SMITH: It is generally known that Creoles marry after they have children and that East Indians marry before they have children. Therefore there are differences in kinship patterns, that may be relevant for other differences between the two groups. The bias of the investigator is important for the outcome of his analysis. What societal model does he use, integrationist or pluralist? A society must be looked at both statically and dynamically. If we look at American sociology and British anthropology, it seems that the sociologists tend to take the unitary point of view, while the anthropologists view societies as pluralistic and changing.

SKINNER: I feel that it is better to see things from the point of view of change.

SMITH: The problem is one of developing a model for analyzing an amalgam. What is the case in Java?

COMMENT: In Java there are many groups that share in the governmental process. The term ethnic group may be applied to them.

SMITH: A plural society exists only when there is a small dominant group that is preoccupied with maintaining power over culturally discrete sections of a society. If there are many groups that share in the government and power, then a simple plurality exists.

SKINNER: The United States sociologist's definitions of majority and minority are particularly poor for universal application. On the world scene the majority group is not numerically predominant, as it is in the United States.

SMITH: Since the concept does not seem to apply in British Guiana, it is not very useful for this area.

[The discussion then centered on the American definitions. Simpson and Yinger, American sociologists, were cited to indicate that the term majority is not used to mean a numerical majority, and that this usage has been current for some time.   It was felt, however, that this definition is contrary to ordinary usage and experience.   The need for proper definition in scientific work was emphasized.]

COMMENT: I should dislike to see this discussion terminate on a quibble over a definition.   Definitions are not crucial, but problems are.

COMMENT: It is a good thing to have a difference of opinion concerning definitions in sociology and anthropology.

Printed in the United States of America